Inside the Family

Toward a Theory of Family Process

David Kantor
William Lehr

INSIDE

THE

FAMILY

Jossey-Bass Publishers
San Francisco • Washington • London • 1976

INSIDE THE FAMILY
Toward a Theory of Family Process
by David Kantor and William Lehr

Copyright © 1975 by: Jossey-Bass, Inc., Publishers
615 Montgomery Street
San Francisco, California 94111
&
Jossey-Bass Limited
St. George's House
44 Hatton Garden
London EC1N 8ER

Library of Congress Catalogue Card Number LC 74-27910

International Standard Book Number ISBN 0-87589-250-7

Manufactured in the United States of America

JACKET DESIGN BY WILLI BAUM

FIRST EDITION
First printing: May 1975
Second printing: March 1976

Code 7506

The Jossey-Bass
Behavioral Science Series

To Meredith and Ellen

Preface

We shall understand families when we understand how they manage the commonplace, that is, how they conduct themselves and interact in the familiar everyday surroundings of their own households. To date, family therapists and researchers have concentrated on extraordinary family phenomena, such as the generation of psychosomatia, social deviance, and schizophrenia. As a result, many of them have overlooked an obvious truth: families, even those families which suffer from serious schism and disablement, devote most of their time to everyday affairs. We emphasize this truth partly to counteract the somewhat distorted perspective provided by the cumulative abundance of studies devoted to family pathology. Although we do not wish to deny their importance, we believe that disabling processes occupy a considerably smaller subclass in the universe of family events than the literature of family pathology might lead us to believe. As a result *Inside the Family* concerns itself with the basic issues confronting all families as families. It seems to us that if a theory or model of family behavior is to be viable, it must be applicable to "healthy" or "normal" family processes as well as to pathological ones. Consequently, our primary concern throughout this volume is to focus on the intrinsic nature of family process itself rather than on its pathological aspects.

Since the 1950s, the study of family interactions has become a discipline in itself, but a number of basic conceptual problems remain. Over the years an increasing number of family investigators have tended to think of the family as a "system." The use of the term *family process* to describe the totality of family interactions reflects this growing systemic orientation. To designate the family as a system, however, raises as many questions as it answers. Perhaps the most basic question is, "A system of what: of roles? of acts? of levels of communication?" Different investigators have approached the problem from varying perspectives, many making significant contributions to our understanding of family. The multiplicity of their observations suggests that this system is a complex network of many different parts, but no one has yet suggested a conceptual framework that successfully demonstrates precisely the way in which these parts interrelate.

A related problem is that no scheme of measurement currently available is both reliable and significant. In other words, family analysts have not had a sound conceptual basis for determining which family interaction variables are important and which are trivial.

A third important problem in family research is the need for a typology that differentiates families in accordance with distinctively different whole-family processes. Classification of a family based on the behavioral characteristics of an individual member— for example, "the alcoholic's family," "the delinquent's family," "the schizophrenic's family"—has proven inadequate as a description of a whole family.

Finally, as each of these problems suggests, researchers and therapists are in great need of a unified theory or model for discussing and explaining what happens in families. The development of such a conceptual framework is perhaps the key task currently confronting the field of family research. Only when a viable model is proposed and gains general acceptance will there be a common vocabulary for discussing family-system events, so that researchers, therapists, and other students of family can know with some certainty what each other is talking about.

In an effort to help resolve these important issues, we are presenting in *Inside the Family* a descriptive theory of family process. This theory is applicable to other social systems as well, because, although the family has certain unique characteristics, it also shares many features with other social collectivities. Our model has been devised in an attempt to answer the basic question about family systems, "A system of what?" Its purpose is to identify the basic component parts of family process and to show how they relate to one another in carrying out the provisions for regulating the actual and metaphorical distances each family must evolve in order to survive as a social entity. The primacy of these distance-regulation aspects of family behavior is demonstrated by the model. Consequently a viable system of measurement for determining the relative significance and triviality of various family-process variables is suggested.

In short, our goal is to reveal the major themes and components of family process and to show how they are employed in regulating members' behavior. The model is based on our observations of a number of different families. Indeed, we have been strongly influenced by our remembered experiences and relationships within our own families of origin: Kantor, the senior author, was the fourth of five children growing up in a tenement section of Depression-era Brooklyn, and Lehr, the younger son of a brewery foreman, was raised two decades later on the south side of St. Louis. No doubt some of our ideas have been generated by the personal need of each of us to understand more fully the events that took place in the parental family—events that continue to influence interactions in our present-day families. A second group of families that have provided us with valuable data are those that Kantor—a family therapist himself—has encountered in his clinical work. A third, and in a sense an "official" set of families guiding the development of our ideas were the nineteen urban and suburban Boston area families, categorized by class, ethnic group, and religion, who constituted the sample for "A Study in Vivo of Disturbed and Normal Family Milieux," an investigation begun in 1965, funded in part by the National Institute of Mental Health.

In our analysis we proceed from a study of the microlevel of acts and sequences of acts to an examination of the reasonably stabilized interactions among the major elements influencing family process. These elements correspond to the five major components or facets of our theory. In our presentation, we have correlated theory with empirically observed family behavior to place our concepts in perspective. Thus each of the major components of our model represents a conceptual reality.

The plan of *Inside the Family* is to present as systematically as possible a balanced and comprehensive description of family process in which certain elements of general systems theory are combined with a naturalistic study of family life. Chapter One is a survey of our research and thinking on families. Chapter Two is an introduction of several key concepts of modern systems theory and the ways in which we apply them to family. Our theory of family process consists of five major components, which we delineate in Chapters Three through Twelve. The first is the network of family subsystems and the interfaces at which these subsystems interrelate (Chapter Three). We suggest that family process is most clearly understood if we think of it as the interactions of these various subsystems, both with each other and with the world outside. The second and third components of our theory, when taken together, constitute a six-dimensional social-space grid on which family interactions take place (Chapter Four). Three of these six dimensions are access dimensions (the second component), and the other three are target dimensions (the third component). We propose that all family traffic takes place on this social-space grid and can be analyzed as the efforts of members to gain access to targets. An elaboration of the access component of family process is provided by a detailed set of access mechanisms in which we attempt to delineate the tasks confronting all families as families (Chapters Five, Six, Seven and Eight). The fourth component can be viewed as a classification of three distinct family types (Chapters Nine and Ten). We describe each type in detail, analyzing both its goals and its structural means for attaining those goals. The fifth component of our theory is the configuration of four player parts members enact in their various interactional patterns (Chapters Eleven and Twelve). The different parts and the operational importance of each are examined, and we suggest ways in which they reveal and express the psychopolitics of family process. In Chapter Thirteen, we survey these five components and unite them into a single comprehensive framework for understanding family process. Within this framework we relate all the parts of our theory to each other and to the whole. Finally, in Chapter Fourteen, we offer some speculations on how families evolve over time by focusing on how individuals leave their families of origin to find mates with whom they can begin families of their own.

We have already suggested that, in order for a theory or model of family process to be viable, it should both emphasize and explain such commonplace events as the following: *A small child stands outside his parents' bedroom door on Saturday morning. He knocks on the door. Both parents hear it. Mother says, "Come in." The boy enters and goes directly toward the bed where he hugs his still half asleep father, who groggily hugs him in return.* We examine this sequence in detail in Chapter Thirteen.

The purpose of the book as a whole is to identify the complex transactions governing such deceptively simple family sequences, so that each process variable in the sequence can be identified and its relationship to all other variables understood. Our twofold aim is to provide a systematic framework that is applicable to the multifarious and often bewildering experiences of families and simultaneously to provide the empirical evidence for our model of family process that will make it accessible.

The primary focus of our research and of *Inside the Family* is the way in which families work. Toward this end we have developed several empirically derived concepts and the beginnings of a theory explaining the interrelationship of these concepts. We have not, however, systematically asked the question of why families work the way they do. In other words, we have not been concerned with ultimate causes, but rather with immediate cause-effect-cause phenomena. A great deal can be said about how families work if we limit ourselves to the structural present. Indeed, some family analysts would probably argue that one need not pose questions on ultimate causes. The contemporaneity of cause and effect is sufficient, they would say. We believe, however, that an examination of visible or nearly visible operations is not sufficient for understanding the totality of what we mean by family process. We believe that there is a relationship, though not necessarily an immediately visible relationship, between immediate cause-effect-cause phenomena and ultimate causal phenomena. In addition, we believe that this relationship between present, past, and future should be one of the prime fields for future family research.

The formulations expressed in *Inside the Family* are the products partly of our introspection and partly of content analyses —sometimes formal, sometimes informal—of the processes we have observed taking place in all the families with whom we have come into contact. Our ideas are inspired primarily by observations of the evaluation and shaping of events and interactions as seen from the inside of family life, insofar as this has been possible. If these ideas are to have any lasting value, they must somehow reveal an inner actuality—something significantly true about the family as the family "knows" itself to be—and then succeed in relating this inner or felt reality to the intellectual currents of the world at large. We hope that our conclusions will establish a true kinship between the phenomenological reality of the family and the systemic reality of the family as we "know" it and report it to be, and that our ideas will be of value to all students of family, be they researchers, therapeutic practitioners, educators, or, simply, members of a family.

Acknowledgments

During the summer of 1970, we began to hold a two-year series of weekly theory-building meetings with three of our colleagues, Rebecca McCollum, Joseph Mullan, and Michael Glenn. The five of us tried to define a conceptual framework for understanding the complexity of behaviors we were witnessing in the families we jointly studied. Many of the ideas presented in this book were introduced in those meetings. The group itself began to function as a very special intellectual conscience, hovering over each of us as we did our individual work. Our meetings forced and often facilitated the crystalization of hunches and other loose ideas into a viable intellectual framework. The work of the group often helped us to separate the wheat from the chaff—the important from the irrelevant, and the truly essential from the occasionally applicable. Week after week the group functioned as a highly demanding examining board for conceptualizations about family. The advice and encouragement it provided were indispensable to the development of our ideas and the writing of this book. We are especially grateful for the often innovative contribution of Ms. McCollum. Our daily coworker for more than four years, she helped us identify and elaborate many of the subjects treated in this book. Additional tribute must be paid to E. V. Walter, professor of sociology at Boston University; Barry Dym, a colleague and fellow instructor at the Cambridge Family Institute; and Larry L. Constantine, clinical instructor in psychiatry at Tufts Medical School, all of whom read and constructively critiqued various drafts of our manuscript. Finally, we are indebted to our secretary Donna MacDonald, who bore the unenviable burden of turning our often disconnected notes into coherent copy.

Cambridge, Massachusetts   DAVID KANTOR
January 1975   WILLIAM LEHR

Contents

Inside the Family

Toward a Theory of Family Process

Chapter 1

A Study from Within

Our primary focus throughout this book is on the intrinsic nature of family process. The naturalistic study of family households we began in 1965 reflects this concern. More than half of the nineteen families we studied were categorized as normal, by which we meant the absence in these families of any major family or individual disturbance requiring hospitalization. In nine of our research families, an offspring who had been diagnosed as schizophrenic before the onset of our research was present in the household. Most of these "schizopresent" families were drawn from the clinics of Boston State Hospital, but a few of them, as well as all "normal" family units, were approached and selected with the help of community sources. A rough matching sample was used. Families with diagnosed schizophrenics had to meet specific age, diagnostic, and other selection criteria. Those that qualified were then selected according to class, ethnic, and other distribution criteria. Usually, selection of the comparison families followed the study of schizopresent family. The families were roughly matched according to class, ethnic background, family composition, and neighborhood. An attempt was made to study public-housing and working-class families as well as middle-class and more affluent households. Research procedures were essentially the same for all families.

Research in the Natural Milieu

In every research project, the data ultimately uncovered are determined, at least in part, by mode of operation, because the design of a piece of research inevitably represents a value judgment by the investigators about the best approach to a particular subject. Our own study of family interactions has been no exception and is founded on two general assumptions: One is that the systems approach—the study of a family as a system of dynamic interacting components—offered the most sophisticated and appropriate technology for conceptualizing the problems at hand. The second assumption is that the family must be studied in its own natural geographic and social context rather than in the professional office or laboratory, that the natural environment provided the richest possible context for the study of family. In addition, this context has been the one investigated least by other social scientists. The idea that detailed and extended naturalistic observation is the appropriate first step in the investigation of social phenomena is not a new one. However no one, as far as we know, has applied it to the study of the family, except for Jules Henry, who began his visits to the homes of five schizophrenic children in 1957 (Henry, 1971).

Our goal has been to study a limited number of families in as much detail as possible. Throughout we tried to bring our researchers as close as possible to family phenomenology: thus we encouraged them to assimilate what it really felt like to live in a particular family, but without sacrificing too much of the emotional distance required to do fair and objective research. In a very real sense, our research focused on the commonplace in family process—that is, the dynamics and interactions that take place in familiar and comfortable surroundings, the myriad small events that occur from moment to moment in the lives of all families. This emphasis, too, reflected certain value judgments: first, that the commonplace is a check on the dramatic, a warning and testament that conflict and argument are not all or even perhaps most of what a family may be about; second, that the commonplace—the everyday, the habitual

—is the area in which families are usually least defensive about being investigated. Because people lower their defenses in familiar and comfortable surroundings, their conduct in such an environment can reveal important information about the complex nature of their personal and interpersonal functioning.

In order to encompass as broad a range of information as possible, we emphasized the collection of five different kinds of data: participant observer reports; tape recordings (and, on several occasions, videotapes) of family interactions; interviews of the whole family, subgroups, and individuals; projective test results; and self-reports by individual family members. The method chosen for study was a clinical one, and the emphasis on observation rather than on scientific measurement. The techniques employed to gather the data were largely unstructured.

The participant observers were university students. One lived in each family household and attempted to develop a complete and systematic account of the characteristic features of that family's life, including the members' trips outside the household. Observations focused on the communications (both verbal and nonverbal) that took place among family members, but other aspects of family life and culture were documented as well. Observers collected data on the norms and structures that each family developed to define its uniqueness as a system and on the style of interpersonal relationships. The role the participant observer was to assume was that of a person who was privy to all that took place but was not one of the central actors determining the events.

The information an observer sought comprised a wide range of areas, including the following: the family's general stylistic features—how it played, what it laughed about, how members responded to trouble; the members' goals—whether they saw themselves as moving up in the world, down, or not at all; how members expressed affection for one another—whether there was warmth, whether or not expression was overt, and which members were the recipients of affection and under what conditions; the allocation of tasks the performance of conjugal roles by husband and wife, what tasks the children had, whether or not members were content with their jobs; the solidarity of a particular family—whether the family was close, whether members considered it to be close, whether it responded as a unit toward the rest of society; the fostering of dependence and independence—whether privacy was valued, how it was maintained; the maintenance of family ties—whether family and kinship ties were warm or strained, whether the family developed warm ties with neighbors; finally, the designation of authority and responsibility—whether role conceptions were "traditional" or "equalitarian," how discipline was carried out, how parents handled not only the aggressiveness of their children but also their own aggressiveness and hostility toward their offspring and toward each other.

In addition to the presence of a participant observer, microphones were place in all rooms of a household to record the verbal communications that took place among members of a family during waking hours. Observers and/or family members started the machines in the morning and the last person to retire turned them off at night. With these sound-recording devices it was possible to obtain a faithful record of verbal interactions between family members. Although such electronic devices provide a more complete and accurate audio coverage of family life than the human observer can, they were not meant to replace the observer, who was sensitive to movements, moods, and numerous nonverbal communications that cannot be registered by machines. In addition, three sets of interviews were used in an attempt to correlate ethnographic and interactional data on the whole family with personality attributes of individual members. In the family interviews, members were invited to tell members of our staff about their family as they saw it: the history of the family, its strengths, its problems, how members got along with each other, where they felt the family was going, how they all managed their lives. In appropriate subgroups this line of questioning was continued. Both sets of interviews provided valuable descriptive materials for a diagnostic understanding of the whole family. About midway through the period of study, each member of the family was interviewed privately so that we could determine how he viewed both himself and the family, including his position in it. Each member was also administered a series of ten T.A.T. cards, with parents and children being shown the same pictures. Self-reporting was a device that some members voluntarily made use of to uncover events experienced internally. Family members giving such reports were asked to give detailed accounts of their unexpressed thoughts, perceptions, and subjective experiences in regard to certain overt behaviors.

All our research data were processed in forms that were either complete or nearly so. For instance, observer reports and T.A.T. stories were recorded and typed verbatim. Electronic-tape data too were in great part reproduced verbatim. Every audible piece of conversation among members of the family was typed word for word. In addition, family and individual interviewers were debriefed for their observations shortly after each interview. The purpose of such exhaustive processing, particularly of those data reported by the observer and the electronic tapes, was to provide a record of each family that could be of value to researchers and scholars regardless of their approach, since such data were unique in the history of family research, and still are as far as we know.

As we began to analyze our data, we did not know how useful the conceptions about family process available to us from studies by others would be. What did seem evident was that life inside the family, where we were witnessing it, did not conform to the descriptions of family behavior that had evolved from secondary contexts such as doctors' offices and individual interviews. For us and others, such conceptions as double bind (Bateson, Jackson, Haley, and Weakland, 1956), pseudomutuality (Wynne, Ryckoff, Day, and Hirsch, 1958), and scapegoating (Vogel and Bell, 1960) had previously been relied on as satisfactory explanations of family behavior. They had been accepted as being generally applicable despite the fact that they originated from study of behavior occurring outside the normal family milieu.

However, once we were inside family walls, we found those concepts to be less valuable to a comprehensive understanding of family process than they had been in the therapy room. This posed a major problem for us, for we had to observe phenomena in one context and try to give expression to them with borrowed concepts that had been developed in contexts we knew did not directly apply. We very soon learned that new conceptual tools would have to be developed if we were truly to comprehend the import of events that were happening before us in the households we were investigating

—tools that a family's natural setting and the happenings themselves would tell us were right.

Spatial Metaphor

The search for a theory and typology of family is inevitably stimulated and influenced by metaphor. Indeed, any new idea begins with the visualization of a seminal metaphor, which, in turn, is of course rooted in a certain context. It seemed to us that metaphors which could lead to a comprehensive theory must come out of the natural context, the context in which the bulk of family life is actually lived. The metaphor that we shall employ in our attempt to describe and understand the family is that of space; for example, we shall consider the ways in which a family imposes metaphorical or figurative—rather than actual—distance between itself and others. This spatial metaphor had not yet occurred to us when we started our research. In retrospect we can only wonder why it did not, since spatial issues and conflicts abound in the life of a family.

Two families, the Rouges and the Sempers, were particularly important in teaching us the importance of space to family process. Our first early clue came when we observed that Buzzy Rouge, a twenty-year-old daughter, had placed a padlock on the door of her room in the family apartment. This padlock asserted and preserved her right to a personal space within the otherwise chaotic Rouge household. It enabled her to control access to her room, even when she was away at work. This padlock, however extreme a measure it might seem to outsiders, was perhaps the only effective boundary checkpoint within a household otherwise devoid of boundaries. Without it and without the emotional controls she placed on herself and on other members of the family when they approached her, she might never have been free to move in and out of the house as she wished or to escape the intricate web of pathology and disablement her family had woven to prevent any of its members from leaving.

Subsequently the Sempers, who were observed late in the study, convinced us of the primacy of distance and space—both actual and metaphorical. Mrs. Semper and her ten-year-old son Charles were caught up in a pattern of mutually invasive moves that neither they nor Mr. Semper were able to alter. One set of invading behaviors centered around the bathroom. Despite Charles' protests his mother would consistently enter the bathroom when her son was inside. When he took to locking the door, she would bang on it until he opened it. She would then give him a tongue lashing about the danger of locking the door, saying that if he should hit his head and knock himself out, she wouldn't be able to come in and rescue him. As a consequence of this and literally hundreds of other events in various households, in which members attempted to put distance—both psychological and actual—between themselves and others in the family, the conviction that space is the key variable in the investigation of families gradually crystallized. Once it did, we were able to examine data from the clinical and research families, as well as from our own families, with a fresh outlook. We began to ask ourselves two key questions, questions we attempt to answer in the rest of the book: *How does a family set up and maintain its territory? How does it regulate distance among its own members?*

The crucial relevance of space should not have escaped us for so long. A newborn infant's first experiences are its spatial relationships to its immediate environment. Its first language, or efforts at communication, are founded on attempts to cope with and respond to those relationships. When the baby cries and its mother comes near, when it cries and no one comes near, when the child's body collides with another object (whether it be the mother's breast or the side of the crib), the child is immersed in the developmental task of distinguishing inner and outer space, a task requiring a vocabulary of spatial terms. Long after such spatial orientations have been internalized, a cognitive language emerges. When it has developed, the first or spatial lexicon recedes in conscious importance. Yet, it remains a dominant force in its own right, concomitant to verbal behavior. It is governed by its own dynamics and has its own tensions and resolutions. The spatial idiom, we believe, is also a language of the future. Man has demonstrated the technological capacity to enter and explore outer space, yet ours is a space age in another sense as well. Western societies are becoming increasingly aware of psychological and intimate social spaces and are developing vocabularies to understand such inner spaces.

We believe spatial constructs are becoming more prominent

in the evolution of ideas about man, his development, and his behavior. The developmental psychologist Jean Piaget has investigated space as a central aspect of individual perception and cognition (Piaget and Inhelder, 1956). The psychiatrist Richard Rabkin (1970), in his theory of social psychiatry, has stressed the dynamics of inner and outer space and developed a model for locating and treating emotional pathology outside the patient's body in his interactions with other people. The anthropologist Edward Hall (1966, p. 1) has coined the term "proxemics" to describe the study of man's use of space as an elaboration of culture. Ethologists such as Niko Tinbergen (1964) and Konrad Lorenz (1962) have studied the phenomena of territoriality in animals and suggested numerous implications for human behavior. The culture is indebted to all of these men for identifying and discussing the importance of space to social issues. Our own innovation has been to recognize that spatial dimensions are particularly useful in studying and classifying social units, such as the family. Using the spatial metaphor as our guide, we have developed a comprehensive descriptive theory of family process, which we will elaborate in the following chapters.

⸕⸕⸕⸕⸕⸕⸕⸕⸕⸕⸕⸕⸕⸕⸕⸕

Chapter 2

A Systems Approach

What we are offering in this book is a cybernetic-like model for understanding family process. Each succeeding chapter is concerned with an aspect of this model, or a set of issues to which the model can be applied. In this chapter we lay the conceptual groundwork for our presentation by introducing some general systems concepts. The first of these is the concept of system itself. We believe that any workable theoretical presentation of family behavior such as we are attempting can be greatly advanced by the idea that the family needs to be understood as a system. The second is the specific systems concept of feedback control. Feedback concepts are proving to be the most useful tool for understanding the nature and outcome of various communications and interactions that take place among family members. The third is our concept of strategies. With the introduction of this concept, we place our observations of systematic interactions into a more humanistic framework. By focusing on family strategies, we seek to identify how real people in real families conduct their lives.

The Family as a "System"

The concept of process is virtually coterminous with the concept of system. To describe what we mean by "family process," therefore, we need first to clarify what we mean by "system." As does Buckley (1967, p. 41), we understand a system to be a set of different things or parts (such as electrical components, machines, or people) that meet two requirements: first, these parts are directly or indirectly related to one another in a network of reciprocal causal effects, and second, each component part is related to one or more of the other parts of the set in a reasonably stable way during any particular period of time. We are most interested in social systems. The chief characteristic of such systems is an almost continuous interchange not only within the system, but across the boundary between the inner environment and the outer environment. Given this understanding of system, process can then be described as the actions and interactions of the various component parts of a system both within and across its environmental borders. The process model we are presenting views the activity of the family as a complex interplay of systemic structures and forces which elaborate and change in response to both internal and external phenomena. Taking a suggestion from Buckley's work on the evolution of systems theory (1967), we contend that *family systems, like all social systems, are organizationally complex, open, adaptive, and information-processing systems.* Let us now survey each of the items in this statement.

Family systems are organizationally complex. This is a concept fundamental to most systems thinking. Buckley defines organized complexity as "a collection of entities interconnected by a complex net of relations"; he distinguishes this concept from *organized simplicity*—"a complex of relatively unchanging components linked by a strict sequential order or linear additivity"—and from *chaotic complexity,* a vast number of components that do not have to be specifically identified and whose interactions can be described "as forming no coherent pattern other than those associated with the probabilities of absolute chance" (1967, p. 38). In stating that families are organizationally complex, we are asserting that families evolve networks of interdependent causal relations which are governed primarily by the mechanisms of feedback control. In other words, the component parts of a family system are neither fixed and unchanging nor chaotically organized; rather, the relations among the component parts of family systems are circular, that is, reciprocally influencing. The parts themselves, though identifiable in character and determinate in number, can be elaborated or changed in response to forces in the environment.

Family systems are open systems. Mechanical and biological systems are either closed or relatively closed systems. Families and other social groupings are more open systems. That a system is "open" means "not simply that it interchanges with the environment, but that this interchange is an *essential factor* underlying the system's viability, its reproductive ability or continuity, and its ability to change" (Buckley, 1967, p. 50). In other words, open systems manifest a great deal of two-directional traffic with the larger environment. It is clear that family systems share this experience. For purpose of analysis, a system's openness suggests that what is inside the system and what is outside can be redefined, depending upon what part of the system one is focusing on at any one time.

Family systems are adaptive. Closed mechanical systems tend to dissolve under the strain of environmental intrusion. Their functioning is maintained, therefore, by a sealing off of the environment. In contrast, open systems grow and develop as a consequence of their interchanges with the environment. Strain and tension are inevitable, but open systems do not necessarily dissolve, for they are capable of making changes, and of responding productively to stress whether it is internally or externally stimulated. In Chapters Nine and Ten we identify different types of open systems, each of which has its own process style for responding to the strain inherent in the open-system condition, which is one of frequent interchanges with the environment.

Family systems are information-processing systems. The fact that open systems can elaborate and/or change their action patterns and structure is due to the information-processing capabilities inherent in the open type of system. Informational interchange is selectively mapped and coded in families and other complex social systems. It is a principle fundamental to the analysis of systems that as one moves from mechanical systems to more complex open systems, the emphasis shifts away from the flow of energy required by the component parts of the system in order to interrelate, and toward the transmission of information. The information transmitted "is not a substance or concrete entity, but rather a 'relationship' between sets or ensembles of structured variety" (Buckley, 1967, p. 47). The significance of this shift from energy flow to information flow is that a small amount of energy or matter from one component part of the system can set off a large amount of activity or behavior in other components. This "triggering" effect seems "to overcome limitations of temporal and spatial proximity as well as availability of energy," a way of saying that the component individuals of such systems "need come into physical contact in a manner of mechanical systems only or principally in sexual union and physical combat." The structure of an information processing system "becomes more and more 'fluid' as it merges with process—the communication process which is its predominant feature" (Buckley, 1967, p. 48). On the basis of our intensive empirical observation of families in their natural setting, we feel confident in asserting that *the information processed by the family system is distance-regulation information.* We believe that family systems seek to attain their goals by continuously informing their members what constitutes a proper or optimal distance as relationships among members, and between members and specific events, become established and fluctuate. In Chapter Four we present a model demonstrating the simultaneous transmission of six different kinds of distance-regulation information.

Feedback and Family Communications

The key systems concept for our purposes, the one to which the preceding four concepts all point (and, we think, the major contribution of systems theory to all social theory), is that of the feedback loop. Systems theory asserts that complexly organized, open, and adaptive information-processing systems are purposive and goal seeking, unlike their counterparts, the mechanical systems. The basic principle underlying such purposive or goal-seeking activity is feedback, a process by which a system informs its component parts how to relate to one another and to the external environment in order to facilitate the correct or beneficial execution of certain system functions. Social scientists have long employed the concept of an open-loop causal chain to illustrate the position that the effect (behavior) depends on the cause (stimuli), but not the reverse. More recently, the idea of a closed-loop causal chain has evolved: it differs from the traditional open-loop concept in that it describes behavior as one of the causes of that same behavior. It asserts that matters of cause and effect can be traced all the way around a closed loop. Not only does effect depend on cause, but cause is equally dependent on effect. The *feedback loop*, including its component parts, is a refinement of the concept of a closed-loop causal chain.

Figure 1 is a modified version of a prototypic feedback loop as proposed by William T. Powers (1973, p. 352), following the work of Norbert Wiener (1948). It shows how a signal is processed

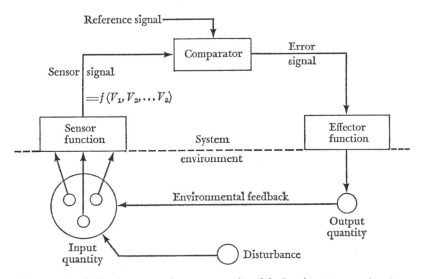

FIGURE 1. A basic control-system unit of behavioral organization.

through a feedback loop in a human behavior system. The loop begins when a stimulus, or disturbance, occurs in the social field, generating an input signal. Between this signal and its response, Powers suggests, a number of important operations take place. These operations are hypothetical constructions, because in reality they cannot be seen. Only the stimulus and response are seen. Nevertheless, Powers' diagram suggests how a particular stimulus or input signal sets in motion a system's response. The *sensor function* receives an input signal from the stimulus and transmits its own sensor signal on toward the system as a whole, alerting it to the quantity of the input signal. This sensor signal is then compared with a *reference signal* of unspecified origin, which states the system's desired state of regulation. The *system comparator* emits an error signal, which is based on the discrepancy between the sensor signal and reference signal. This error signal actuates the system's *effector function* to produce the system's response to the original stimulus in the social field. The output, a part of the environment, provides a feedback link to the input stimulus.

Systems theory asserts that both positive and negative feedback loops are necessary to the survival of any living system. A negative feedback loop is generally understood as an error-activating process designed to maintain constancy or a steady state in response to environmental alterations. The ordinary thermostat is often cited as the prime example of a negative feedback control system. A preferred temperature reading is set, so that the thermostat is required to activate heating equipment whenever the temperature falls too low, or cooling equipment when it climbs too high. In addition to maintaining structure, however, every living organism must at times change its basic structure and adapt to environmental change. Such adaptation is accomplished by the process of positive feedback loops, loops whose purpose is to amplify variety and deviation and either to maintain or increase system disequilibrium. Positive feedback loops therefore produce system mutations that are better able to respond to environmental change.

The terms "positive" and "negative" feedback loops are not as precise as one might like, especially if applied to family systems, within which positive rewards can be and are used to maintain constancy. For instance, an eldest son may be rewarded with an allowance for cleaning his room, taking out the garbage, or cutting the grass, all of which may be defined as his regular chores by the family. Are such positive rewards a part of a negative or a positive feedback loop? Their purpose is clearly that of a negative feedback loop, and yet a significant confusion of words is readily apparent. To eliminate this confusion we suggest that family analysts use the term "constancy feedback loops" in place of negative loops, and "variety feedback loops" in place of positive loops. This will allow us to talk about the constancy and variety feedback purposes of negative rewards without undue confusion.

Thus far we have been talking about the usefulness of systems concepts, particularly that of the feedback loop, for describing and explaining process in complex organizational structures. Our primary interest, of course, is family process. In order to describe and explain family process, we have developed a distance-regulation model in which the concept of feedback loops is applied to family interactions. Our model works in basically the same way as the feedback loop diagrammed in Figure 1, but we have identified the feedback loop signals associated with the entire family system as distance-regulation signals. In short, we contend that the principal activity of family process is distance regulation. Succeeding chapters elaborate in detail the component parts of the family system associated with each part of the feedback loop distance-regulation model. The basic components of our model of family process are the subsystems, the target and access dimensions, the mechanisms, the typal design, and the interactional player parts. In general, our concepts of subsystems and the access dimensions and mechanisms correspond to the sensor signal, the target goals to the reference signal, typal design to the comparator, and the four-part interactional model to the effector function of the feedback loop illustrated in Figure 1. As shown in the succeeding chapters, each of these parts reveals a special aspect of the total distance-regulation process.

Strategies: Interactions in Context

As theoretically sound and informative as the systems process and feedback loop concepts are, they remain general and rather abstract. To bring our model of distance regulation down to earth, we need to talk about family strategies, the recurring patterns of interactional sequences. Strategies emerge whenever two or more people are living in the same social field. They are evolved by the persons in that field to regulate and shape the relationships between and/or among themselves. Similarly, strategies emerge in the family for the same purpose. The concept of strategies allows us to link the principles of systems process with phenomenological reality—the reality people feel as they experience everyday family life. It permits us to extend the concept of distance regulation into the field of palpable family interactions. Strategies thus provide a vehicle for studying relations rather than structures. Because they comprise process, transition, and change in flexible structures, strategies provide a means for looking at the dynamics of family behavior.

Our concept of strategies starts with the conceptualization of the "act" as part of the basic interaction process of family. We define an act as a manipulation of the environment that has "meaning" only in terms of context (formally defined or not) and others (whether they are present or not). In short, we restrict our consideration of acts to social acts, executed in participation with others. Although we recognize that every social act has a private aspect concealed within the individual and thus inaccessible to others, this private aspect does not concern us here. What does concern us is that a social act functions simultaneously as a signal to others, a response to an antecedent signal, and a signal to the self. In other words, the social act is not an isolated event, but a relation taking place in a specific field of shared experience, one of six fields, or dimensions, which we identify in Chapter Four. Within these dimensional fields, the family actions that emerge can be viewed as processes of feedback control that are in fact methods of distance regulation—that is, the manipulation of objects, events, and individuals in order to increase or modify associations, or "distances," between one another.

The social acts we are primarily interested in take place in families in which the behavior of members has become truly interdependent. The unmistakable reality of this interdependence is the empirical basis for viewing family system behavior as consisting not only of acts or actions, but of interactions as well. The interactional approach to family process and family strategies is founded on the notion that all actions and interactions in families subsist in multiple-part systems, each part producing the contextual ground for the other and vice versa. As we shall see in Chapters Eleven and Twelve all family members contribute behaviors to keep an interactional sequence of events going. Even an observer is a contributor and may be a central player in a continuing sequence as long as he or she is defined as part of the action field. Thus, the "act" for us refers to the act of acting on, the act of taking in, and any other event that is felt by those participating in the sequence to be a potential source of subsequent action.

A sequence is a series of acts and interactions. The more extensively families are observed, the greater the variability that is perceived in the acts and interactions they display. When acts and interactions are observed in sequences, their variability declines somewhat as they arrange themselves into patterns or uniformities that can be seen to repeat themselves. These recurring patterns of interactional sequences are the strategies. Thus, the identification of a strategy gives definition to the series of acts and interactions constituting an interactional sequence. The beginning, the end, and the theme of a sequence is demarcated by the particular strategy being employed. A strategy can be seen but not always comprehended by an outsider, for only when the pattern of movement, or the relationship of acts, is perceived can the strategy itself be known. To the uninitiated observer, a series of strategic acts may appear to be unrelated. Indeed, many strategic movements go unnoticed even by the participants who are directly caught up in them. In particular, nonverbal exchanges might not be noticed or understood, nor would those actions occurring when the strategy is the sequence itself. Such a strategy might dictate that a son not speak before his mother, who is in turn not allowed to speak before her husband.

It is not always an easy task to determine the beginning, end, theme, or goal of a specific strategy. Different behavioral sequences often overlap, making it difficult to determine the precise starts and stops of particular strategic interactions. A second difficulty is posed by the fact that not all strategies are played through to their conclusion. A strategy may be aborted at any point in the course of its sequence. A third difficulty is raised by the lapsing of time within sequences. This kind of problem occurs in those strategies in which the acts that follow each other in sequence do not occur in immediate succession, but only after significant periods of time have elapsed. Despite these difficulties, a sensitive observer will discover behavioral sequences whose patterns are repeated again and again in a family's life. It is through the observation of such repetitions of sequence that one usually begins to recognize a family's typical movement patterns. Indeed, strategies that do not produce frequent sequence repetitions are usually not very significant.

We define a family strategy as a purposive pattern of moves toward a target or goal made by two or more people who are systematically bound in a social-biological arrangement. This is not to suggest that family members behave like automatons or even like football players who know exactly how they are to execute their maneuvers at the snap of a ball. Such tightly structured relationships occur rather infrequently in the family. Neither do we mean to imply that family strategies are inherently legitimate or are consented to by all, or even any, of a family's members. It is clear that institutionalized patterns must be recognized as including deviant and maladaptive values and operations as well as worthy ones. What we do mean to suggest is that family strategies are patterns generated by the family, which both family members and sensitive observers can recognize as important to family purposes, because they manifest themselves in various recurring contexts. Some people think of the term "strategy" as referring to individual motivations. Many others use it only in reference to relations between adversaries. Our concept of family strategies is much more complex and subtle. We believe that family strategies, whatever their specific intent, manifest the following five basic features.

Family strategies are purposive. Though not necessarily rational themselves, strategies function in a rational framework. They have a purpose, a reason for being. As such they cannot be logically separated from the family's goal structure. Rather, they are the family's intentional means (that is, "intentional" at some kinesic, motoric, or cognitive level) for implementing its goals.

Family strategies are accompanied by members' awareness of such strategies (systemic awareness). Observation has demonstrated that members respond to each other's verbal and nonverbal cues in reasonably predictable ways, a fact that leads us to believe that members know at some kinesic, motoric, or cognitive level the parts they are expected to play in family strategies. Even though they can't always label the parts they play, they feel compelled to play them. "I can't help it, I have to do it," is a frequent explanation. We have noted that when we point out to family members their own strategic patterns, they usually acknowledge the validity of our observations. Such acceptance provides a marked contrast to members' frequent denials of observations about their motivations.

We do not mean to suggest that families always accept observations about their strategic patterns. Obviously they do not. Nevertheless, we believe that members' awareness of family strategies offers therapeutic practitioners a more fruitful avenue of exploration than does a preoccupation with deep-seated motivations, often removed phenomenologically from the reality of everyday affairs.

Family strategies are processes of collaboration. In our view of the family system, strategies involve the participation of all members, even those members who may be shamed or harmed by the strategy. Even strategies which feature competition and conflict remain collaborative, because each member either voluntarily or involuntarily agrees to play his part. Even if a member refuses to play the part assigned to him or opposes the pattern of moves associated with the strategy, his participation can still be viewed as collaborative, providing his refusal or his opposition fails to alter the strategic pattern of moves. Only when refusal or opposition successfully modifies or changes strategic movements do the movements cease to be systematically collaborative. On such occasions, of course, the other members collaborate with the new strategy.

Family strategies entail shared responsibilities for their outcomes. The individually oriented family observer will often focus his attention on processes of scapegoating and victimization. Though we accept the validity of such observations, we would also assert that the scapegoat shares a systemic responsibility for his vicitimization. We do not introduce the concept of shared responsibility as a moral responsibility but as a strategic phenomenon, because we believe that victimhood is itself an aspect of process, that is, one part in an overall strategic pattern. From the systems point of view, we affirm the reciprocal nature of controls. Systems control individuals, but individuals, in turn, control systems. It is within this framework that we suggest that all family members share some responsibility for family strategies.

Family strategies allow for contingencies in the playing of parts. The "contingencies" inherent in the strategic process are of three types. Contingency number one is that an individual is usually free to vary his movements as an active agent in a complex and ongoing event. For instance, a strategy may require a family player to say "no" to another player, and yet permit him to move in a number of different ways provided he executes the "no" requirement. The second contingency is that there are degrees of freedom in the interrelations of parts. For example, two players may interchangeably execute the same move in a family strategy. In other strategies, various parts may be eliminated without alteration of the basic pattern of movements. A third and final contingency exists in the freedom to decide *not* to play the parts or to make the moves assigned by a strategy. In other words members can oppose and alter family strategies. The conditions under which such strategic change can occur varies from system to system as well as from one period of time to another one within the same system.

We believe that all family strategies are designed, at least initially, to enable members to achieve the goals they seek. As we all know, however, families do not always succeed in fulfilling their purposes. Indeed, in their moment-to-moment strategic responses, a disabling chasm between what is sought and what is actually experienced can appear. This discrepancy between the ideal and the actual illustrates a very important truth about strategies. In all strategies, individual as well as collective, something is risked in order to gain something else. Feelings of guilt, shame, loss, frustration, and depression can accompany repeated strategic failure. Strategic success, on the other hand, can and does generate feelings of pride, acceptance, security, and confidence. Given these stakes, the risks inherent in social strategies can be very great indeed.

Though a multitude of different strategies are potentially available to a family system, all of them may be identified as belonging to one of three basic classifications: maintenance, stress, and repair. On an abstract, theoretical level, these three strategic categories represent different possible types of relationships among the component parts of a social system. Strategies of maintenance preserve the relationship of parts as is. The structure of the system is believed to be worthy of preserving by the proponents of maintenance strategies. However, tension among the parts is a natural condition of life for social organisms. The family is no exception. Through its boundaries, new inputs are constantly being admitted for processing. Pushes and pulls on the interrelationship of parts is the inevitable result. Strategies of stress accentuate and accelerate this tension and occasionally push the family's relationship of parts into confusion and turmoil. Systems may intentionally generate stress, usually in the form of a competition for goals. Normally, what is intended is a period of stress followed by a natural recovery, but a continuing acceleration of stress can and does occur. Strategies of repair offer the family a chance to modify itself in order to remain a liveable, workable system, responsive to members' needs, particularly when maintenance strategies preserve self-destructive activities, or when strategies of stress continue to accelerate to such an extent that all chance for natural recovery is eliminated. Repair strategies thus alter or reconstruct the relationship of parts, a necessity occurring from time to time if the family, or any social system, is to survive in a world of rapidly changing realities.

All three types of strategies are complex distance-regulating operations and as such are essential to an operational understanding of family process. If one hopes to compile a comprehensively complete and detailed portrait of a single family, one must identify and analyze its strategies. In order to analyze a strategy thoroughly, however, one has to examine its many distance-regulation features. In actual experience all of the features of a strategy may appear to be blended together since they occur simultaneously. In Chapters Three, Four, Eight, Ten, and Twelve of this book, however, we will examine a small number of strategies, extract and analyze a specific feature of each strategy, and demonstrate how it can be illuminated by an understanding of the various component parts of our family-system model. Each part is itself a system of parts, and the whole a system of systems. Likewise, each strategy contains a number of different features, each of which helps illuminate a different part or component of the total family system. The reason for including our comments on strategies is that, although we have one family system model, we have two quite different descriptive statements to make, one theoretical and the other operational. These comments allow us to make an operational statement at each stage of our theoretical model until we bring the two threads to culmination in Chapter Thirteen.

In summary, our distance-regulation model constitutes a comprehensive descriptive approach to the subject of family. Its analysis of family process relies on the concepts of systemic control, feedback—the primary ingredient in the systems notion of organizational process—and family strategies as a means for labeling systemic interactions. Our model of family is not limited to the concepts of systems theory, however. Its development has been equally influenced by observations of families in both clinical and natural contexts. The contribution we hope to make toward a universally acceptable model of family systems derives from the interplay of these two sources.

Chapter 3

Three Subsystems

Many family analysts make the mistake of taking a part of the family system and treating it as the whole. Like the three blind men who try to describe an elephant to each other, researchers and clinicians have focused on different aspects of family life, and, on the basis of data pertaining to these particular aspects, tried to describe and define what families as a whole are like. In this chapter we introduce the first component of our descriptive theory. In essence, we propose that *the family system is composed of three subsystems that interact with each other as well as with the world outside: these are the family-unit subsystem, the interpersonal subsystem, and the personal subsystem.* Although it may seem a luxury to investigate operations within each of the subsystems and at their touching points, one can be seriously misled unless he does so or, at the very least, recognizes that he should. It is precisely because families tend to vary their style of organization from subsystem to subsystem that the formulation of conclusions about the whole based on the examination of a few parts can be hazardous. This chapter, then, is more than an attempt to describe a family's subsystems: it is an injunction that families must be studied in full.

Interface Phenomena

A discussion of subsystems invariably entails a discussion of interface phenomena. An interface is a meeting ground of two or more systems or subsystems, each with its own boundary, each with its own set of interrelated parts, and each with its own rules and metarules for governing how its parts are to work in various contexts. Interface experience becomes meaningful only when at least one system or subsystem recognizes that it is in a meeting ground with another system or subsystem. Once such recognition is made, each system's traffic can be regulated in relation to the traffic of the other system, particularly as each system's members see what they might gain from members of another system or transmit to them. Meetings at interface thus result in a shaping and reshaping of each unit's space, including the thickness of its boundary walls. Those inside each unit use their experiences in meeting members of another unit to define who and what they are as a unit among other units. In this way, interface always provides a system with information about the differences and similarities between it and another system. Let us illustrate one type of interface—that of the family-unit subsystem and the exterior world.

As the Orange family moves into its new neighborhood, it encounters a complex set of ongoing social conditions and institutional arrangements. At the interface of their family-unit subsystem with the outside world, family members become aware of how the new neighborhood differs from their previous one. The location of such institutions as the library, gymnasium, school, and town center are discovered and mapped out for future reference. So, too, are people in the neighborhood. Conversely, those already living in the community begin to assess the newcomers. The mailman who passes their house each morning, the kids on the corner looking into the backyard, and the local welcome wagon committee all get a good look at them. Both neighbors and the new family cue each other, signaling certain persons to come closer and informing others to remain at a distance. Before long, the relations between the family and its new community begin to crystallize. Family members become receptive to certain elements in their new culture and unreceptive to others. Likewise, various members of the community are attracted to different family members for different reasons.

As we can see from the preceding example, the conditions of interface create the necessity for two or more systems to develop strategies for interacting with one another. Within the operations of such strategies, the interactions of a given interface really take place. Once each system has recognized and analyzed both its own and the other system's cultural patterns and images, its members must decide whether they want to approach or avoid the other system and its members. Under normal social conditions, an outsider cannot enter the family's space until a boundary decision is made to admit him. Thus, for each system the following questions arise: Shall we admit members of another system into our own? Do we wish to gain admission into theirs? If so, on what terms? And how fast? Toward what ends? Each member must decide to what portions of the other system he wishes to gain access, and, correspondingly, what access to his own system's life he wishes to grant outsiders. The parents in the Orange family, for instance, might choose to invite their new neighbors into their house, but only for small, informal dinner parties on specific evenings rather than for whole days, and might never suggest joint excursions into the town.

In Chapter Two we introduced our concept of the spatial metaphor. The metaphor is a useful device for resolving the confusion that can so easily arise between the *architectural* boundaries of a household and the *social-space* perimeter of a family. The two often overlap since families use the structural boundaries of their apartment, house, or backyard fence to establish and maintain their metaphoric social perimeter, but they need not be identical. The figurative boundaries that a family imposes are nowhere more apparent than on occasions when the family leaves its household. Whether on a picnic, at a ballgame, or out fishing along a stream, families signal those around them just how close others may come, sit, or pitch a tent before trespassing on the family's "territory." Though there are no physical walls to block one's entrance in such instances, the sense of bounding out and binding in is nevertheless evident.

People, families, and cultures have their own characteristic ways of dealing with both the physical and metaphoric walls of their systems and subsystems. Many families seek to regulate the outsider's approach by checking his credentials, that is, his legitimacy or fitness to negotiate entrance. They in effect say, "Hold on. Back up. Approach more slowly." In another kind of family, an outsider can feel a little like a trespasser because he has been inducted into a family's social space without any negotiation, perhaps even without his own intention. Important signals can be transmitted by the physical perimeter itself. Peepholes, cameras, and other unfriendly apparatus tend to signal the approaching visitor that he barely has a right to knock on the door, that, merely by standing before it, he is violating family territory. At the other extreme, whether by means of a literal sign or a decorative design, a perimeter passageway can say, "Come on in. Sit down. Amuse yourself." Still other doorways announce by means of a handsome knocker or bell that an outsider has a right to ask for entrance, but admission may not be granted.

Once inside the family perimeter, the outsider remains a stranger to the interpersonal system within the family. The fact that he has been admitted into the family unit's space does not mean that everything within is accessible to him. Rather, the outsider must discover what his new prerogatives are within the family's interior subsystems. More specifically, he must locate the boundary of the next subsystem, the family's interpersonal subsystem. The boundary of this subsystem is even more abstract than the family-unit perimeter tends to be, but is no less real. Patients of physicians and therapists who have offices in their homes know this phenomenon well. Even if patients must walk through the household to get to the doctor's office and, in so doing, meet members of the family, they are excluded from the interpersonal system of the family. Normally, no one invites or expects them to participate in activities or relationships among family members. Clients in this position find themselves passing through a family's social intraspace, that is, the space between the family perimeter and the boundaries of its interpersonal system.

Official visitors of all kinds (salesmen, estimators, political volunteers) are usually confined to this social intraspace, neither visitor nor family expecting anything more than to conduct some piece of intersystem business. However, another kind of official visitor can place considerable stress on family, especially poor families: for example, a welfare worker or social worker enters the social intraspace by legal decree rather than by the usual route of social negotiation, and begins to demand access to the family's interpersonal system. Strain may also be placed on a family by such visitors as grandparents and in-laws who have at one time been intimately related with one or more members of the family and now seek to regain such interpersonal contact during a short visit. Such relatives may be kept inside the family intraspace, but be prevented from reviving an interpersonal relationship with their "loved ones," because the family (or at least one of its members) fears conflicts would arise if a more interpersonal relationship were available.

Visitors who seek admission to the interpersonal subsystem experience a period of "prenegotiation" while they reside inside the family's social intraspace. A new interface ring is defined by both family and visitor. Largely by a transmission of images and nonverbal metacommunications, but also by direct verbal communication, family members both assess their visitor and begin to transmit cues of their own, defining the social range in which that person is to be permitted to roam. In order to gain further access, the visitor must first locate the boundaries, or metaphoric walls, of the interpersonal system and then find a way to cross them. The layout of these walls varies from family to family.

In one family pattern we have observed, the family-unit perimeters and those of the interpersonal subsystem are almost spatially identical. Thus a visitor, upon gaining access to the family space, is invited to enter the interpersonal system as well. In effect, the family says, "Come in. Here we are. Know us." Such families virtually eliminate the social intraspace. In a second pattern, the interpersonal subsystem is diffuse in shape. The metaphorical outside wall of this kind of interpersonal subsystem is difficult to find. In effect, the family says, "Since you happen to be here, find us. If you can." Members of such an interpersonal subsystem move around a lot and may be absent at strategic times. Their relationship is often unclear. As a result, the visitor may not be sure whether he is occupying the social intraspace or whether he has stumbled into the family's interpersonal subsystem. Such a space without walls, where walls are culturally expected, can be highly disorienting to the outsider. In a third pattern or layout we have identified, the wall around the interpersonal subsystem is clearly delineated. Upon entering such a family, the visitor may very quickly locate the interpersonal subsystem's walls, which he recognizes as thick and initially impregnable. The family's signals can be interpreted as, "Here we are. There you are. You may enter by invitation only." The size of the social intraspace is clearly marked in such a family as are the options of what a visitor is allowed and not allowed to do. Admission to the interpersonal sphere is rare and difficult to attain. Not all families present interface consistency, however. Process variants can and do appear from one interface to another. For instance, in a commune visited by the senior author, one could enter the social and physical interior virtually at will. Yet, life went on around one, keeping one out of the commune's interpersonal subsystem. In effect, the commune said, "You have a right to be here, but we have no obligation to entertain you."

Intraspace negotiation can be even more important for family members than it is for outsiders. When a family member places himself in the position of being inside the family perimeter but outside the interpersonal subsystem, he establishes for himself a different experiential domain from that of other members. A member who encamps himself in the intraspace can become a source of frequent irritation for the family as a whole, leading other members to identify him as "the stranger," "the outsider," "the different one," or even "the crazy one." The intraspace member then has to decide whether he agrees or disagrees with the family's label of his behavior. Not all members stay in the family intraspace by choice. They can be maneuvered there by their families and kept in a position in which they are not allowed either to leave the system or to participate in its interpersonal activities. Such deliberate relegation can be both traumatic and disorienting for an individual. We believe that the confinement of individuals within the social intraspace is a potential source of serious emotional disorder. What we are suggesting is that "madness" can be an index of disjunction in social situations. When either an individual or a family system feels that its relationship with the other has been somehow disrupted, it usually follows that the dislocated party will feel cut off from the experiential field and communication code of the other. The result is that each can be mystified by the other. From a theoretical standpoint, then, the intraspace concept suggests a systemic framework for understanding processes of "mystification" as identified by R. D. Laing (1969).

Once the boundaries of the interpersonal subsystem are located, the visitor can begin to negotiate for position, and so can the subsystem he seeks to enter. Here, as at the perimeter, strategies for regulating access emerge. Persons on both sides of the interpersonal interface must ask themselves certain questions: "How close do we really want to get to each other? How much time do we want to spend together? Do we really like the other person(s)? Do we feel comfortable together? Is (s)he the kind of person we want to be associated with? What do we have to gain?" These questions at the family-unit–interpersonal interface are similar to the kinds of questions asked at the family perimeter. They vary, however, in that at this interface the issues of admission are more closely tied to the goals both sides seek to attain. There is usually more at stake. Also issues and responses are constantly being reformulated as both sides go about the business of negotiating access. Most of us have had the experience of finding another social group attractive as we approached them only to find out that, as we moved closer, their behavior made them far less appealing, and compelled us to alter our course.

An important distinction must be made between the interpersonal subsystem as a whole and the personal subsystems of the individuals who group together to form and maintain it. Each person in an ongoing interpersonal subsystem leads a kind of double life, one as "member" and the other as "self." It is important for guests, researchers, and therapists who seek access to personal systems to keep this in mind, for the dual lives of "member" and "self" are experienced simultaneously. Expressed in another way, all members of an interpersonal subsystem share a collective responsibility for developing and maintaining their relationships. Yet each individual also has a responsibility to act in accordance with his own self-interests, meanings, and desires. Consequently, in response to any input contributed by a player to an ongoing interaction, it would be fair (and theoretically astute) for an observer to ask, "Is that action an expression of you as a member of your group or is it an expression of you as yourself?" In asking this question, one seeks to determine in which capacity an individual is primarily acting at any one time. A visitor or, for that matter, a therapist who has gained access to the family's interpersonal realm and now wishes to approach an individual member must learn to distinguish which part of the individual's behavior is group behavior and which part is unique to the individual himself. The family member—from his position on the interface of the interpersonal subsystem and his own personal subsystem—must in turn try to decide whether the visitor is approaching him as a person (including that aspect of himself that does not belong to the group), or approaching him solely as a member of the group. Both visitor and member can become very confused, and it is possible to interpret a set of behaviors one way when in fact they have been intended in the other.

The following example may help to illuminate the way in which such confusion on the interface of the interpersonal and personal subsystems arise. Let us assume that a male college student named Tom is visiting his roommate Bill Green's family for a holiday weekend. One evening Tom and the whole Green family—parents, roommate, sister, and kid brother—play a frolicsome game of Monopoly. Throughout the game Tom and his roommate's sister Joy, who is sitting next to him, engage in a running banter and repartee. Indeed, the entire family seems to enjoy a similar style of interaction. All present help provide Tom with anecdotes about the family's private life, including certain aspects of its sexual life. Afterwards, as Tom finds himself sitting alone with Joy by the fire, he notices she has "cooled" toward certain of his behaviors which earlier, as a member of her family, she had helped sanction. In particular, she no longer seems to find certain of his stories and innuendos funny. She starts to leave for her room. When Tom tries to follow, she suggests he would be "ever so much more comfortable by the fire."

Another type of interface confusion occurred at the initial meeting between the adult members of one of our research families and a staff interviewer. The interviewer's task was to recruit the Baxter family for study and to devise a contract that would be agreeable to both family and research staff: After some very brief social amenities, the interviewer was invited into the adults' interpersonal subsystem for a discussion of just how the processes of that subsystem functioned, particularly in respect to family decision making. The interviewer was very careful not to take the side of any one person in the conflicts of the interpersonal subsystem, trying as much as possible to stay in his official position as mediator at the family perimeter. When it became time for each adult to give his or her consent to the research proposition, the wife, who had previously been "the holdout," said to the interviewer, "Hey, I really dig you!" The tone and various unspoken signals conveyed the implication, "Yes, I will consent to the research so long as you come into our household and live with us. Yes, especially if you sleep with me." Publicly, the interviewer ignored this communication, though he may have smiled at being found sexually desirable. Privately, he had to say to himself that he didn't understand what was going on except that the family seemed to be giving its consent to be studied. Only later did he fully realize that the wife was not treating him as a representative of a staff of family researchers, but as a man and a possible partner for sexual activity. In reality, she had been extending an invitation to him to come into her personal space. In subsequent discussions the other adults acknowledged their recognition and silent support of Mrs. Baxter's personal invitation.

Approach and negotiation of access to the personal system is always a two-way procedure. Both approacher and approachee cue the other as to the conditions under which access may be negotiated, in much the same way as they do at the interface of the family-unit and family-interpersonal subsystems. Again each party asks certain predictable questions of himself: "Is what the other person wants what I want? How much of myself do I really want to share with the other person? How highly does (s)he value me? How highly do I value him/her? Can I control and alter those parts of him/her I do not like and will not want? Are our styles for attaining intimacy compatible? Will my present life be enhanced? Is there any promise of a lasting future? Am I free to be me and make my private feelings known?" As these questions suggest, negotiation at the interpersonal-personal subsystem interface is concerned with gaining mutual access to goals that are even more important than those at the family unit-interpersonal subsystem interface.

Strategies at Interface

Thus far in this chapter we have been concerned with the three subsystems of family, and their interfaces with one another and with the world outside. We have drawn upon the spatial metaphor to describe the basic issues and experiences that occur at the touching points of two or more family subsystems. In order to keep the discussion as simple as possible, we have approached the subject of subsystem interface from the point of view of a visiting outsider, progressing from the quite public interactions to those occurring more deeply within the interior of the family. Family traffic, however, moves outward from the inside, as well as inward from the outside. The three concentric interface rings we have delineated call attention to the fact that *family activities involving one subsystem will at the same time involve at least one other subsystem. Consequently, in turning to the subject of family strategies, we find it necessary to think in terms of the simultaneous strategic interaction of two or more subsystems at interface.*

The different subsystems of family interact both cooperatively and competitively with one another: the personal with the interpersonal subsystem, the interpersonal with the unit subsystem, and the unit with various exterior systems. Other important interfaces include those of the interpersonal subsystem and the exterior, the personal subsystem and the exterior, and the personal and the unit subsystem. From these interactions a family develops strategies for delineating each subsystem's boundaries and goals. Intrasystem strain is usually the result of incompatible intent between two competing subsystems, each pursuing its own ends simultaneously. For example, a disabling symptom in a child might be precipitated by chronic parental disagreement (personal—interpersonal interface), which the child is required to monitor. It might also be a product of a change in neighborhood, and the new and unfamiliar peergroup demands (personal—exterior interface), or it could be a product of an overcrowded and chaotic household (personal—unit interface). In order to comprehend this kind of complexity, both family researchers and therapists will have to learn how to conceptualize and negotiate effectively at these various subsystem interfaces. Only then will they be able to understand the mutually causal effects of family interactions.

The following sequence illustrates this complexity: After dinner, Linda Weber, a fifteen-year-old girl who wishes she were eighteen announces that she is going out shopping and "won't be back until late." Mother replies, "You'll be back on time, young lady. Tonight's the night we set aside to see our vacation movies." Linda glances toward her father who turns away and says, "I think

Mother is right." Linda's younger sister Elise interjects, "Yeah, we wanta see our movies." "All right," Linda agrees rather unhappily. "I'll be back on time." She returns late, however, forcing a postponement of the movies. Mother says, "Since you don't know when to come home, you're grounded for the rest of the week."

This interaction takes place primarily at the personal-subsystem—unit-subsystem interface of the Weber family. It is clear from the narrative that both subsystems fail to attain the goals they seek. Linda loses her freedom, and the unit loses its sense of togetherness, largely because the unit and personal subsystem goals are in this instance discrepant. In order for one to be attained, the other must be disregarded, or at least compromised. Such discrepancies are an inevitable cause of strain and conflict in families, and a stimulant of claims and counterclaims about what the family as a whole and each of its members require. Righteous indignation about the obligation of one subsystem to sacrifice its goals for another, combined with a frustration over strategic compromises and impasses, not infrequently results in subsystem goal discrepancy.

One can also infer from the Weber sequence that the family's interpersonal subsystem is deeply involved in the interaction. This third subsystem seems to be split by various interpersonal coalitions. Father is attempting to be a good husband by publicly presenting a united parental front to their children, but he is also in a necessarily covert alliance with his daughter Linda, whose search for freedom he secretly applauds. Meanwhile, Mother's espousal of unit togetherness reflects her interpersonal effort to move emotionally closer to her older daughter. The sister is very sensitive to her mother's needs and does everything in her power to ally herself with her mother. Thus, to focus in this way on the interface of the personal and interpersonal subsystems helps to enlighten further the strategic sequence, and particularly the Weber family's covert or latent aims. Indeed, *distinguishing overtness and covertness usually means nothing more than a focusing on different subsystem interfaces, which, when done, makes manifest a system's latent or covert aims as well as its clearly announced ones.*

Therefore the concepts of subsystems and interfaces offer family analysts a working framework for discovering all of a family's aims and goals. This approach removes some of the pejorative and sinister connotation from the label "covert family processes" by suggesting that all family members, as a very function of their living in a family, simultaneously feel different and often conflicting subsystem allegiances.

It has been our experience, both in our research and in the therapy room, that all family strategies are originally devised with good intentions. We believe that each family strategy is developed to maintain or improve a family's functioning in a specific area. Yet somehow strategies often produce unforeseen and/or unintended results—"unforeseen" because disablement occurs in a section or sphere of the family other than that for which the strategy was developed, and "unintended" because the actual results are not the intended results. Therefore, we regard the destructive effects of family strategies as *ironic displacements*. We introduce this descriptive term to counter the tendency of professionals to formulate certain capsule generalizations: for example, that a "bad" mother or a "bad" father or a "bad" family has produced a disabled victim; or that a victim himself is "guilty" or "evil" because of his condition. We assert that such labels are a misrepresentation of reality and of the way in which systems actually operate. They are usually counterproductive as well in that they tend to arouse defensive denials by family members and thus prohibit them from altering course and developing new strategies. Needless to say, we do not mean to suggest that people do not do evil things to each other in families. Rather, we mean to assert that their moves initially have a benign goal, however disabling their ironic displacements.

A theorist or practitioner who concurs with our view of family as a complex multisystem will accept each subsystem's rationale for being the way it is. In the Weber example, Linda might be seen by some analysts as an oppressed victim or perhaps even a scapegoat of her family's strategy of presenting a united opposition. Other analysts might view the family as a system that is being denied its goals by an unresponsive holdout. In addition, Father could be seen as a weak betrayer, Mother as a selfish dominator of the entire family scene, and Elise as an inveterate follower of the party line. Each of these summations, in our view, represents a moral or quasi-moral judgment, and is founded on a misunderstanding of the complexity of family strategies. Those making such assessments focus on the unhappy outcome of actions and in part ascribe guilt retrospectively. Furthermore, they ignore what we regard as the benign intentions of each subsystem in the Weber family, especially the unit's search for togetherness and Linda's search for freedom and individuality. If we insist that the intentions of each subsystem were benign, how then do we explain the disabling outcome? First, we need to remind ourselves that strategic interactions take place at the interface of two or more subsystems. In the Weber family, the interaction is one between competing subsystems. Ironic displacements occur because families choose to pursue the goals of one subsystem and as a consequence sacrifice those of at least one other subsystem. Thus, in electing to advance unit togetherness, the Webers limit Linda's freedom. Ironically, they also lose the desired goal of togetherness, because in choosing this goal in the way they do, they prevent a voluntary and shared family gathering from occurring. By the end of the evening, the Weber family members are alienated from one another.

The notion of ironic displacement is based totally on the concept of a multiple system that we have presented in this chapter. Only by adhering to this concept does one begin really to understand family strategies and the complexity of family process that such strategies reflect. In sum, we believe that systemic interactions are at root interface phenomena that affect two or more subsystems of family simultaneously. To understand any process fully, then, one must recognize at which particular interfaces a given operation is taking place. Explanatory statements about family that do not identify the two or more subsystems affected by the operation are at best limited propositions and at worst misleading ones.

❦❦❦❦❦❦❦❦❦❦❦❦❦❦❦❦

Chapter 4

Access and Target Dimensions

In this chapter we present the second and third components of our theory of family process, the access and target components. In our conceptual model, the family has two sets of dimensions. The access dimensions describe and include the physical aspects of family members' quest for experience. They are the quantitative means through which members' need for safety and participation are actualized. The target dimensions describe and include the conceptual aspects of family members' quest for experience. They are the qualitative means through which members' need for specific life goals are thematically actualized. Before we get to a more detailed description of specific access and target dimensions, we need to define what we mean by the term "dimension." In our family system model, dimensions are physical and conceptual fields of interactional activity. Within these physical and/or conceptual fields, families regulate the activities of people, objects, and events. Each specific access and target dimension we delineate in our theory regulates a somewhat different category of social relationship. Taken together, these access and target relationships constitute the framework in which the totality of family process takes place.

Six-Dimensional Field

All family interactions involve issues of gaining or losing access to some target, be it person, object, or event. Every waking minute, but particularly those minutes we spend with our families, each of us is engaged in seeking, permitting, denying, or being denied access to one thing or another. In the material world, what we seek may be a pen or a dollar bill or a cold glass of beer. In the abstract what we seek are the targets of affect, power, and meaning. In whichever way we attempt to realize them, we all seek certain goals: (1) affect, that is, intimacy and nurturance—that sense of loving and being loved by someone in our world; (2) power, the freedom to decide what we want, and the ability to get it—whether it be money, goods, or skills; (3) meaning, or some kind of philosophical framework that provides us with explanations of reality and helps us define our identity—so that we glean a sense of who and what we are, and perhaps even who and what man is. These—the concepts of affect, power, and meaning—are the target dimensions, and they categorize conceptually all or nearly all the interactional behaviors manifested by family members as they move toward their target destinations. The target concepts are not the only factors of family process, however. The access dimensions of space, time, and energy are the physical media through which each family system marks off its pathways for attaining the targets it seeks. It is through these dimensions that access to targets is regulated. This then is our basic thesis. *Members of families gain access to targets of affect, power, and meaning through the way in which they and their families regulate the media of space, time, and energy.*

The totality of a family's experience takes place within these six dimensions of a family's social space, that is, its aggregate physical-conceptual field of interactional activity. In theoretical terms, social space is the enclosure within which family process takes place. Each of the six dimensions represents an aspect of this metaphoric family field. Usually, of course, family traffic spans at least one access dimension and one target dimension as when, for instance, Mother moves physically closer to Father in order to gain some affection from him.

Our model of family process addresses the basic problem confronting every family system: How do interacting individuals *regulate*—that is, assess, interpret, act upon, and check—the actions of people, things, and events in face-to-face social situations? In the course of pursuing a family's substantive and qualitative group goals, a theory of family process must also answer a correlate question: How do interacting individuals maintain a system of behavior among themselves and between themselves and the environment in response to both internal and external boundary strain? Our concept of distance regulation embraces the idea that a six-dimensional structure of family organization is constantly being called upon to maintain, repair, or reconstruct itself as it solves the problems of regulating traffic within and across various family boundaries. Using the feedback principle of distance regulation, we are able to conceptualize this six-dimensional structure of family as a complex informational field. Each dimension is not merely an abstract category but a field of complicated interactional processes in which mutual assessment of self, other, unit, and environment takes place.

Our notion of distance regulation encompasses the systems concepts of feedback loops, goal-seeking behavior, self-awareness, self-direction, and information processing. If we subscribe to recent systems thinking, it becomes clear that what distinguishes family systems from mechanical and biological systems is that "the relations among the parts are primarily psychic, involving complex communicative processes of information exchange" (Buckley, 1967, p. 43). We extend this idea, using the concept of distance regulation to show what specific kinds of signals the family system transmits in its problem solving, boundary maintaining assignments while directing traffic toward specific goals. More specifically, the concept of distance regulation can be used to explain the family system's complex and variable arrangements of association and dissociation, among persons, objects, and events within the six-dimensional field of family process. In short, the concept of distance regulation establishes the substance of family system organization. It is the mediating concept integrating the six dimensions of family process into a systemic relationship, as illustrated by Figure 2.

On the basis of the diagram, we can now revise our thesis as follows: *Through the transmission of matter and information via energy in time and space, family members regulate each other's*

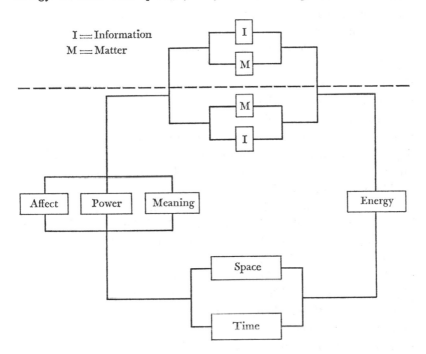

FIGURE 2. A self-regulating model of six dimensional goal seeking activity (after Larry L. Constantine, personal communication, 1974).

access to the targets of affect, power, and meaning. As the diagram shows, the matter (M) and information (I) that are transmitted may originate on either side of the dotted line, that is, either from within or outside the family. Whether verbal or nonverbal, the information transmitted has a distance-regulation signal attached to it. As used here, "information" refers not to content in and of itself, but to content about relationships between and among elements in specific fields. Generally speaking, matter in and of itself is of no importance to family process. It only becomes important when it is recognized as being relevant to some component part of family. For example, the planet Pluto might only become relevant to family interactions when the youngest child in a family, upon learning of its existence as the planet in our solar system farthest away from the sun, brags to some rather skeptical siblings that he intends to become an astronaut and explore it someday. As this example also suggests, every interactional event involving matter is at some level also an informational event. Since man is a conscious, thinking being, any movements by people and objects that he is aware of cannot help but generate some distance regulation information. The diagram also suggests that energy has a dual function in the transmission of distance-regulation information from one dimension to another, for information transmission is dependent upon the existence of some sort of carrier energy. Without such a carrier, even information about the energy dimension could not be transmitted.

Though all six dimensions of a family's social space are interrelated, those dimensions within each of the two major sets of dimensions bear a special relationship to one another. The access dimensions—space, time, and energy—are the spheres of activity in which family process takes place. Without space there can be no place for an event; without time, no sequence; without energy, no vitality. These three, then, are the media in and through which families move. They are initially experienced at boundary, at the edge of a system or subsystem, especially when that system meets or interacts with another system or subsystem. It is at boundary that the three access dimensions regulate traffic between two or more systems, between two or more subsystems, or between a system and a subsystem. When one system or subsystem approaches another, it immediately encounters the spatial, temporal, and energic rhythms of the other system, rhythms which must be taken into account in regulating access. Mother and baby learn to anticipate each other's rhythms very early in their life together as nursing takes place to meet the hunger needs of the newborn child. Also, fathers and children, brothers and sisters, husbands and wives, siblings and friends, families and communities all learn to anticipate each other's rhythms, for unless people manage to occupy the same social field, spend time together, and devote energies to the same activities, they cannot hope to develop suitable conjoint affect, power, and meaning targets. Let us now examine each of the six dimensions in turn.

Space

Each subsystem of family has to negotiate two kinds of spaces—interior spaces and exterior spaces, that is, inside areas and outside areas. Traffic goes out and comes in, and it is regulated in some fashion by the family and its subsystems. Basically, the question on space that a family has to answer for itself is twofold. First, how does it develop, defend, and maintain its system and subsystem territories? Second, how does it regulate distance among its own members? To return to the first question on territory, each family must determine the extent to which its members can feel safe within the system's social space. This issue assumes a particular resonance at the family perimeter and outside it in the exterior space. Often, a family will attempt to create a safety zone in which family members can move without having to fear harm. Backyards, driveways, sidewalks, courtyards, and even streets may constitute the actual physical space of such a safety zone, as long as these areas can be easily patrolled and defended either by the family or its community representatives.

An examination of the safety zone can reveal much about a family's relationship with its community, because within the safety zone, a regulation of the distances between system members and outsiders takes place. The community or outer system learns how close it can come to a family without violating the smaller system's sense of territory, while the members of the small system learn how far they can go outside the perimeter into the world and still feel protected by the family. For many families, the zone of safety may not extend very far. Some inner city families, for instance, have the sense of being unable to defend any space outside their walls. Others fear they will not even be able to defend the household space within those walls, should the criminal elements of the community desire to break in. Those who live on farms or suburban estates may have radically different experiences. Whereas the inner city family may feel impinged upon and crowded, the rural or suburban family may feel isolated. In addition to the actual physical circumstances, the community's view of the family, the family's view of the world outside, and the family's means of regulating access to and from this outer world can each affect the size and quality of a family's safety zone. These three variables may dictate the manner of a system's territorial defense as well as its feelings about safety itself. Additional safety zones are developed at the edges of the interpersonal and personal subsystem territories. The issues in these areas are somewhat different, however, because the purpose of these safety zones is usually the protection of property, privacy, and the relationships among family members, rather than the guarding of actual physical safety.

Within the interior of a family's space, members confront the difficult task of trying to develop and maintain optimal spatial relationships with one another. From moment to moment they must decide how close to move toward each other, and how much to move away. The actual physical size and design of a household may have a strong effect on how such closeness and distance is attained. A house in which each child has his own room poses physical problems that are quite different from those of a house in which two, three, or four children must share the same room. Yet, the main spatial issues of family process remain the same. How do we come together to share the same space for common or overlapping activity? How do we establish distance from one another without either deserting each other or losing our place in the common society? Within the family interior, certain places tend to become more important than others for each subsystem of family. The parents' bed, the children's treehouse, Father's study, the nursery, the rug in front of a fireplace, the TV room, the recreation room, the dining room table, and the back porch can all become special gathering places for members. As such they can become *central regions* of family, regions in which the most intimate and meaningful activities of a family's life take place.

Time

The movements of family members can be traced across two different kinds of time structures: clock time and calendar time.

The day and the week are probably the two most important time cycles to examine in order to gain an understanding of a family's basic rhythmic patterns. Within a family's daily experience, getting up in the morning, getting out to daytime locations, the returning of members back home, the gathering to eat, and the putting to bed are all important recurring events. Similarly, in the course of the week, the cyclic passage of weekdays and weekends—work times and play times, busy times and leisure times—is basic to family life. To understand a family's time movements fully, one also needs to get a sense of the progress of the system's life cycle. One must know something of the family's history—the direction which it has been taking—and the direction in which it thinks, or at least hopes, it is going. Family members erect temporal boundaries as well as the spatial ones, and regulate access to one another and to the world at large. People can avoid each other on the basis of time as easily as space. In one of our research families, only one person occupied a room at any one time. When one person left a particular room, another went in, but not until then. In many other families, certain times were set aside for bringing members together for some kind of joint activity. Dinnertime is often such a time.

The primary question confronting both the family as a whole and each of its members is, "How is time to be used?" Then follow a host of subsidiary questions. When and how often should certain events occur? What should be valued from the past? What do members collectively and individually envision for the future? In their behavioral answers to these and countless other temporal questions, members establish whether their rhythms are in phase or out of phase—with each other, and with the movements of the world at large. The term "in phase" suggests a considerable overlap or similarity in the clock and calendar schedules among family members or between members and outsiders. "Out of phase" is a condition in which there is very little overlap or contact. Thus, two members may be out of phase even if they eat dinner in the same room if one finishes his meal before the other begins, or if the one thinks and talks about the past while the other reflects on the future. It is important to note that the terms "in phase" and "out of phase," like close and distant, are descriptive rather than evaluative. Thus, to be in phase with a particular person or group is not necessarily a more desirable condition than being out of phase. Indeed, large amounts of time which one person may find himself devoting to one other person or a specific activity may produce even more ill will or worse results than would very short or infrequent periods.

Energy

Energy is both static and kinetic in families, static in that family members have supplies of stored energy available to them, and kinetic in that members actually expend these supplies. Though each family's use, deployment, and restoration of its energies will vary somewhat, a general pattern of charging and discharging energy operations is common to all families. By charging, we mean the accumulation of energy and, by discharging, the expending of it. If either activity alone—charging or discharging—repeatedly takes place at the expense of the other, a family can find itself in serious difficulty. To expend energies without ever refueling can leave a family feeling depleted and depressed, whereas constant refueling, without development of any meaningful outlets for its energies, can leave a family feeling jammed and frustrated. Though crises may temporarily upset such a formula, each member of a family as well as the family as a whole ought to have ideally a nearly even ratio of charge to discharge in the course of time. To accomplish this goal, families inform their members how to acquire and expend their energies, whether they are inside or outside the family.

The concept of energy enables one to identify the intensity of family experience. In general, the more energy that is involved in a sequence, the more intense the sequence. Intensity in the abstract is a difficult subject to conceptualize. Usually, it is more useful to talk about the energy dimension's interfaces with the other dimensions than about energy alone. The energy sphere's interface with the time sphere, for example, allows us to gauge the amount of energy and intensity present in a family at the beginning, middle, and termination of events. Some families (and persons) have high impetus, but make little or no impact. They are forever starting, but almost never finishing things. Other systems may experience difficulty in starting projects. Still others experience difficulty with their momentum, with carrying forward through the middle of a project, when initial inspiration is forgotten and the end point is not yet in sight.

In applying our distance-regulation concept to the energy dimension, what we are measuring is whether each subsystem is energically in balance or out of balance, that is, whether it has enough energy to meet its demands and enough demands to utilize its supplies or not. In making such assessments on the balance between energy supply and demand, we must ask the following questions: Does the family expend enough energy to meet the demands placed on it? Does it overextend itself, undertaking more demands and expending more energy than it can hope to supply? Do legitimate energy demands go unmet? Do members have satisfying outlets for their energies? Are family energies squandered?

Space, time, and energy, then, are the physical media. The movements in such media are quantifiable, particularly the movements in time and space. They can be measured in seconds or feet or in whatever temporal or spatial scale of measurement is deemed most appropriate. Measuring family energy is more difficult because the common energic units, such as horsepower, footpounds, and ohms, appear to be irrelevant in the family context. Nevertheless energy phenomena remain quantifiable: one can talk fairly readily about a high, medium, or low energy level in families and be understood.

If space, time and energy are the media of family process, affect, power, and meaning are the end points that are sought— that is, the targets of such process. Obviously these three target dimensions are of a different conceptual and experiential order than the access dimensions. For one thing, no scales of measurement exist that enable us to quantify them. Despite these inherent differences, we believe that both access and target issues can be conceptually linked to our notion of family social space. We believe that in a context involving experientially meaningful events, there is invariably a person or object or event that becomes the bearer of affect, power, or meaning. The access dimensions focus on these various bearers in terms of how and when and where and with what energy they move. The target dimensions focus on the bearers in terms of what they represent to family members.

We have found it useful to think of the interior social space of a family as an enclosure, such as a sphere or a cube. Within this three-dimensional physical analogue, most, if not all, of a family's substantive transactions take place. We have divided these transactions into separate affect, power, and meaning categories, three different kinds of distance-regulation events. We conceive of affect events as lateral relations, power events as vertical relations, and meaning events as depth relations. Distance regulation within the interior of the family social space is in effect the regulation of events along these three intersecting axes. When we focus on specific social realities, however, we conceive of each dimension as a field with its own spatial, temporal, and energic boundaries. In the following discussion, the "space" of each dimension is examined in terms of its axis, its primary target goal, its polar limits, its major content issues, and its typical crises.

Affect

Distance regulation in the affect dimension can be seen as the regulation of transactions laterally, along the horizontal axis of our three-dimensional physical analogue of the family's interior social space. Affect dimension transactions encompass all behaviors relating to sentient experiences and moral expressions, in both the social and personal realms, that are evaluated and experienced along a continuum of the positive to the negative, of good feeling to bad feeling, of friendliness to unfriendliness. The equation of such affect dimension events analogically with laterality not only has literary and poetic precedents but the support of our common language as well. Indeed, it is difficult to conceive of people transacting their emotional relations of loving and hating, attachment and antipathy, sympathy and disdain, fondness and estrangement in terms other than those relying on images of joining and separating, of people approaching and moving away from one another in a horizontal plane.

Affirmative intimacy and nurturance are the primary targets of the affect dimension of family life. The specifics of what constitutes nurturance and intimacy vary, no doubt, from family to family and from individual to individual within families, but nearly all families claim that they seek to provide those two emotional qualities. We define intimacy as a condition of mutual emotional closeness, often intense closeness, among peers. Nurturance is an exchange in which one or more family members receive emotional support and encouragement from another member or members. Thus, whereas intimacy involves a two directional emotional exchange, nurturance implies a primarily unidirectional flow of affect.

In regulating its exchanges of the heart, a family determines how its members shall join and separate from one another. As we use them, "join" and "separate" are descriptive distance-regulation terms. They are not substitutes for love and hate or some other evaluative scale. In fact, although members' joinings may be based on affection, they may also be based on hate and result in serious emotional conflict. Similarly, separations need not signify dislike. Rather, they may suggest an absence or sparsity of emotional exchange. All kinds of issues are raised by the ways in which a family regulates the emotional distances among members. Affiliation, loyalty, emotional acceptance, and affirmation all involve complicated joining/separating maneuvers.

In emotional distance regulation, the ideal of the family is to satisfy its members' needs for intimacy and nurturance. Realization of this ideal is complicated, however, for the emotional distance which affirms one member may violate another and leave a third feeling relatively unaffected. For example, when a father closes the door to his study or flinches when it is opened, he is signaling his family that he considers it neither the appropriate time nor place for joining together. Similarly, if he should embrace his wife and child before dinner, he may be communicating his desire for emotional joining to begin. A child's grimace at his forcefully exuberant hug may, in turn, mean that the father is exerting too much energy for the child to feel comfortable joining him. In this way, family members are forever learning from one another how and when joinings and separations are tolerable, optimal, or intolerable.

Because nurturance and intimacy are matters of singular importance to the human organism, unsuccessful movements toward

these targets generate crisis situations. Fusion and alienation suggest
two highly disabling resolutions of affect regulation crises. Affect
fusion is a condition in which emotional joining is pushed to the
point at which virtually no differentiation of individual participants
or subsystems remains in family interactions. It is an extreme emotional unity, in which boundaries are diffused. As a consequence of
such boundary conditions, options to separate are simply not available, and intimacy with peers outside of the family, as we normally
conceive of it, is not really possible. Emotional alienation occurs
when affect separation is pushed to a point at which the interacting individuals or subsystems are locked into such positions that all
moves for joining are obstructed. Sustained alienation may leave
family members feeling so completely out of touch with one another
that they no longer feel even remotely related. Such extreme boundary resolutions as alienation and fusion can occur either at a single
interface or at numerous subsystem interfaces throughout the family.
In one family, the boundaries of all members may be fused; in
another the parents may be emotionally alienated; or one member
—a child or an adult—may be cut off from the others. If a family
analysis is to be accurate, the particular subsystem boundaries experiencing affect crisis must be clearly delineated.

Power

Distance regulation in the power dimension can be viewed
as the regulation of transactions along the vertical axis of our three-
dimensional physical analogue of the family's interior social space.
Such vertical issues in family systems refer to transactions relating
to voluntary or conative powers and faculties, that is, to matters
of individual, conceptual, and intersocial volition. Such issues inevitably bring into focus a system's ends, the actions and social arrangements that are designed to achieve those ends, and the requirements
and opportunities for autonomy from and subservience to either
means or ends. The association of images of verticality with issues
of dominance, submission, and mediation, hindrance and further-
ance, opposition and cooperation, competition and association, option
and necessity, and superiority and inferiority is virtually explicit in
the idiom of our culture. Moving up, getting to the top, going down

for the count—that is, the entire realm of rise and fall—suggests who holds power and who does not. Skyscraper architecture, with its room at the top set aside for the boss, expresses this vertical relationship even more explicitly. The vertical axis permits ready use of such explicit images in conceptualizing distance regulations in the power dimension of family process.

The primary target within the power dimension of family life is the ability to effect what the system wants, to get done what it wants to get done: this target is called constructive efficacy. Few conditions are either more pathetic or tragic than an awareness of what is wanted or needed combined with the lack of ability or freedom or confidence to attain it. Metaphorically, the power dimension represents the muscle and sinew of a family. Learning, exercising, and striving for a mastery of skills are all part of a family's efforts to be effective. Without the development of such skills, members can grow physically, socially, and intellectually flabby and thus find it difficult to attain their goals. In short, vertical relations are the crucial factor in a family's ability to get things done.

Power relations focus on the aspects of freedom and restraint within family organization, and it is to these aspects that we apply the distance-regulation concept. In any given situation, then, one can measure a family's social traffic by quantifying the degree of freedom or restraint in members' movements. Many families formalize their vertical relations in such a way that a power hierarchy, both official and unofficial, is created. Such formalizations are used by families to determine situational distance-regulation issues. For instance, if Daddy is "boss" he probably has the right to tell Junior what to do. Situational distance regulations may be, and often are, at variance with official formulations, however. Situationally, a young child may be allowed to interrupt the movements of others, demand nurturance and affection, or be exempted from the restraint of family chores even though his formal status as "baby" relegates him to a low place in the power hierarchy. In short, a family's power regulations determine who and what will move freely, and who and what will be restrained.

Status in the family hierarchy, decision making, concepts of property, of rights and responsibilities, and attitudes of dominance and submission are all important power issues, and as such they fall within the distance-regulation framework. For example, in a dispute about how the family wants to spend a weekend holiday, Father may be freer than either Mother or the children to determine the activity; and Mother and the children may feel more constrained to accept Father's choice than he is to accept theirs. Similarly, on questions of property, one child may be free to use the television or the stereo whenever he wants to while a younger member may be restrained from watching certain TV programs or from manipulating the stereo equipment without supervision.

By means of its power relations, then, a family demands, rewards, protects, punishes, and tries generally to shape the social traffic of its members. Conflicts over the extent to which the family should be allowed to control individual lives invariably arise. But if family traffic is marked by either extreme freedom or extreme restraint, other potential problems arise. Thus if members feel totally free to do whatever they wish, anarchy can result, the movements of each subsystem disrupting and/or violating previously agreed upon family goals; at the other extreme, traffic that is totally restrained can produce conditions of tyranny, in which members are not allowed to do what they want, choose what they want, say what they think, or, for that matter, even dare to dwell on what they start to think. The extreme power resolutions of tyranny and anarchy are not here highlighted to suggest that power should ideally be regulated near the center of the freedom-restraint axis. That ideal balance will be the one which allows each subsystem within the family, as well as the family unit, to be most effective in gaining access to the targets it seeks.

Meaning

Distance regulation in the meaning dimension can be viewed as the regulation of transactions transversely along the depth axis of our three-dimensional physical analogue of the family's interior social space. The meaning dimension encompasses all those actions and transactions relating to ideas and the communication of ideas about the family and the various worlds (social, spiritual, conceptual, and material) to which it relates. The family's depth regulations refer to the maintenance of its identity as a living entity by the transmission of ideas about itself ("us") and the world ("them"), and by the management of sameness and difference in the organization of its shared conceptual life. In regulating such transactions family members inevitably become concerned, at least indirectly, with issues of belief and doubt, concordance and diversity, gullibility and skepticism, clarity and vagueness, explicitness and ambiguity, literality and figurativeness, manifestness and latency, and revelation and concealment. All of these issues can be readily associated with conditions of depth—with the perception of distance from front to back, from the clearly visible to the shadowy and largely obscured.

Purposeful identity is the primary target of the family's meaning dimension. That identity can be defined as the self-knowledge of a system or subsystem plus the ability to represent that self accurately to others. For an individual, to have an identity means to have an integrated sense of direction and destination, an awareness of who one is and what one would like to become. It is the antithesis of uncertainty, confusion, or disorientation. Like individuals, families strive to develop identities, usually by emphasizing the unity and solidarity of members in a common cause or purpose, and the existence of a meaningful "we," even if the "we" is a collection of individuals who agree never to interfere with the individual freedoms of one another.

Metaphorically, the meaning dimension represents the mind of family experience. Ideas, credos, values, ideologies, world views, and a sense of good and bad and right and wrong all fall within its province. Despite the diversity of specific issues in the meaning dimension, the distance-regulation concept remains applicable, the primary measurable quality being the degree to which a depth-oriented axis is shared or unshared. By "shared" we refer to those meanings held in common and, by "unshared," those not held in common. Useful as it is, however, the shared—unshared axis fails to measure satisfactorily all interactions of the meaning dimension. For example, some meanings that appear at first to be unshared are in reality different. Thus we use the term "different" to draw attention to those meanings that are held to be true by one or more subsystems but which simply may not *exist* for another or others, whereas in the shared-unshared axis, the meanings *exist* for all subsystems but are not necessarily *accepted* by all. To employ a spatial model, we might imagine a shadowy or nearly invisible axis extending parallel to the shared-unshared axis in the depth plane. This is the axis of meaning difference.

If meaning regulation is forced toward any of the three distance-regulation end points, serious problems can ensue. Such rigidity at these extremes can produce conditions of conformity to absolute meaning, of conceptual isolation, or of intellectual irrelevance. For example, shared meanings can be so strongly emphasized by a family that they are the only meanings members are permitted to hold or express. Such conformity, if it is genuinely adopted, can be stultifying and oppressive; or, if the conformity is only pretended, the person's adherence to that meaning can become totally devoid of conviction. Other families, of course, can emphasize unshared meanings to such a degree that a subsystem, an individual, or a faction of the family can feel constantly isolated from or opposed to the meanings, values, and ideology of the rest of the family. As a result, such isolated members may feel obliged to reject whatever ideas or meanings are proposed to them, regardless of the merits of the meanings themselves. Still other families permit or even encourage individuality of meaning to such an extreme that members find themselves, their views, and their experiences irrelevant to the views and experience of the rest of the family circle, or even of the world at large. Members of such families may find themselves unaccepted by outsiders, and their intellectual contributions rendered eccentric or inapplicable to reality.

It is almost impossible to overstate the importance of family meaning regulation in a society that is intellectually concerned with the meaning or meaninglessness of existence. A world as complex as ours puts extra strain on both individual and family identities. Like the caterpillar in *Alice in Wonderland*, it is forever asking, "Who are you?" If a family fails to offer itself and its members a model, or variety of models, on which the individual can base a purposeful identity that enables him to answer this basic existential question, or if it offers a model that is inappropriate for prevailing reality, it fails to fulfill one of its most important functions.

Dimensional Interfaces

Most family events do not transpire solely within the confines of a single dimension. We have already suggested that at least one access and one target dimension are almost always jointly involved. The social-space event takes place at the interface, or meeting point, of the dimensions and can be labeled as, for example, a spatial-affect event, a temporal-meaning event, or some other access-target event. However, many events have more than one access or target component. For instance, an event may take place at the energic–affect-power interface. This means that the event raises important issues about distance regulation in the energy, affect, and power dimensions of family process. Certain key events, requiring distance regulations in all six dimensions, might even be said to take place at the spatial-temporal-energic—affect-power-meaning interface. To be sure, all social space events touch upon issues involving all six dimensions, but usually one or two interfaces are emphasized more than the others. The paragraphs below suggest some of the more important dimensional interfaces of family process. We include interfaces of two dimensions within the same set as well as interfaces across the two sets of dimensions.

AFFECT-POWER INTERFACE: Through its regulation of affect-power interactions, a family works out its members' sense of belonging and place. When members feel they are loved, they can usually go off into the world with a strong sense of self-confidence and optimism about what the world has to offer. The effects of a family's affect-power relations are not always so benevolent, however. A system may soothe and caress some of its members as a means of keeping them in a low position on the family hierarchy. How a member feels about the place accorded to him by his family can be expressed by heated conflicts within the family. If a person feels he has been assigned too low a place in the family hierarchy and is desirous of more freedom, he may become very hostile to the other members of the system, however much he may try to suppress such feelings. For instance, a housewife who is required to take complete charge of all household tedium may develop difficulties in responding sexually to her husband.

AFFECT-MEANING INTERFACE: If effective loving can empower one and give one a sense of power, it can also be used to affirm and validate oneself and one's meanings. The affect-meaning interface is no less important than the affect-power interface, for here the head and the heart meet and tug with one another. Through its regulations at this interface, a family determines which of the lifestyle meanings of its members it will accept, and the degree of acceptance of each. Not all loving leads to meaning affirmation and validation, however. If an individual with high propensity for meaning autonomy grows up in a family with a high push for intimacy, he may find that only some and not all of his lifestyle meanings are affirmed by the family. At this important interface, the family also expresses its feelings about its meanings and identity. Such feelings provide a primary clue as to whether a family's meaning-dimension regulations are functioning for the benefit of family members.

POWER-MEANING INTERFACE: At this target interface, the primary issue is a potential conflict between members' individual rights, particularly the right to think and believe what they wish, and the rules which are enforced by the family unit either to support or deny such rights. Many families use power to arbitrate the truth or falsity of different meanings, frequently punishing deviance and rewarding conformity. The salient power-meaning issue in each family is the extent to which members' places in the hierarchy of the family are compatible with the family's and individuals' definitions of self. The struggle to reconcile these two components is one of the major ongoing struggles in any family. Indeed, the power-meaning interface is the ideological battleground of family life. Distance regulation here can be the most prevalent source of conflict in the family, particularly when one or more members challenge family practices and beliefs, thus putting the fairness of the system to test.

ENERGY-AFFECT INTERFACE: Affect and energy meet in numerous contexts. To experience one is often to experience the other. Every emotional experience has an energic component attached to it. Words like passion, fulfillment, satiety, and ennui are all linguistic attempts to describe complex energy-affect configurations. When distance regulation at this interface approaches the ideal, members can feel good about one another. At other times, serious disagreements about the amount of energy that should accompany a particular emotion can develop. At still other times, members may find their attempts to join and separate supported by little or no energy at all.

ENERGY-MEANING INTERFACE: On the meaning side of this interface, the intensity or conviction behind family images is the key issue. All families have beliefs about what is important and not important in the world. One way of finding out just what is important to the family is to identify the amount of energy or push behind each of its meanings. The more important the meaning, the greater the amount of energy that will be invested in it. It is here at the interface of energy and meaning that families and their members state who they truly are. There will often be an icon in the family's space to symbolize a family's highly energized meanings. The family Bible, pictures of the Virgin, report cards, and other family artifacts can be used as symbols to invoke or reinvoke the meaningful image and generate or revive the energy attached to it. On the energy side of this interface, the key issue is whether or not family meanings facilitate or frustrate members' attempts to replenish and discharge their energies. For instance, meanings and beliefs which permit no spontaneity tend to deplete a family's energy resources.

TIME-MEANING INTERFACE: Key issues at this interface include the consistency of statements and the durability of ideas and concepts about the world. Meanings and identities that are not adjusted in accord with the passage of time, and with the changes that inevitably result from growth and decay, soon lose their purposiveness and, indeed, become unworkable in the real world.

There are, of course, many other important dimensional interfaces. Events taking place at each interface provide important information about the complexity of family interactions. Family-process issues are seldom isolated issues. Rather, they revolve around complex operations that reverberate throughout the six behavioral dimensions we have outlined in the preceding pages.

Thus far in this chapter we have stressed the sequential nature of dimensional operations. We have stated that family members gain access to targets, thereby implying that access concerns and operations sequentially precede target concerns. This need not always be the case. Access-dimension operations are as affected by target-dimension designs, expectations, and experience as target destinations are affected by access operations. A closed-loop effect-cause-effect relationship exists between experience in the two sets of dimensions. Consequently, family members may, at any given time, be seeking and striving after targets within the access dimensions. In a situation where family members are disaffected with one another and preoccupied with extrinsic or even irrelevant concerns, a family's affect relations may be seen as preceding its time relations. Thus, spending time together to eliminate the impediments in their affect relations may become a family's primary target. Protection of space, getting energically turned on, finding time to do things—all of these may be a family's primary target for a temporary period of time.

If, then, the target dimensions can serve as access routes to targets within the access dimensions, as well as the reverse, is there any validity in designating space, time, and energy as the access dimensions, and affect, power, and meaning as the target dimensions of family process? We believe there is. Our experience is that, even when a family's targets seem temporarily to reside within the access dimension, those targets are in a sense "pre-targets" for gaining additional access to primary target-dimension goals. For instance, a family whose members feel strong affection for one another, may want to protect each other's space, spend time with each other, and expend their energies together in order to enhance these ties.

Access and Target Strategies

The dimensional component of our systems model reflects our suggestion that family strategies are characterized by a minimum of two dimensions at interface, one access dimension and one target dimension, and are generally directed toward one of the major target-dimension goals: nurturance/intimacy, efficacy, or identity. We also state in this chapter that family strategies are purposive distance-regulation patterns. Why then speak of strategies at all? Why not just speak of distance-regulation patterns? The reason is that the term "distance regulation" refers to the more abstract and systemic features of family process. "Strategies," in contrast, has a more dynamic and phenomenological connotation. It is a term family members can usually accept as relevant to their behavior, for it represents a process which can be directly and immediately experienced. In addition, "strategies" is a term that highlights the goal-directed aspects of distance regulations. The dimensional component makes clear that strategies are developed to attain specific target goals.

The six-dimensional social space field we have delineated in this chapter grounds family process in thematic content, the subject matter of family life. A family's major goals are inclusive. They are broad and somewhat abstract in scope. In one way or another, all families strive after them. Everyday activity may point in the direction of one or more of these goals, but it nearly always focuses on a subtarget within them. For instance, in pursuit of the general goal of purposeful identity, family members might seek to achieve ideological solidarity, ironic sensitivity, uniqueness, integrity, sophistication, or some other subtarget. In pursuit of efficacy, they might strive after liberation, discipline, object acquisition, productivity, frugality, nobility, or competence. In pursuit of nurturance and intimacy, families might try to foster cheerfulness, emotional cohesion, physical pleasure, amusement, loyalty, or generosity. Temporary targets or pre-targets may also be found in the access dimensions. Subtargets associated with the energy dimension include excitement, friction, vitality, inertia, forcefulness, violence, and strength. Subtargets associated with time include punctuality, spontaneity, durability, speed, newness, conservation, and dependability. Spatial subtargets include separation, physical closeness, exclusion, expansion, physical security, and inclusion. We call all of these and other subtargets "themes."

Themes give content to a family's strategic intentions, content around which family strategies take shape. Strategic themes, like the distance-regulation patterns associated with them, reoccur frequently throughout a family's life. Together, these strategic patterns and themes constitute a family's style of relating. Within the concept of theme, means and ends overlap. A theme does not exist apart from an action but, rather, it is embedded in the action, and has a dynamic relationship with the goal of that action. Thus, a theme such as ideological cohesion may be both an end in itself and a means toward the further end of purposeful identity. A theme is never exclusively actional. The actional components of a strategy derive both from the subtarget or theme and from the access mechanism(s) with which it is most closely associated. We shall discuss access mechanisms in some detail in the next four chapters.

In the comments on strategies we made in the preceding chapter, we noted that the dominant competing themes in the

Weber family were emotional cohesion and individual freedom. Recall that the teenaged daughter Linda's desire to be free to move and do as she likes came into conflict with the family unit's goal of togetherness. Linda, however, is not the only Weber interested in preserving and extending individual freedoms in the family, as the following episode demonstrates.

Mother suggests that the family spend the day sailing on Father's boat. Father and Elise very quickly agree. Linda announces, "I'd rather spend the day in town with my friends." The others keep urging her, however, to spend the day on the boat with them. Finally, Linda gives in, agreeing, "All right, if it's so important to you, I'll come along." When they get to the dock, Father reminds the family they'll have to do some work on the boat before putting it in the water. "Great!" Linda comments in a sarcastic tone. Elise says, "Well, let's get it done fast." Mother makes lunch. Afterward, she asks, "Can we take it out now?" Father replies, "Hilda, there's still a lot of things I have to do. The rudder isn't working right." He continues to work into the afternoon, enjoying the chance to work with his hands. The others are less happy as they sit around waiting. Linda shakes her head and complains, "All the things I could've done today. I have to waste my time out here." "You should've brought a book like me," says Elise, settled down with a copy of *Gone with the Wind*. Hilda repeatedly interrupts Father: "Franz, is the boat ready yet?" "No, it's not," he replies. Meanwhile, Elise puts down her book and goes to the back of the car. She starts playing with several of her dolls, making up an adventure story for them to act out. Linda hears her and mutters, "God, this is all we need." Hilda once again approaches her husband. "She's playing wth her dolls again, dear. Can't we save some of the repairs and put her in the water?" "I'm doing my best," Franz replies. By late afternoon, the Webers do get the boat in the water, but no one is particularly happy. In fact, by this time everyone is thoroughly angry with everyone else.

The strategy for emotional cohesion portrayed in this episode is rather prototypic of the Weber family's time–affect–power impasses. The basic strategy is to gain access to intimacy through the medium of time. Except for contextual changes from one episode to another, the sequence of moves and the general form of the strategy remain fairly constant. The family's investment in emotional close-ness is often impinged upon by power-dimension issues. In this se-quence, the key power issue is individual freedom, an officially espoused subgoal of the family. The Webers experience very little conflict at the power-meaning and affect-meaning interfaces of their family. Members can spend a lot of time in discussion with each other, sharing each other's meanings and learning from each other. When affect targets become dominant, however, complications at the affect-power interface are experienced.

Individual freedom, though collectively espoused, means something different to each of the Webers. For Franz, the issue is one of maintaining private time and space within the family. In this episode, he has to struggle with his individual need to think and work by himself while not relinquishing his desire to have a "close" family. His definition of "close" differs from his wife's however, whose affect needs require a more intense and a much more con-tinuous emotional exchange. For Hilda, freedom means having the power to regulate closeness so that the other person does not arbi-trarily leave the emotional field. Her concept of perfect freedom is to be in a situation in which everyone voluntarily wants to be joined so that control need not be asserted. In the recurring strategy for fostering family cohesion, she is usually the person who designs the affect field and determines what goals are to be pursued. Her moves are coercive and she is often disappointed. Her requirements for freedom (as she defines it) are no more fulfilled than her husband's.

Linda poses a particular threat to her mother's affect goals. She shares the family's goal of emotional closeness, but "close" for her is very "distant" for her mother. Whereas Hilda needs to spend a sizeable portion of time with another person in order to feel joined, Linda can feel emotionally joined to another person even if they only share a few moments with each other and separately move on. But Hilda, in pursuit of her personal emotional affect ideals, suppresses Linda's freedom to pursue an individual lifestyle outside the family. Since Linda tends to consider anything limiting her choice of lifestyle as illegitimate coercion, the oppositional part she plays in the strategy is a result not so much of her not wanting to go with her family as it is of the feeling she has to go with them.

For the twelve-year-old Elise, a similar freedom-of-choice

issue arises. Unlike Linda, she is the academic achiever her family wants her to be. She is loyal to the family, she is intellectually competent beyond her years, and she is everyone's ally in the family. Only occasionally does she slip back into the fanciful and spontaneous behavior of the childhood she prematurely left behind. In this episode, we see both of her versions of freedom—the freedom to function in the emotional field as everyone's ally, and the freedom to follow her interests by acting the child she in many ways remains. Unfortunately, she gains access to this second freedom only when a system strategy fails. As a result, the others have come to regard her playing with dolls as an indication that things are not going right.

In summary, the overall goal of the Weber family strategy is to increase family intimacy. The strategic theme delineates the more specific subgoal of emotional cohesion. Progress toward this goal is obstructed when the Webers' time-delay access strategy is put into effect. This strategy generates conflict at the personal-interpersonal subsystem interface as each person's power goal of individual freedom is placed into jeopardy. Consequently, instead of the desired emotional joining, ironic displacement occurs and the result is a distance-regulation pattern dominated by separation in the affect dimension.

Many strategic themes are rooted in the past, yet these origins continue to have influence over present-day distance-regulation operations, as the following brief histories suggest. Though now a professional mathematician, Franz was a disappointment to his father, a European philosophy professor of some renown. As an adolescent, Franz rebelled against his father's intellectual demands, expressing his rebellion by symptomatic school failure. Memories of his adolescence continue to remain profoundly painful to him. Now, in his own family, he both understands and deplores his daughter Linda's indifference to academic achievement. Franz describes his mother as an oppressively solicitous woman whose demands for emotional closeness exceeded his father's demands for academic excellence. Thus, while alienated from his father, he was simultaneously trapped in an emotional claustrophobia by his mother. Throughout his adolescence, Franz felt uneasy whenever his mother entered the same room he was in. Hilda entered into marriage with a not unrelated theme, drawn from her own family of origin. Feelings of emotional deprivation dominated her adolescence. Her mother died suddenly and unexpectedly. Despite the good intentions of her stepmother, Hilda's feelings of loss remained. She herself acknowledges that her need for emotional security and her images of how a family ought to live together derive from these early experiences.

If we introduce historic themes and trace them through two or more generations, we take our dimensional discussion of strategies into a new realm, away from the observable and verifiable to the presumptive and often unverifiable. Historic themes are generated by past events, even distant past events, involving previous generations. They are often rooted in prototypic scenarios or strategies that have affected the lives of their participant-carriers in highly significant ways and, as a result, continue to have influence on the activities of the present generation. Many historic themes are based on events which either did not take place at all or were radically different from the way in which they are remembered. What is most important about historic themes is not that they resurrect past events as they actually happened, but that the content and processes associated with such themes recur in the present. Consequently the participant-carriers get caught up in strategies that produce outcomes associated with the original theme. For the family analyst, historic themes have the same kind of continuity as a plot in a novel. They connect a family's history and its present ongoing processes with its destiny, and can thereby greatly increase one's longitudinal understanding of family. They allow one to summarize the basic strategies of three generations or more: family members' motivations and intentions can be delineated, complicated situations coherently described, and outcomes predicted. Thus, not only are family strategies, including their embodiments of both present-day and historical themes, eminently fascinating transactions, but also they are the most instantly enlightening conceptual tools at the family analyst's disposal. They are the concise dramatizations of family themes, scripts in which the politics of distance regulation are worked out and recorded across all six social space dimensions. The following examples, chosen at random from among many, will suggest the variety of ways families regulate access to specific target themes, especially those themes competing with each other.

The attorneys Mr. and Mrs. Wolf are proud libertarians who have resolved that their three sons should follow them into zealous public service. The Wolfs' two older sons Peter and Bill readily consent to the family's ideals about "equal opportunity" for everyone in the country as well as to the paradoxically authoritarian style the parents maintain within the household. Their younger brother John, a privatistic person who prefers meditation to political action, is the family's rebel, the one who manages consistently to get caught up in its machineries of control and punishment. One evening at dinner, John announces that after his high school graduation he plans to travel to Argentina with a group of modern day spiritualists. His parents express grave disappointment. They had hoped he would take a job as a tokenly paid volunteer in a local mental hospital, a job arranged by a fellow member of the community mental health board. The senior Wolfs refuse to advance John the money he needs for his trip. John insists that his parents are hypocrites. "You're always preaching personal autonomy. This trip is part of my quest for freedom," he says. "If it is, it's a selfish quest," Mother retorts. Father adds, "A few months ago when we mentioned Dr. Rose's idea, you said you might be interested. We have gone to great lengths to bring it about." John's two collegiate brothers express sympathy for his "personal" cause, but urge him to reconsider his plans inasmuch as it seems really to upset their parents. John feels he has only one choice: to refuse.

The result: John finds himself in a familiar impasse, in which he feels alienated and alternately angry, trapped, and guilty. In desperate frustration he breaks the impasse, cashing in some bonds on which he has forged his parents' signatures. The family broker, instantly recognizing the clumsy fabrication, telephones the parents. John's punishment: forced labor for the entire summer as an apprentice in his father's law office. In this strategy, the themes of personal autonomy and public service, a central concern of the Wolf family identity, compete. The ironic displacement is that one family member is denied access to autonomy, a power goal the family genuinely endorses and seeks to make available to all members of the community. In the Wolf household, the routes to autonomy are chosen by the family, not by the individual. Distance regulations in the power dimension are scrupulously guarded.

Situations of emotional joining present very difficult issues for the Anderson family. Mr. Anderson and the family's twin sons Lenny and Benny, both thirty years old, experience a sense of disorientation whenever they enter the presence of Mrs. Anderson. Twenty years younger than her husband and twenty years older than her sons, Mrs. Anderson is a lovely, but emotionally fragile woman who harbors a great many fears, including the fear that her sons will die of starvation if she doesn't feed them. To protect himself both from his mother's fears and sorrows and from her tendency to smother him with undifferentiated affection, each of the twins has taken to staying on the fringes of the Anderson family's social space. Benny now locks himself in his room and refuses to come out except when the family is out of the house. At dinner each evening, Mr. Anderson takes a trayful of food upstairs where he leaves it just outside Benny's door. Only when Mr. Anderson has gone back downstairs does Benny open the door and pick up the tray. Meanwhile, Lenny fills his plate and eats quickly. By the time his parents enter the dining room, he has finished his meal and leaves the room to watch the evening news on television. Once the parents have sat down to eat, Mr. Anderson holds the afternoon paper in front of him, obstructing his wife's view of him. In sum, the three male members of the Anderson household regularly avoid Mrs. Anderson in both space and time, thus denying both themselves and her any access to emotional intimacy. They have chosen to protect themselves and her from the disorientation and hostility that inevitably result whenever an attempt at joining is made.

The Budges are a family who like to do things together whenever they can, but particularly on weekends when Father is at home. Several months ago they moved out of a city apartment to a house on an acre lot in the distant suburbs. Since then, they have been devoting their free time to fixing up the house and getting to know their new neighbors. The Budge parents, however, do not believe in coercing their two sons into doing things they don't want to do. They believe in the viability of voluntarism. Early one Saturday morning, Peter Budge, the older of the Budges' two teen-age sons, receives a telephone call from Joe Carter, a friend who invites him to join the Carter family for a weekend of camping in the mountains. Peter says, "It sounds great, but I have to ask my parents. I'll call you back." "O.K., but hurry," replies his friend. "Mom, can I go camping with the Carters?" asks Peter. "It's all right with me," replies his Mother, "but isn't your father expecting you to help him plant some trees in the yard?" Moments later, Father comes striding into the kitchen. "Dad, I've just been invited to go camping with the Carters. Can I?" The enthusiastic expression that has been on Father's face disappears. "I thought we were gonna do some work together today," he remarks. "Yeah, I know I promised," Peter replies, "but I didn't know Joe was gonna call." Father reluctantly agrees to let Peter go. He says, "If you really want to go, Gordy and I can plant the trees by ourselves." "You don't mind too much if I go, do you, Gordy?" asks Peter. "No, not too much," answers Gordy. On the way back to the phone, Peter passes his mother who says, "You know, I think they really want you to stay." "Yeah, I know," says Peter, who proceeds to call the Carters and tell them he can't go. Later that morning as they are planting an apple tree in the front yard, Mr. Budge says to his son, "Peter, I know it was hard to do, but I think you showed a lot of maturity in keeping your promise to me." "Yeah," says Gordy, "I'm glad you decided to stay."

This sequence takes place primarily at the Budge system's personal-interpersonal interface, with task solidarity as the interpersonal subsystem theme and integrity as Peter's personal theme. Peter's choice reduces to a dilemma over which kind of integrity he is more interested in gaining access to: the integrity of keeping his promises or the integrity of doing what he wants to do. His choice of the more traditional integrity target heals the personal-interpersonal schism and opens up access to an identity the interpersonal subsystem can enthusiastically support. Such a resolution is predicated of course, on his not feeling coercively restricted by the other family members.

In conclusion, family systems are constantly engrossed in the task of regulating traffic in accord with their goals. Thus, when different targets and subtargets compete for dominance in the family, different distance-regulation patterns in the form of strategies also compete. For instance, if competent achievement is the theme of a particular strategy, one distance-regulation pattern may evolve, but if emotional integrity is the accepted subtarget, another distance-regulation pattern might be dictated. Stress occurs in the family whenever different distance regulation patterns compete. What follows the appearance of stress is obviously of great important to families. On some occasions, the result is an enrichment of the entire system. On others, stress may produce communicational and perceptual distortions. It has been our experience that many communicational problems in families can be traced to dimensional interface stress that has occurred because competing strategies have either collided head on or have fused into some kind of mutually disabling hybrid. Such distance-regulation fusions increase the possibility that a sustained family impasse will develop, denying members the family's preferred target destinations and its means for gaining access to them.

Chapter 5

※※※※※※※※※※※※※※※※

Methods of Access:
Space

In this and the next three chapters, we present a detailed elaboration of the second major component in our theory of family process, the access component. Taken together, Chapters Five, Six, and Seven constitute a taxonomy of the family system's mechanisms and submechanisms for regulating interactions within its space, time, and energy dimensions. Chapter Eight takes a more general overview of the family's access interactions. It suggests how families develop traffic plans and strategies to carry out the functions of their mechanisms and submechanisms.

The detailed taxonomy we present in this and the next two chapters represents our attempt to identify all the elements of access inherent in family process. We are making this attempt for several reasons. First of all, our naturalistic study of family households provided us with a unique opportunity to observe variables of process that are not often identified, conceptualized, or used by either researchers or clinicians operating out of laboratories and offices, but which nonetheless are important to the everyday functioning of the family. Our taxonomy seeks to call attention to these overlooked variables. Secondly, we believe it important to demonstrate that all families, whatever their styles, goals, or economic stations, have certain access-regulation tasks in common. Our taxonomy attempts to articulate precisely what these tasks are. Thirdly, we are attempting to make the detailed complexity of family interactions more comprehensible. Many observers and analysts have found the totality of family process a subject too complex to cope with and understand. To be sure, the immense amount of data a family provides can indeed appear overwhelming. In the following discussion of the mechanisms and submechanisms of family process, we attempt to make such immensity finite.

We are aware that our account of the access mechanisms and submechanisms is not a definitive one. It is a first attempt and will no doubt undergo revisions based on both logical and empirical evidence. We are also aware that some readers may not feel it necessary to examine all the details of our discussion in this and the next two chapters. Such readers should feel free to concentrate on the major space, time, and energy mechanisms as a preparation for the rest of this book, which is devoted to the more dynamic aspects of family interaction.

To begin our discussion of the family system's access mechanisms, we need to define what we mean by the term "mechanism." Family mechanisms are patterns of organization that support, defend, and implement the family system's traffic control functions at the interfaces of its access and target dimensions. As this statement implies, we believe mechanisms are "structures" as well as "process." When we think of mechanisms as structure, we regard them as abstract constructs, not to be distinguished from the ongoing interactive process, but to be viewed rather as definitive representations of such process. By designating mechanisms as process, we regard them as the actions and interactions of the component parts of an ongoing family system. Mechanisms, then, can be understood as a family's "structures of action," as abstract concepts which become tangible in operation. A family's mechanisms are those operations it must carry out in order to maintain itself as an ongoing system, much as a single human organism requires respiratory and circulatory mechanisms to maintain itself.

Bounding

Bounding is a mechanism in which families establish and maintain their territory within the larger community space by regulating both incoming and outgoing traffic. In its most general sense, "traffic" means movement—of people, objects, events, and ideas. In physical space, it is easy to see how a family regulates traffic across its borders. Gates, pathways, doors, and hallways all determine where people must walk if they hope to get in or out. Analogically, ideas and events are regulated in much the same way. Members of a family decide what kinds of things are allowed to enter the family space and under what conditions, and what kinds of items are simply not permitted admission. Inevitably, bounding issues are issues of safety, of providing an enclosure for the protection of family members against external danger. In bounding, a family demarcates a perimeter and defends its territory. In short, a family says, "This is ours. We are safe here." If a family system fails to develop a territory, it virtually ceases to exist, for it becomes indistinguishable from the larger space. It is in the working out of its bounding activities, and marking off how it is the same or different from those around it, that a family operationally defines itself to the community. Let us now examine some of the submechanisms a family makes use of in its negotiation of numerous bounding issues.

MAPPING: A ten-year-old girl is told she may invite some of her friends over to the house, but not others. Similarly, she is encouraged to go to ballet practice, but warned against ice skating on a local pond.

In such a way, each family develops its own "map," or picture, of the exterior culture—one that indicates the ways in which that culture resembles and differs from the interior family, as well as those people and items outside that are safe or worthwhile for family members, and those that are not. In some families, this map is quite uniform for all family members, and in others each member has a different map. In doing its mapping, a family seeks to recognize and label what is outside the family space in order to guide members' traffic. The ten-year-old girl's family in the preceding example labels the local pond and certain of her friends as "dangerous and to be avoided." Ballet, on the other hand, is mapped as a cultural good, as are her approved friends. In this way all items of experience are checked and tested against the map. The map, too, is tested by experience and often altered by it, as the relationships between interior and exterior events develop and fluctuate.

Each major family mechanism in our model has a submechanism which references information about the workings of that mechanism, including the workings of each of its submechanisms. Mapping is the referencing submechanism of bounding.

ROUTING: Two brothers know that they must check in at home before going anywhere else after school.

Routing is the directing of traffic to designated interior or exterior spaces. The relationship between the submechanisms routing and mapping is very close. Routing is the organization of movement along pathways. One's expectations are that such pathways will correspond to the pathways designated and approved by the system map. In actuality, however, traffic may follow disapproved or even uncharted pathways. In routing, families seek to regulate their members' traffic outside the family. The two brothers in the example have their way home from school charted for them. Should they stop and play ball, pick flowers, or drop in on their friends, they violate the routing directives they have received from their family and are trying instead to establish their own routing prerogatives.

SCREENING: A family of sunbathers must decide whether to construct a three-, six-, or nine-foot fence around their property.

A new, sexually provocative book is published. The parents read it first before allowing their teenagers to examine it.

A family living in a high crime area must decide whether all or only some of its members above a certain age should have a key to the apartment.

In defending its territorial borders by determining who shall be allowed to come in or go out, families carry out a submechanism of bounding we call screening. In screening, families filter both incoming and outgoing traffic, permitting some people to pass and prohibiting others. The family of sunbathers, the parental censors, and the family in a high crime area all deal with issues of screening. Fences, locked doors, cultural taboos are some of the means employed for keeping certain kinds of traffic out of the family space, or at least for inspecting them before allowing them to enter. Then families set up checkpoints or filters through which traffic is expected to flow. The front and back doors are obvious physical checkpoints for regulating the flow of physical traffic. Not all checkpoints are physical, however. Concepts, rules, and customs are all conceptual checkpoints.

PATROLLING: A toddler is not allowed outside the house unless accompanied by a parent or other sibling.

Each member of a teenage girl's family is awake, making note of her return home from a Saturday night date.

Screening checkpoints alone are ineffectual without a patrolling of the perimeter wall. Family border guards oversee the flow of incoming and outgoing traffic to make certain it conforms to family desires. Often such patrolling is performed by a person or group of persons, but it can also be performed by a watchdog or household pet, an automatic camera, or other device. The toddler's companions and the teenage girl's parents and siblings serve as guards who protect the family's space from intrusion and possible harm. Without such guarding, screening decisions could not be enforced, and claims of "mine" or "ours" would be rendered operationally void.

Linking

Linking is the regulating of distance, that is, the physical and conceptual associations and dissociations of all persons within the family's spatial interior. Linking operations, because they directly affect interpersonal relations, are much more closely connected with target issues than are the bounding operations, which take place at the family perimeter. Nevertheless, the focus of linking mechanisms is not on the targets themselves but on members and their movements as bearers of targets.

BRIDGING: A child asks his mother to give him a cookie.

A teenage girl calls to her two angry brothers, one of whom is reading upstairs while the other punches a beanbag in the basement, and asks them to come to the living room for a game of Scrabble.

Bridging is a bringing of members into closer voluntary contact with one another or with objects. Bridging may be unilateral. One person may cross over to hold a conversation with another person or to pat him on the back. "Crossovers" may be invited. The injunction "Please sit near me" is an invitation for the other person to cross over and come into closer contact. It is an example of bilateral bridging. Not all bridging is confined to two parties, however. Bridging in families often involves three or more. For instance, when two members of a family become estranged from each other, a third may create a situation such as a parlor game to attract the two to a space in which they can come closer together. Sometimes three-party bridging consists of two people and an object, as does the child's request for the cookie from his mother. If a family has no bridging mechanisms for bringing members closer together, feelings of alienation are bound to develop. The ability to relate is itself contingent upon effective bridgemaking. Experience simply does not occur until some relationship or contact is established between two or more persons or objects. Therefore bridging is one of the primary conditions for learning, in which people make, or are helped to make, meaningful connections in their total experience. Bridgemaking phenomena, then, are particularly important for the targets of affect and meaning. Without the ability to make physical and conceptual bridges, we can neither love nor learn. Bridging is also important for gaining access to the target of efficacy. The child or adult can acquire competence and skills, and thereby efficacy, only in areas for which he can obtain, or be helped to obtain, the appropriate tools.

BUFFERING: As Mr. Jones enters a room in which his wife is sitting, Mrs. Jones picks up what she is doing and leaves the room.

An elder son asks his little brother not to take their father's book off its proper shelf, suggesting that their father would prefer that his books not be taken away without his permission.

Buffering is a maneuver in which different persons or persons and objects move farther apart or voluntarily separate. Buffering is the obverse of bridging. It puts physical or conceptual distance between people or between people and objects. Unilateral buffering occurs when a person, such as Mrs. Jones in the example, puts some distance between herself and another person, event, or object. Dodging, escaping, avoiding, and distancing all suggest unilateral buffering tactics. Many other buffering operations are more complex, in that three or more parties are involved. The elder son who asks his younger brother not to take their father's book off its shelf sets in motion such a buffering action. When his father is absent, he acts as the library's protector, not letting his little brother harm any of the books. We must emphasize the importance of the voluntary aspect of buffering, which is the shared realization that something or someone needs to be protected from harm, at least temporarily. When such voluntary participation disappears, buffering is no longer operable.

BLOCKING OUT: As Mr. Jones enters a room in which his wife is sitting, Mrs. Jones picks up what she is doing and starts to leave. Mr. Jones says, "I forbid you to go." She stares at him a moment, and then leaves the room anyway.

An elder son asks his little brother not to take their father's book off its proper shelf, suggesting that their father would prefer that his books not be taken away without his permission. The little brother takes the book and is slapped for doing so.

Blocking Out is a coercive or involuntary separating of persons or persons and objects. Sometimes the coercion is obvious, as it is when the boy slaps his younger brother. Blocking out may be more subtle, however, because the involuntary or coercive elements may be covertly rather than overtly communicated. For example, a mother may grimace every time a father tries to change their baby's diapers. The person who has been blocked out in some way may feel terribly angry and frustrated, for he does not share the blocker's view of the target bearer's need for protection.

CHANNELING: A child asks his mother to give him a cookie. She gives him a glass of milk along with it, saying, "A balanced snack is better for you."

When she notices that her children still haven't done their homework, Mother orders them to their desks.

Channeling is the involuntary or coercive bringing together of people or people and objects. It involves the pushing of another in a specific direction or toward a specific destination. The mother who produces the glass of milk along with the requested cookie and the mother who orders her children to their desks both perform channeling movements. As these examples suggest, channeling operations are those performed by someone when he feels justified in pushing someone else toward certain targets or goals that he has selected for him. The channeling mechanism is usually employed in order to get things done, even if no one particularly enjoys doing them. Reality being what it is, a family based solely on voluntary bridging without any coercive channeling is probably a utopian's dream, though certainly a family based solely on channeling directives without any bridging, offers a bleak and brutalizing alternative, one likely to produce revolution by some of the members.

RECOGNIZING: A child asks his mother to give him a cookie. She gives him a glass of milk along with it, saying, "A balanced snack is better for you."

An adolescent boy enters a room in which his father is seated, reading the paper. He walks nervously through the room several times, turns on the stereo, fidgets with some playing cards, stares at his father for several minutes, slams the cards down on a table, and storms out of the room. His father continues reading.

Recognizing is the referencing submechanism of linking. Recognizing establishes the relevance of all linking phenomena—of bridging, buffering, blocking out, and channeling activities. Each member has his own perception of what goes on within the family, among the others, between himself and the other members, and within himself. Such perceptions are difficult to measure for anyone but the perceiver himself except when he chooses to reveal them. Many families gain from communicating their awarenesses. Indeed, the sensitizing of awareness itself can be encouraged and fostered by accurate and articulate recognition.

Simple recognizings include the labeling of people, things and events as good or bad, right or wrong, better or worse. The mother in the preceding example above labels the activity of drinking a glass of milk with the cookie when she tells her son, "A balanced snack is better for you." Positive recognition generally validates the other person and affirms the relevance of his actions. Negative recognition tends to invalidate both an individual and his actions. Positive and negative labeling can be extremely important operations, for they affect how people think about themselves and each other. Nonrecognition can be important, too. The father's nonrecognition of his adolescent son in the previous example, coupled with the son's recognition that he hasn't been recognized, reflects the absence of a precondition of relatedness. Without recognition that the other exists, there can be no relationship with the other. Habitual nonrecognition can even cause one to wonder if he actually exists or, at the very least, to question seriously whether his own recognitions bear any relationship to reality.

Centering

Every family generates general guidelines for organizing the total space in which it lives. The mechanism of centering consists of the developing, maintaining, and transmitting of spatial guidelines for how traffic should flow within and across its borders. It includes the assessing of whether such traffic flows in accordance with the guidelines or whether they should be modified to accommodate the traffic. How a family carries out its centering operations profoundly affects the ways in which it bounds off its space and binds members to it. Without spatial guidelines, members may not know how to bound, who and what to screen out and in, or where to go and where not to go. Without them, they certainly will not have a rationale for making such decisions. These guidelines are also the basis on which members form a coherent view of themselves and of the family, and so determine what they and it stand for. In performing these tasks, the guidelines, and the centering operations supporting them, can be the glue which binds members together into a cohesive and coherent whole.

LOCATING: A black family, anxious to safeguard its identity after moving into a white neighborhood, turns its dinner hour into an occasion for pinpointing the racial demands of its new community.

Locating is the referencing submechanism of centering. Specifically, it is a scanning of the family field to locate what is working well or ill in and for the family. If the family model is threatened by some event, it is the function of the locating mechanism to discover it. If traffic isn't flowing in and through the family according to design, it is again the task of the locating mechanism to make the discovery. It is also the task of the locating mechanism to find things or events which, though they aren't currently a part of the family's design, could foreseeably enrich the family's life according to the intent and purpose of its design. The black family mentioned above consciously tries to locate and sort out the white middle-class culture's threats to its blackness. For the members of such a family, making certain changes of design, such as wearing suits and ties instead of dashikis and inviting only white friends into the neighborhood to visit them, even though they would help win the approval of new neighbors, is to give up too much of their identity and cohesion.

GATHERING: After the teenage son in a "liberal" white family gets busted for smoking marijuana at school, the family initiates a series of meetings to decide if its life style and rules are still valid.

All families have the problem of bringing people together to locate and identify what is right and wrong with their systems. The black family cited in the preceding discussion uses its mealtimes to gather its members together. In other families, meetings, bedtimes, and even outings provide the context for a gathering of members. In still others, members never seem to come together at any one time. For them, blackboards, memos, and letters can serve as the gathering vehicles. Some families may never gather at all, or may gather so destructively, that their abilities to develop, maintain, and spread a design for family living is highly diminished. Gathering can be a key mechanism for maintaining the design of a system, but it can also be a vehicle for questioning and challenging the system. The "liberal" family in this example uses the crisis of a son getting busted as a gathering call to reexamine its design and possibly to change it. In other families such a gathering might include only some members, a kind of inner council, rather than all of them.

DESIGNING: When a financially successful middle-aged engineer is let go in a major organizational reshuffling, he and his family are forced to consider how they can each help raise additional money while cutting individual expenses.

Designing is in a way the primary centering submechanism. Designing gives birth to the articulated and unarticulated purposes of the family. It is the formulation of the desired shape of a family's space, a shape which emphasizes how traffic should flow through both bounding and linking mechanisms, that is, across its borders and within its own space. Designing is the formulation of a general style in which the family desires to live. Certain members, of course, may be far more important than other members in developing such a design. Indeed, they may be the only ones to gather for such a purpose. In the engineer's family, each member participates in the probe to determine how each can increase the amount of money coming into the family until their financial crisis is over. They agree to alter the shape of their lives. Explicitly, their crisis is financial; implicitly, it can be stated, "How does our financial crisis threaten the shape of our design for living together?"

ARRANGING: A couple, anxious for their children to be admitted to name colleges, decide to move to a suburban community noted for the academic excellence of its schools. Once there, they urge their children to meet the right people socially and to involve themselves in those extracurricular activities most likely to impress a college admissions board.

Father bawls Mother out for picking up their youngest son's undershirt after him. She responds, "I can't just let it lie here." "He'll never learn to pick things up for himself with you around," he retorts. She breaks down and cries, and he apologizes. Later, he proposes, "Everyone should take care of his own stuff. Otherwise, it goes in the rubbish." The next day Mother finds her husband's shoes in the bathroom and throws them in the waste basket.

Arranging is a working out of an accommodation between the design the family has developed for itself and the situation in which it finds itself. Sometimes a family will try to make events conform to its design, and sometimes it will alter its design to conform to events. The couple who want their children to be admitted to prestige schools work out accommodations that they feel will actualize their design. By its arranging operations, the family regulates its members' experience—externally by changing its geographic location, and internally by channeling members' energies in specific directions. In the second example, Mother's action of throwing out Father's shoes demonstrates that not all arranging need be rational.

SPREADING: When a son asks if he can have money to buy a state lottery ticket, he is told by his mother, "No, we don't believe in gambling. You should know by now that we don't throw our hard-earned money away on foolishness."

Spreading may be defined as a disseminating of the desired shape of a family space to all its members. In many families, it is the most readily observable of the centering submechanisms because most parents are anxious to pass on not only their design itself but also the morality and culture of the design. Teaching and preaching are often used "to spread the word," to make members aware of the family's spatial design. In the example the mother, by her negative injunctions concerning the purchase of lottery tickets, tells her son what the family design is and is not. Her message is that money is not to be wasted.

The spatial mechanism of centering has a special link to the target dimension of meaning. Centering submechanisms are employed in family members' attempts to gain access to all three target dimensions. Regardless of the targets being sought, however, a family's centering phenomena are accompanied by certain key meanings, often credos or central family beliefs. Meanings and actions are often inseparable as families seek to focus and design their lives around certain ideals. Whereas the bounding mechanism controls spatial perimeters and the linking mechanism controls spatial interiors, centering is concerned with spatial essences, with where and how members' traffic should ideally flow in order to create the best of all family lives.

Chapter 6

꒚꒚꒚꒚꒚꒚꒚꒚꒚꒚꒚꒚꒚꒚꒚꒚꒚꒚

Methods of Access: Time

Time is a variable of behavior that is often taken for granted by theoreticians and clinicians in the behavioral sciences. Perhaps it is because time is at once so ever-present and yet so differently experienced that it is seldom dealt with in detail as a locus of interest unto itself. Novelists, poets, musicians, and dramatists have been far more successful than the rest of us at both grasping and conveying the idea that the phenomenon of time is one of the most important ingredients of the human condition. As a result, no conceptual model with which we are familiar makes any attempt to explicate how time affects relations either in the family or in other social systems. Our own view of time as a social variable is based on the distance-regulation concept of "in phase and out of phase," which we introduced in Chapter Four. The temporal mechanisms and submechanisms we delineate below represent an elaboration of this basic concept. They are the family-system functions in and through which members move in phase and out of phase with one another as well as with events in the world at large.

Orienting

Orienting is the selecting, directing, and maintaining of attitudes and behaviors toward the past, present, future, and nontemporal realms of experience by emphasizing one or more of these realms or of the particular relationships among them. Where a family lives in time is as important as where it lives in space. Objectively, everyone lives in the present, but in actuality not everyone is oriented to the present. Three people can be in the same room, but one can be recalling the past, another planning his future, and the third checking to see if he has bubblegum on the sole of his shoe. A fourth could walk in thinking about *King Lear*. All four, though living in the present, could be oriented toward different time spheres. Such orientings determine the temporal field(s) in which members are to gain access to the targets of affect, power, and meaning. A family's temporal orientation thus works as a filter for members' experience in the present. The operational strength of such a filter may represent nothing stronger than a slight set toward past, present, future, or nontime experience, or, in other families, it may be nothing weaker than an actual predestining of ongoing experiences. Needless to say, individual members of a family may find themselves in or out of phase with one another because of conflicting orientations.

PAST ORIENTING: A mother of two grown sons, now in their thirties, has collected and preserved in her desk every paper, examination, and sketch her sons ever brought home from school, beginning with kindergarten.

A husband and wife find themselves further estranged from each other since he has acquiesced to the wife's getting a new tile floor for the kitchen. He only enters the kitchen when compelled, preferring instead to spend most of his time in the antique parlor.

Past orienting is a remembering, re-experiencing, or reenacting of something that has already taken place or existed. The goal of such orienting is to retrieve or hold onto that which has been. Past orienting is always concerned with history, family history especially. The mother who has saved all her sons' papers has preserved a plethora of artifacts to help her reconstruct and relive the past. All she needed to do was to go to her desk and open a drawer to help make the memories and history come alive. She, like the husband who feels estranged from his wife's remodeled tile kitchen, seems to live only partly in the present, preferring instead a nostalgia for the past. Without some past orienting, neither a family nor its members could experience any sense of continuity or of learning from the past. However, to immerse oneself totally in such orienting seems highly disabling, and anyone who does so probably requires some exterior support in coping with the exigencies and pressures of the present.

PRESENT ORIENTING: A mother, angry at her son, shouts, "If your grandfather could see you, he'd roll over in his grave." Her son replies, "Ma, I couldn't care less. These are the 70s, not 1910."

Present orienting is an orientation to the here and now, to what people are actually sensing, feeling, experiencing, and doing. Families for whom such orienting is dominant emphasize the spontaneous. They ask themselves, "What do I want to do now?" giving little consideration either to past or future. As the son tells his mother in the example above, "These are the 70's." Without some present orienting, a family's experience would be austere and uninspired. Indeed, it would be unable to maintain itself. It is difficult to conceive of anyone who is even remotely aware of what is going on around him who doesn't display at least some present orientation. A total immersion in the present, however, suggests an inability to learn from the past or to apply one's experience to the future. Extreme present orienting thus excludes both tradition and vision.

FUTURE ORIENTING: "What do you want to be when you grow up?" asks Aunt Jane. "I don't know. It's so far away," responds Jimmy. "If I were you, I'd want to be a lawyer. That's what I always wanted to be," says his aunt. Father chimes in, "If you're going to become a lawyer, you've got to plan ahead."

Future orienting is emphasizing what is to come by anticipating, imagining, and/or planning for it. Historians have suggested that the middle class has been dominated by a particular kind of future orientation, of deferring present gratification for future success. This postponement is not the only kind of future orienting that takes place in families, however. Members may anticipate the future with anything from intense excitement to boredom or dread. If the question of the past is, "Where have we been?" the question for the future is, "Where are we going?" Without any future orienting, a family would be lacking in vision, unable to conceive what might happen next week or next month or next year. A family that oriented itself exclusively to the future would, of course, be totally cut off from the here and now. Its dreams would tend to be unrealistic, if not completely unattainable.

NONTEMPORAL ORIENTING: The Shore family is worried because their oldest girl, who is approaching puberty, prefers playing with her dolls to being with people. Though she knows her family doesn't approve, she stays in her room with a pair of stuffed bears named Jack and Marie and acts out imaginary adventures.

Past, present, and future orienting all take place in relation to the calendar. Nontemporal orienting, however, is a submechanism composed of events unrelated to calendar time. Nontemporal orienting features fantasizing, dreaming, meditating, in private time unbound by past, present, or future calendar time constraints. In the example, the girl who invents and plays out stories for her stuffed animals is engaging in a nontemporal sphere experience. Her family is worried that she is too involved in such experience and uninvolved in other spheres, that is, in calendar time. Their fear, in short, is that she will be locked into her private nontemporal experience and unable to leave it to participate and live with other people, including the other members of her own family. In Western culture, people in such a position of orientation are often thought to be hallucinatory or pre-hallucinatory. Yet artists, thinkers, and creative people in all areas enter into fantasy and meditation in the nontemporal sphere in order to play and invent and increase their own understanding of things. The hallucinogenic and psychedelic drug culture is an attempt to explore further this realm of nontime. Many have been willing to cut their ties with calendar time to facilitate such exploration, but not without risk, since calendar time orientations function as conceptual anchors on experience. One of the hazards of a predominant nontemporal orientation is that the explorer may never return to the normal temporal frame of reference.

INTEGRATING: A father tells his children that Abraham Lincoln was always known for his honesty and fair dealings with people, that he once walked miles to repay several pennies he had overcharged a man. "Boy, I wanta be like Lincoln when I get big," little Joey exclaims. "Then you'd better stop mooching chocolate off your friends," his sister says, "You'll never get to be a great man that way."

Integrating is the referencing submechanism of orienting. It enables families to organize their experience of past, present, future, and nontemporal events into a pattern for interrelating events experienced in different time spheres. Such patterns may be chronological or historical. They may also be associational or even mythical. In the example, the little boy who wants to become like his father's description of Lincoln is reminded by his sister that he had better start acting like Lincoln in the present if he wants to be like Lincoln in the future. She suggests that the future is determined by ongoing present-day behavior, that if one wishes to change the future one must start by changing the present. Although a family could probably survive without integrating strategies, its orienting would suffer great impoverishment as a result. Without integrating processes families lack an awareness of where they are in time in terms of either immediate or external temporal events. Second, such families lack a temporal perspective from which to restabilize should they lose control of their own processes.

Clocking

Clocking is the regulation of the sequence, frequency, duration, and pace of immediately experienced events from moment to moment, hour to hour, and day to day. Whereas orienting is a mechanism concerned with calendar time, clocking is concerned with the daily cycles of time, or with those cycles occurring within a day. Clocking phenomena are among the most immediate, poignant, and (unlike many orienting phenomena) observable influences on family behavior. If people are out of phase with one another, they may not even be able to be home together at the same time, much less make love or fight with one another. Every experience is affected in one way or another by the way in which the family regulates its members' clocking. Whether a person feels his day has been well spent, whether a man and a woman make love satisfactorily, whether a family spends any time together at play, are all in part a question of clocking.

SEQUENCING: A large family on a picnic cannot agree

whether to go swimming before having lunch, to have lunch before going swimming, or to lie down on the grass and rest for awhile before doing either after a hot, unpleasant drive from the city.

The submechanism sequencing is employed by families to develop and maintain an order to events. In the example, the family on a picnic cannot decide what to do next—whether to go swimming, to eat, or to rest. In its sequencing operations a family determines its ad hoc priorities, that is, what activity it considers most important to do at any one moment. Certain family rules are built into sequencing to help illuminate and stabilize certain priorities, such as who will speak first in certain situations, what activities (for example, taking out the garbage) must immediately follow other activities, and what activities (such as playing ball) may not take place until other activities are completed. The sequence of events can affect the quality of an experience as much as the specific content of the events themselves. Thus two different families might do the same things but in different sequence— Family I in the sequence ABAAC, FamilyII in the order CBAAA. The ordering of the same general events in these two different ways can create two entirely different experiences.

FREQUENCY SETTING: A new father and mother are observed to have tremendous patience in helping their young child repeatedly put one foot in front of the other in order to learn how to walk. Three times a day they allow time to encourage this exercise.

Frequency setting is a submechanism concerned with the question of how often events are repeated. In setting the frequency of events, families develop and maintain patterns of repetition. The parents who teach their young child how to walk display a great tolerance for repeating the same event over and over again, perhaps because they know that their young child must learn by repetition and reinforcement. Repetition is a factor in all learning, but it can also produce boredom. How often people see each other, play a certain game, watch television, go out, or read a book depends on a decision about frequency. For one person, doing something three times in the course of a day may be sufficient; for another, 103 may be just the beginning. If these two people live in the same family they will probably often disagree about the frequency with which a particular activity or task ought to be done. In this way the setting of frequency can cause people either to come closer together or to move farther apart. Also the extremes of either constant repetition of an activity or its total absence can destroy the boundaries of time and meaning. We humans require a certain degree of repetition to perceive order in the world around us. Without it, experience becomes a blur and we learn nothing from it. The system of a family, too, requires repetition. Mealtimes, worktimes, sleep times, and recurring schedules of other specific activities can all help a family cohere. Indeed, the repetition of ordinary events is one of the most significant of all family phenomena, for it is in its handling of such everyday events that a family makes and reinforces its declarations about itself and the world.

DURATION SETTING: The exercise periods set aside by the young couple are usually so long that the child becomes exhausted and grumpy toward the end of each period.

In duration setting families determine how long events will last. They develop and maintain time limits. The couple in the example set a length of time for their child's activity which is too long for him to enjoy. Their experience demonstrates that negative or at least diminishing returns result if events are carried on too long. But if events are too short, not lasting long enough to meet a person's needs or expectations, futility, anxiety, and frustration can ensue.

PACING: When Grandpa comes to visit the Brown household, he is usually amazed and excited by the speed with which his grandchildren move from one thing to another, but he knows he can't keep up with them.

All families determine in part the speed or rate of events they experience by regulating how fast things happen. This is what we mean by *pacing*. Thus Grandpa lives at a much slower pace than his grandchildren. He doesn't move as fast as they do, nor does he experience as many different events over the same period of time. Pacing is the regulation not only of an absolute rate or speed of events, however, but also of the variations in speed from one point in time to another. Such variations, if repeated, form rhythmic patterns. Pacing rhythms constitute a very complicated temporal field in which members of families move in and out of phase with one another. Each of us has no doubt had the experience of learning something more quickly or more slowly than somebody else or of progressing at a pace that is different from that of a coworker on the same job. In either type of situation, the slower persons have the task of catching up, a task that can generate considerable anxiety. The faster persons may have as difficult a time: waiting for slow-paced persons to catch up, they can become anxious to move on. Eventually they can feel blocked, frustrated, and even enslaved by the more slow-paced persons. In general, the smaller the space within which people of different paces try to live and the greater the amount of time they hope to spend together, the greater their task of regulating pacing differences is.

SCHEDULING: When Johnny and Peter Bowen notice that their parents have accepted yet another drink at their neighbors' home, they remind their parents that it is already past the time when they had promised to take the kids home.

Not all clocking is designed on an ad hoc basis. Families schedule many events in order to regulate their sequence, frequency, duration, and/or pace. Such scheduling is done in advance, before the commencement of an event, and is the referencing submechanism of clocking. Much scheduling is the establishment of deadlines for the completion of goal-oriented tasks. Schedules have the dual function of reminding and prodding families about what needs to be done, and prodding them to do it. In the example, the Bowen parents schedule a time at which they will take their sons home. Their boys demonstrate that the scheduling submechanism also includes a check on whether or not events are taking place in accord with the time plan established for them or whether a new schedule has to be made. Families frequently reschedule in an effort to establish time structures that more adequately accommodate members' access clocking patterns.

In a very immediate sense, the way in which a family clocks its movements determines its members' access to affect, power, and meaning. From infancy—when the length of time it took our mothers to respond to our hunger cries was an indication of our access to nurturance—we have been receiving clocking messages, not only about access to nurturance and affect, but also about when to start and finish things, how fast to move, and even how much time to give to specific events. It is no overstatement to suggest that a family's clocking patterns operationally reveal what the family considers most important.

Synchronizing

Synchronizing is the temporal equivalent of the spatial mechanism, centering. It is a mechanism through which a family develops and maintains a program for regulating the family's total use of time, including the ways in which members clock and orient their movements. Synchronizing includes the creation and execution of temporal guidelines, much as centering includes the creation and execution of spatial guidelines. Perhaps the major synchronizing questions facing the family can be expressed as follows: "How do we spend our time so we can get the maximal amount of what we want out of life? Which targets are we going to devote our time to pursuing?" Operationally, these may be translated, "How much time do we want to spend together? How do we manage to spend the time together we think we want to spend together?"

MONITORING: The oldest son in the Green family notices that his father seems grumpy every morning, and he passes this information on to his mother. That evening she approaches her husband and asks him whether he thinks he is working too hard.

Monitoring is the referencing submechanism of synchronizing. It is the recurring assessment of whether the family's use of time is beneficial. Monitoring may be done primarily by one person or by the family as a whole. It may be crisis-oriented or it may be ongoing. In the Green family, the oldest boy acts as monitor and passes on his perceptions to his mother, who in turn raises the issue with her husband. Families often get into time ruts, thereby doing things habitually, without real cause or perspective. Monitoring helps restore perspective and, as a result, sets into motion a potential for change. Virtually all families have devices for monitoring their movements in the course of time. Crises frequently make these devices visible. This is not to suggest that all monitoring takes place directly. For example, one member may initiate the monitoring process for a family by succumbing to psychosomatic illness.

Whether visible and direct, or invisible and indirect, it is by means of its monitoring that every family assesses the degree of satisfaction it is experiencing as a consequence of the life it has been evolving. It thus decides whether its program and priorities are being carried out, or whether the program itself is a good one or not.

PRIORITY SETTING: A young couple who have attended several "happy hours" in their apartment building, and have had divergent experiences, argue whether they should spend the next evening at a cocktail party or at home by themselves.

Monitoring operations lead somewhat naturally into another submechanism of synchronizing. In setting priorities, families determine what kinds of events are most important for family members. As the example suggests, priority setting nearly always generates some conflict. Even when people generally agree, the exigencies of life, combined with members' individual time-regulation differences and their separate visions of target possibilities, would seem to make complete agreement nearly impossible. Which of several target visions and styles of temporal regulation will gain priority is mediated by power operations in the family. It is in priority setting that the time and power dimensions are most closely interrelated. Many of the most important continuing decisions a family has to make include the determination of its temporal priorities.

PROGRAMMING: Mister Gore, the breadwinner of the Gore family, has a nervous breakdown, attributable at least in part to the workload he has taken on to advance himself at his law firm. During the father's convalescence, the parents and children decide to slow down the pace of their lives, to build more fun and relaxation in to their everyday experience, and thus to alter their hitherto single-minded pursuit of material and social advancement.

Programming is the developing of guidelines for how to use time in pursuit of a family life plan. Programming produces a conception of who and what the family wants to become, a conception that is nearly always articulated, or that it is at least possible to articulate, in one form or another, though not necessarily with pure logic and reason. The Gore family in the example radically alters its temporal program from one of working hard and deferring gratification in the hope of eventual achievement to one of much greater enjoyment in the here and now. Likewise, each family develops its own idiosyncratic life plan for attaining its goals in the course of time. In some families programming phenomena may occur only infrequently. A tradition-bound family, for instance, may not feel the need for new programming since its life plan is firmly established. In other families, whose life plan is less structured or more alterable, a great deal of programming activity may take place. In short, the amount of change a family will consider making in the ways it spends its time is directly related to the operation of its programming mechanism.

COORDINATING: In attempting to preserve family unity and cohesion, a group of married sisters hold a reunion of their three separate families for two weeks in August every summer. Within each of their families, members are obliged to forego their own projects at this period of the summer, a task the husbands and children complain about.

Coordinating is that submechanism in which a family organizes and adjusts its members' movements so that they are in some synchronization with each other, and in accord with the family program. If programming is basically a planning activity, coordinating is clearly an implementing one. In the example above it is the married sisters who assume primary responsibility for coordinating their families' movements so that the annual reunion takes place. Without some coordination, no program or life plan, however well designed, is likely to be effected. Coordination may be implicit or explicit. That of the sisters in the example is quite explicit. In other families, members' deviations from program norms may be greeted with silence or a special glance. Whether coordination is explicit or implicit, its purpose is to get family members moving in time with the program in such a way that they do not hinder or obstruct each other, but rather facilitate one another's activities. In some families, this type of facilitation is fostered by gathering in order to do things together, whereas in others it is accomplished by moving apart to do things separately.

REMINDING: When the husbands and children complain about the family reunions engineered by the three sisters, they are each reminded of how important the reunion is for all concerned, including themselves.

Reminding is a submechanism in which families make their

members aware of what their life plan program is, its origin, the way in which it is to be maintained and enforced, and how it can be altered. In this example, the sisters keep each of their families openly conscious of their annual reunion. Not all reminding need be verbal however. The routine of a program itself and the concomitant dislocation that is felt when such routine is broken are less overt but may be no less effective reminders. Discontent is often the stimulus for reminding activity. When one sees a family experiencing discontent without reminding, however, one can begin to suspect either that the family fails to use the reminding mechanism or that there is no program felt to be viable and worth reminding members about. The connection between these submechanisms, programming and reminding, is especially close in the traditional family, in which the life plan is essentially nonmodifiable. In such a family, the programming experience of the younger-generation members consists solely in their reminding and being reminded.

One's satisfaction with existence is closely dependent on whether he feels he is getting what he wants out of life, a goal irrevocably connected with the utilization of time. As we have seen, the various time phenomena of family are orchestrated by the mechanism of synchronizing. In establishing and maintaining a program or plan for how members should clock and orient their movements in time, synchronizing plays a significant part in regulating each family member's access to the targets of affect, power, and meaning. If a family's centering operations can be said to inform its members what the proper targets of life are and where they are to be found, synchronizing tells them how to utilize their time in order to attain them.

Chapter 7

Methods of Access: Energy Mechanisms

There is perhaps no subject more difficult for us to write about than a family's energy mechanisms. Though everyone might agree that energy is a key ingredient of life, people are often at a loss to articulate just what they mean by the term "energy." As far as we know, there are no social or psychological studies concerned with the energy of families. Furthermore, there are very few models that we can use to describe the flow of energy other than the models of physics, models from which we have necessarily had to borrow, but which in general we regard as inappropriate to family experience. All the scales of physical measurement and quantification, such as those for conversion, absolute limits, and sources of regeneration, are phenomenologically different entities when they appear in a social system framework.

The psychoanalytic notion of cathexis is perhaps the most famous attempt to define and understand psychological energy. The term "cathexis" itself was borrowed from the study of static electricity and has been used to describe the attachment one person feels for another person, or idea—and the energy invested in that person, object, or idea. Sigmund Freud's chain of conceptualization went from electrical to biochemical to energy phenomena. He proposed on a somewhat mythical basis two types of mental energy: creative (libidinal) instinctual drives and destructive (death or thanatos) instinctual drives. Though we have also borrowed from Freud in our conceptualization of energy, our primary interest is not instinctual drives. Rather, we are interested in the mechanisms and strategies families employ to regulate the flow of their energies. In Chapter Four, we introduced the concept of charge-discharge ratio, emphasizing that the primary energy issue in families is the regulation of energy flow to attain energic balance or imbalance. Families in great distress are often those which have failed to balance out their members' energies. Waste, failure to mobilize for change, chronic chaos are all potential results of energy imbalance, occurring when families develop disabling strategies in their attempts to carry out their energy functions.

All of the energy mechanisms we shall discuss in this chapter are social mechanisms. Family energies may have a biochemical as well as a social component, but as long as the energies are regulated by social processes we are interested in them. Thus, at a family meal, for which hamburgers are served, a biochemist might investigate the number of calories and nutrients in each burger and study the effect of metabolic rate in each member on the conversion of calories into energy. In comparison, we would want to know whether the family is acquiring or expending energy at its mealtime. We would study the family's social process to determine the context in which the hamburger is eaten. In one family, mealtime might be dull and unappealing, leaving its members bored and uninterested in what transpires. A second family may turn such a mealtime into an exciting occasion by having its hamburgers cooked over an open fire in the back yard. Both families could be acquiring the same amount of biochemical energy, yet one family could be experiencing social charge while the other experiences an actual drain in social energy. One can easily imagine a third slightly more complex example in which the social relations of a family help to regulate members' actual biochemical intake by burning the hamburger, by giving out skimpy or uneven portions, or by putting such a strain on mealtime that either no one feels like eating or members overeat to avoid recognizing the strain. In this way, a family's social processes can affect the total charge-discharge ratio of its members.

Fueling

Fueling regulates the acquiring of energy. Perhaps no other major family mechanism is as difficult to observe—much less measure—as fueling, because so much of a person's acquisition of energy takes place internally, invisible to an observer. For instance, a person can be sitting in a chair reading a book, and yet he may be obtaining the energy he needs to enjoy the rest of an evening. Another person reading the same book may actually be experiencing an energy drain. How can there be such a difference in fueling experiences? If one pulls an auto into a service station, he is able to note precisely how much fuel he is getting. Social fueling, however, is a far more complex phenomenon. Every social item or event is energically inert until it is experienced. Individuals may not draw on such energy until they actually experience the item or event in their own idiosyncratic ways. The potential energy that can be acquired from an event thus varies from individual to individual. Clearly, the acquisition and accumulation of energy is a vitally important process for any family. A social unit might be able to survive on biological energy. Should it rely exclusively on such energy, however, it would condemn itself to a rather bleak and uninteresting future.

SURVEYING: Looking for something to do, Johnny Mason turns on his radio. Finding nothing he likes, he picks up a novel. After reading a few pages, he puts the book down and decides to raid the refrigerator. On the way to the kitchen, he passes through the living room, where his parents are watching a movie on television. He lounges around, watching it for awhile along with them until he decides it is so inane that he goes into the kitchen and stuffs himself with leftover food.

Fueling begins with surveying, that is, with locating the sources of energy. In the example, Johnny expends energy in various directions as he tries to locate a viable source of social energy. When various social alternatives fail to charge him, he heads into the kitchen to fuel himself with an intake of biochemical energy. The search for energy sources may range from very passive to very active prospecting in families. It would be a mistake to assume that more active surveying inevitably results in finding more or greater sources of energy, however. Less adventurous families may receive great amounts of charge, if they locate and hold to the best sources. In general, family members' surveying operations are linked to their curiosity about themselves and the world. Families and members who are curious tend to explore their space either more widely or more fully and with a great deal of drive. In searching for more energy, the curious tend to extend the human boundaries of any particular access or target field. In so doing, they do not fear to expend significant amounts of energy, because they expect to receive significant amounts back in refueling.

TAPPING: After a dinner, devoid of any conversation, the three Dierkers gravitate to different rooms of the house. The son goes to his room to look out the window where he wistfully watches a sandlot game on a nearby field. Father goes to his den to look at the latest edition of *Playboy,* and Mother stays in the kitchen to phone several friends and invite them over for an evening of canasta.

In tapping, families try to hook up with the sources of energy they have located. At its extremes, tapping may be indiscriminate and all-inclusive, or very discriminating and highly selective. Neither way is necessarily better than the other. Indiscriminate tappers may try to hook onto everything and wind up exhausted, whereas the too selective may deny themselves excessively. Many critical family battles are fought over how or in what ways fueling is to take place, especially over what sources members may tap and what sources they may not. In the larger culture, whole schools of morality and ethics have formed and divided over just these questions, especially that of fueling from sources of lust and violence. The family is no different. What sources members tap often turns into a discussion of both individual and group morality.

CHARGING: Bob Jordon loves to play Monopoly. He pesters his reluctant sister Joan into playing with him. After awhile Joan starts winning and gets excited about the game herself. Mother hears her daughter cheering and moves in to watch her children play. Father, however, hates Monopoly and goes upstairs to listen to some music.

Charging is an actual taking in of energy. It increases the amount of energy available to a system. In this example, charging takes place quite smoothly. Bob acquires energy simply by playing the game, Joan by winning, Mother by watching her children happy and excited, and Father by leaving the scene to listen to some music. It doesn't take much imagination, however, to envision how such a scene could turn into a battleground. Suppose Joan were losing instead of winning and wanted to stop playing. Suppose Mother had to break up a fight instead of watching two happy children. Suppose Father, as a way of preventing future fights, forbade anyone in the house to play Monopoly for the next month. In such a situation family members might acquire energy but of a quite negative nature. In observing fueling phenomena, then, one must ask not only in what ways fueling takes place, but also in what amounts the charge is occurring, and in what direction (positive or negative). The goal of most families is to gain at least a small surplus of biochemical and social energies, a surplus that will allow them to grow and develop beyond the mere maintenance of the status quo. Without such surplus, social growth and developmental change may not be possible. However, the goal of obtaining energic surplus is not in conflict with the overall energy goal of achieving a nearly even ratio of charge to discharge, because what is initially surplus energy can become a needed expenditure for growth or for meeting a crisis.

STORING: The Hadleys make it a point to see all the new "in" movies and plays, buy paintings by the artists currently in vogue, read all the "right" books, and collect contemporary slogans, fashions, and rumors, which they proceed to name and to converse about with enthusiasm whenever they are invited out to dinner or to a party.

Families experience storing when they develop and maintain a reservoir of available energy in the forms of meanings, images, feelings, and/or body responses. In the above example, the Hadleys store their surplus social energy in order to expend it later for their own social gain. Not all storing is so self-serving or as consciously undertaken, however. All remembered items are stores of individual and family energy. Some items, of course, store much more energy than others. Traumas, for instance, can be remembered in ways which store for future release tremendous amounts of energy. In general, the kind of energy a family stores reflects the kind of experience each family has. A family that is predominantly athletic and given to expressions of physical energy, for example, will tend to store energies in muscular reflexes and images of physical competition while a more cerebral family might store its energies in ideas and images of intellectual dialectics. Amounts of stored energy are also important. A family whose energy reserves are low may have difficulty meeting crises, because its members may not be able to act when they need to act. Correspondingly, a surplus of stored energies may seem overwhelming or inappropriate to other persons when it is finally expended.

REQUISITIONING: Early one morning the Segals are invited to go on a picnic by their neighbors, the Willards. The Segal children are excited by the prospect, but Mr. Segal is not. "I wanted to watch the game on TV this afternoon," he protests. "You can watch the game next week," his wife replies. "The rest of us want to go on a picnic."

Requisitioning is the referencing submechanism of the fueling mechanism. It is the submechanism in which family members comment about their fueling processes. Requisitioning operations consist of the making of plans to set up, maintain, or alter the acquiring of energy. As the Segal example suggests, not all requisitioning is based on agreement. Obsolete requisitioning, based on measurements that are no longer relevant or true, may lead either to significant conflicts among family members, or to stratified ruts if everyone unquestioningly continues to follow them. By its referencing operations, a family's requisitioning can perform either a beneficial or a disabling function. It offers the possibility of checking and reshaping fueling strategies that don't seem to work, but it also creates a vehicle for potential distortion and poor fueling planning.

Investing

Investing is the regulation of expending or discharging energies to targets and bearers of targets, whether they be people, objects, or events. Whereas fueling phenomena are often very difficult to observe, investing operations are usually recognizable. Energy investments provide a unique portrait of who and what a family is. Common sense tells us that what a family considers important is not so much what it claims is important, but what it commits its energies to. Investing as a term implies expenditure, not just for expenditure's sake, but for some return. The ideal energy investment is one in which family batteries are recharged as well as discharged. In practice this may often mean doing what members want to do or working at what they want to work at. "Drudge work" usually refers to work that one does not want to do, work in which one expends energy without being recharged.

RECONNOITERING: A family arriving in a big city takes out its maps and guidebooks to figure out where it will go on the first evening of its vacation.

Investing begins with reconnoitering, with locating and selecting targets for family energies. The example portrays a rather pure reconnoitering phenomenon. Most reconnoitering is more closely related to the routines of daily life, in which the choice about how family energies ought to be invested is minimal because so much energy is committed to habitual maintenance tasks. Wealth increases the range of a family's reconnoitering choices. Even with wealth, however, the momentum of habitual and unconscious commitments can restrict the selection of new or different targets. At another extreme, of course, families can lose all perspective in continuing efforts to expend energy in a new or different way. Such families can spend the bulk of their energies in mere reconnoitering, without ever making a commitment. Families who find themselves unsuccessful in their reconnoitering operations often reflect either an inability to recognize targets appropriate to their interests and energies, or a lack of knowledge about how to go about the process of reconnoitering. The end result of either can be the relinquishing of hope for a better life.

ATTACHING: A big fight has just taken place in a family, involving all members. The still irritated members each treat a pair of surprised visitors to a vicious game of "get the guests."

The attaching mechanism focuses on the way in which families direct their energies to specific targets. Thus the guests in the example become the targets of a great deal of negative energy from a family that has just had a lacerating fight. Each member of the family seizes the guests as a target for his own anger and disgust. Energic attachments may be strong or weak, welcome or unwelcome. There is no general right or wrong way to make energic contact with a specific person. A passive emotional attachment on the part of one person may lead the recipient to think, "He says he loves me, but it doesn't feel very strong," whereas an attachment that is expressed more aggressively may cause the other to decide, "This isn't love—it's control." Attaching operations are a fertile ground for family conflict. Which ideas, beliefs, people or causes one ought to choose as targets for one's energy inevitably produce differing opinions and conflicting actions.

COMMITTING: After two miscarriages, a wife finally gives birth to a healthy first child, and the new parents now give as much of themselves as they can to the child, even to the point of never going out in the evening.

Committing is the devotion of energies to targets. In the example above, the twice disappointed couple makes an overloaded energy committment to its newborn. The infant becomes virtually the sole target of its parents' energies, including the energies earmarked earlier for the child's two aborted siblings. Patterns of seduction and betrayal, in which all of one person's energies are devoted to attachment, and little or none to commitment, are sources of another kind of committing crisis. Even without such deception, however, even when people are dealing as honestly as possible with each other, committing phenomena can lead to intense and difficult conflict. Serious difficulties develop whenever members are required to commit more energy to a target than they wish or are able to devote, or when they are not permitted by family regulation to commit the amount of energies they wish to. In a very basic sense, every positively charged commitment toward a target is a commitment for survival. Persons commit energy to other persons, ideas, and events because they want those persons, ideas, or events to continue to live, perhaps to grow and develop and expand, but certainly not to die. Validation of personhood is intimately linked to such commitments. A commitment of negative energy, however, is at root a commitment to destroy, to do away with a part or the whole of a target, be it person, idea, or event.

DETACHING: In the Cooper family, Father and Mother talk a lot to each other at table. Whenever their daughter Peggy interrupts, Father discontinues his conversation with Mother to converse with Peggy. Afterward, he resumes his conversation with Mother. Whenever their son Jimmy interrupts, however, Father and Mother continue talking, pausing only long enough to ask him to wait until they are finished.

Detaching is a disconnecting, a removing of energy, either in whole or in part, from targets. It is the reverse of attaching. Like all other family mechanisms detaching may be employed for positive or negative ends. Detaching from destructive causes and processes can be an important tactic in preventing family tragedies. But unwanted detachments can be experienced as intense emotional deprivation. Another kind of deprivation can be experienced when a family detaches in a seemingly fickle way from all its commitments, even recent ones. Also, if detaching is based on arbitrary and non-negotiable rules, as it is in the foregoing example, members can feel irrationally regulated and robbed. Still another type of problem arises if detachment cannot be executed because of compulsion or fixed ideas. Finally, complete and universal detachment is destructive, because it represents an emotional withdrawal from all social interaction.

ACCOUNTING: Mrs. Cochran gets up with her eight-year-old Benny twice a week before dawn to feed him his breakfast and drive him to the oversubscribed local rink for peewee hockey practice. She returns home grumpy and tired and slips back into bed. Father, still in bed, remarks, "Marian, I think these early morning hockey practices are getting to be too much for you." She replies, "I don't see you doing anything to help, John."

The bickering between John and Marian is a form of accounting, that is, a keeping track of energy commitments in order to determine whether they are sufficient, and whether they are beneficial to the family. In its referencing capacity, accounting can function as a perceptual and conceptual checkpoint and safety valve on a family's investment strategies.

Mobilizing

By means of its mobilizing mechanism, families develop and implement guidelines for regulating the total flow of energy in a family, including how energy should be acquired and expended.

Every family has its own energy mandates—either implicit or explicit—concerning what its proper rhythmic patterns ought to be. How the family's energy guidelines are first of all designed and then executed determines a family's energy efficiency. Even with low amounts of biochemical energy at its disposal, a family may, if it operates efficiently, become more effective than a family with great funds of biochemical energy that it can't seem to regulate satisfactorily.

GAUGING: A father makes the judgment that his lackadaisical collegiate son does not have enough drive or "get up and go" to get himself into a prestigious law school.

Gauging is the referencing submechanism of mobilizing. It is the taking of an inventory to determine how much energy is needed. The father in the example takes a reading of how much energy his son has available and is willing to expend, and then compares this reading with the amount of energy he thinks a student will have to commit in order to qualify for entrance into a top law school. Gauging need not always be so carefully plotted out. Body responses, such as fatigue or listlessness, are gauging signals, as are emotional crises of one kind or another. When the family's own gauging processes are ineffectual, gauging judgments may come from outside the family—from friends, physicians, neighbors, even bartenders and beauty shop operators. Gauging distortions occur when families make errors in judgment by thinking they have more energy than they actually have, or by underestimating the amount of energy they have available. Such misjudgments often occur when family members make gauging projections for other family members that are based on their own energy rhythms. For instance, a high-energy wife may undertake countless community projects, for her husband as well as herself to participate in, only to find her husband overcome by fatigue in trying to keep up with her.

BUDGETING: Mr. and Mrs. Scammon have different ideas about how to use their energies. Mr. Scammon feels the family should buy a farm and spend its weekends there, catching its second wind after its week in the city. Mrs. Scammon feels the family should take advantage of the stimulation the city provides by going to plays, concerts, and art exhibits on the weekends.

Budgeting is a submechanism in which families develop a plan for regulating the flow of their energy, including the ways in which members will acquire and expend it. The Scammon family has a problem because the two plans proposed for the family are personal, each serving the individual energy needs of one parent but not both. To implement one proposal at the exclusion of the other may be to violate the energy rhythms of the other parent. Since energy is absolutely vital to life, the formulation of a scheme for adequate two-directional energy flow is one of the most important of all family processes. Much of the quality of life is determined by the appropriateness of a family's plan to the varying energy needs of individual members. The expressions "I am starved," "I am overloaded," "I am bored to death," or "I am simply exhausted" may each represent a personal response to the family's energy budget.

MUSTERING: Their neighbors can't understand how the Woodwards manage to survive one seemingly insurmountable crisis after another. Mrs. Woodward feels the family's secret is its faith in God to pull them through. Mr. Woodward feels they still wouldn't survive without his occasional pep talks exhorting each member to give his all when everything looks bleakest.

Mustering is a submechanism in which family members rouse and focus their energy. In general, families suffer two kinds of mustering crises. The first type is one of energy deficits, and the second, of energy diffusion. A family responds to deficit crises by drawing on its energy stores. In response to energy diffusion, a family may be obliged to bring its energies into denser concentration and sharper focus to develop, at least temporarily, a single-mindedness of purpose. A family's "strength" is often measured by its abilities to muster its energies at critical times as in the example of the Woodward family. Some families reverse the sequence, however, and actually create crises because of the joy and excitement crisis periods bring. At the other extreme, some families deny that crises ever exist and thus prevent mustering from ever taking place. They tend to reduce all experiences, even supreme crisis experiences, to the routine. They have no interest in, much less enthusiasm for, anything out of the ordinary.

TRANSFORMING: In the Spencer family, when members' disagreements escalate and threaten to become physically violent, either the antagonists themselves or the family as a whole ask Grandfather to hear their dispute. Once in his revered presence, they calm down and stop threatening each other. In fact, when Grandfather speaks the rest are silent.

Transforming is a mechanism families use to regulate the level of their energies (high, medium, low), the form of their energies (emotional, muscular, conceptual, imaginative), and the charge of their energy (positive, neutral, negative). The Spencers transform all three qualities: level, form, and charge. First, the ire of the angry contestants subsides in Grandpa's presence, so that the level of discharge is significantly lowered. Also the Spencers regulate form by not allowing verbal emotional energy to become violent physical energy. Finally, they transform energy charge, since the antagonists' negative energy is turned into neutral if not altogether positive energy in Grandfather's presence. As this example illustrates, transforming phenomena determine in large part whether the family system runs smoothly and efficiently or is disrupted by frequent dramatic clashes and crashes.

DISTRIBUTING: Mrs. McGruder instructs her children to tiptoe so they don't wake up their father in the morning. She knows that if he wakes up too suddenly, he will throw a tantum and be grouchy the rest of the day.

Distributing is one of the most readily visible of the mobilizing submechanisms, because it is the assigning and conducting of energy from where it is available to where it is wanted, needed, or attracted. In the example, Mrs. McGruder sees to it that her children's early morning energy is assigned and conducted away from their father. When individual energies mesh appropriately, energy distribution can effectively help to defend and maintain the system and to accomplish tasks that need to be performed. When separate individual energies clash, instrumental family goals are often not achieved, and the defense and maintenance of the system is thereby put in jeopardy. Without an efficient distributing mechanism, everyday maintenance tasks, such as taking out the rubbish, cooking, laundering, and doing the dishes, can either pile up or become arenas in which individual energies constantly clash.

Without enough energy a system cannot survive. With too

much it can become overstimulated, destructive, and chaotic. Mobilizing is the family system's mechanism for designing and carrying
out a plan of energy flow, for determining the purpose and
direction of the family's fueling and investing. Through its mobilizing mechanism the family develops a scheme for balancing its
total charge-discharge ratio so that members have enough energy
available to meet family needs, and also enough suitable targets
toward which their energies can be appropriately released. A family
that fails to budget successfully for either or both of these needs
fails to alert its members to the full potential of life.

Chapter 8

Methods of Access:
Plans and Strategies

In Chapters Five, Six, and Seven, we have attempted to deal with the access mechanisms of space, time, and energy separately and with the submechanisms of each mechanism discretely. In reality a family's space, time, and energy operations overlap and happen all at once. Even our own selected and hypothetically developed examples reflect such simultancity. Thus in the final example of Chapter Seven—in which Mother instructs the children to be quiet in the morning, so that their father will not waken too suddenly and be in a bad mood—we have an excellent illustration not only of energic mobilizing and its submechanism distributing, but also of the spatial mechanism of linking and its submechanism buffering and the temporal mechanism of clocking and its submechanism sequencing. This kind of operational overlap is particularly acute among what we call the modulating mechanisms—the centering of space, the synchronizing of time, and the mobilizing of energy.

Plans of Access

The modulating mechanisms perform a special integrative function for the family system. Within each access dimension, they coordinate the workings of the other two major mechanisms. The modulating mechanisms can thus be examined as a shorthand survey of the range of a family's decision-making processes. Most investigators identify the following stages of the decision-making process: (1) gathering data about what is at stake, (2) judging which data are most important, (3) choosing a course of action, (4) executing a course of action, and (5) maintaining a course of action in accord with the choice. Because they permit an examination of these various stages in the family system's decision-making processes, the three modulating mechanisms can be of particular value to the work of family therapy. They provide a framework within which therapists and family members alike can conceptualize conflicts about how a family can and does operate. The modulating mechanisms also provide a logical progression of tasks by means of which a family can focus on the important job of developing and implementing an access model all members can accept and adhere to.

In order to fulfill its integrative and decision-making functions, each of the modulating mechanisms is concerned with the development and implementation of a family traffic plan. A traffic plan is a design for moving people, things, and events through the family's social space. It is an important part of any access model a family might develop for itself. Each of the three modulating mechanisms develops and implements a traffic plan for its specific dimension. Each modulating mechanism has a range of four basic traffic options. Because of the considerable overlap of options from dimension to dimension, the family itself has four basic plans from which to choose.

The first plan features procentric spatial movements, prosynchronous temporal movements, and meshing (pro-mobilized) energies. A procentric traffic pattern features a great deal of movement toward the center of the family. Members gather frequently together in the morning, at meals, in the evening. They would probably also tend to read the same books and champion the same causes. A prosynchronous family spends a great deal of time together, or at least as much time as possible, blending its various individual schedules and orientations. A family in which energies mesh is one in which members fuel up and invest their energies together, usually in similar ways. They share the same sources and the same targets. To use colloquial terms, the *pro* traffic model advocates "a closely knit family." It is probably the most often articulated family traffic plan.

The second traffic plan is the reverse of the first. It is anti-centric, antisynchronous, and divergent (anti-mobilized). This *anti* model encourages a great deal of movement out and away from the family, particularly away from its center. Members go places away from each other. They do not tend to share the same space. Rather, each tends to develop his own space and move autonomously toward his own ends. In an antisynchronous family, members have highly individualized schedules and orientations, and there is little or no attempt to make them coincide. They tend to spend a minimal amount of time with one another, only enough to establish a common family space. They prefer instead to spend as much time as possible apart from each other on their own projects and activities. Their energies are divergent, in that they fuel up from different sources and invest in different targets. The family subscribing to the second plan might be colloquially described as a "family of individuals," a family that encourages each individual to develop his autonomy as far as possible.

The third traffic plan is one of parallel movement. Such a family's spatial traffic is acentric. Members neither move closer together toward the center, nor do they move farther apart from one another. Certain acentric families may adopt static traffic plans, but this is by no means universal. The members tend to maintain the same distance toward one another, even when they move. Similarly, members' temporal traffic is asynchronous. They tend to spend the same moderate amount of time with one another from week to week. Their energies tend to be disengaged (amobilized). A momentum is established and maintained. Rarely is it altered.

What are the reasons for such parallelism within a system? In some families, the parallelism stems from a feeling that there is an appropriate, moderate amount of space, time, and energy that families should share; that it is undesirable either to withhold or to share too much, and that members should establish the middle ground and observe it quite consistently. In others, centering, synchronizing, and mobilizing are felt to be irrelevant, perhaps owing to a belief in some system of cosmology, by which everything is predetermined and over which humans have no control. A third and much more frequent reason is that paralleling represents a kind of holding operation adopted in response to otherwise unviable options. The couple who have been hurt too often by each other to want to seek greater intimacy, but for whom the idea of separation and divorce is intolerable, may adopt such a model. Often a family executing this third plan is viewed as a "fatalistic" or "dutiful" family. Neither of these two words seems quite as accurate to us, however, as a description of a "parallel family."

The fourth plan is ecentric, esynchronous, and vacillating (e-mobilized). Members' traffic in such a plan sometimes flows toward the center and each other and sometimes away from the center and each other. Sometimes, it may even resemble paralleling. The major attribute of ecentric traffic is its changeability. Similarly, esynchronous time is equally changeable, and members' temporal patterns are unpredictable. Some weeks, the family may spend nearly all its time together; other weeks, members will be almost constantly apart. Furthermore, members' energies will vacillate. Sometimes they will be acquired or expended here, and sometimes there. Again, there is no single pattern. Such a family might be described as "eccentric."

These four prototypic traffic plans are used by families as a basis for developing their actual traffic modes. No one family that we know of totally and exclusively exhibits only one conceptual and operational traffic pattern. Such exclusivity, we suspect, would reduce each of the models to their logical absurdity. For instance, no family could be constantly gravitating toward its center unless members could also move away from it, nor could members move constantly away from the center unless they could also have some opportunity to move toward it. All families then develop some mixture of the four pure traffic patterns, any one of which might prove successful as a dominant overall plan for a given family.

Each plan provides a different means for grappling with the tension of sameness and difference among family members. Each presents "a solution" for this tension, a way of resolving it. It is our contention that there is no one ideal way for all families. Each family has the task of choosing its own "solution." In fact, families may, and customarily do, adopt different "solutions" during different phases of their lifecycles. For instance, a family that has been highly procentric, prosynchronous, and meshing when its offspring are young can adopt an anticentric, antisynchronous, and divergent model for handling these tensions of sameness and difference as the offspring mature.

Needless to say, not all families successfully actualize the traffic models they articulate. Many a family with procentric and prosynchronous *ideals* produces acentric, ecentric, or anticentric patterns *in actuality*. Such patterns develop, in these situations, not by design but as the result of an inability to implement the desired plan, either because members do not really want the ideal they articulate, or because the ideal is against the grain of members' real propensities. Either way members develop strategies that inhibit rather than facilitate the ideal.

Strategies of Access

The primary contribution that the access mechanisms component of our family process model makes to our understanding of strategies is twofold: first it names the action of a strategy and, second, it identifies the action as intrinsic to the family's primary structures for regulating members' access to targets within the affect, power, and meaning dimensions. Every strategy is thus directly associated with one or more of the access mechanisms. All families share the same basic family system functions as delineated by the mechanisms. They need not share the same or even similar strategies, however, because every family develops its own particular strategies to carry out the functions of its mechanisms as it sees fit. Consequently, although the family's mechanisms are limited in number and can be listed in this and the preceding three chapters, there is no conceptual limit on the potential number of strategies families may call upon or invent. A further difference is that mechanisms are evaluatively neutral. They are functions that can be used for good or evil, depending on the quality of strategies a family employs in implementing them, but they are neither good nor evil in themselves.

In order to examine more closely the relationship between mechanisms and strategies, let us examine a couple of family sequences. First, let us examine again the Weber family sailing sequence (cited in the strategy section, Chapter Four), in which the family set out to achieve emotional cohesion by going sailing. With encouragement from her parents and younger sister, Linda, a teenage daughter, was induced to go with them. Unfortunately, the sequence ended with Linda, her sister Elise, and Mrs. Weber feeling unhappy with each other and alienated from Franz Weber, whose delay in getting the boat in the water helped to prompt their unhappy reaction. In structural terms the Weber family was striving to attain the goal of intimacy via the theme of emotional cohesion through the media of time and space.

The primary access mechanisms employed were clocking in the time dimension and linking in the space dimension. All family members cooperated with the family linking strategy to share the activity of sailing together. Even Linda agreed to the bridging requests of the other Webers. Once on the pier, however, the family disagreed over what kind of clocking strategy to follow. Three family members expected to go sailing immediately, but Mr. Weber set in motion a sequence in which repairs came first, sailing second. This was a minor conflict, however. Real disappointment was generated by the family's duration setting, by the amount of time set aside for the repairs. For the three women, Father's repair time lasted much too long.

In one sense, Father played the villain in the Weber sailing sequence. It was he who determined the inappropriate duration setting and it was he who actively blocked out the others from emotional cohesion. Yet, in another sense, the rest of the Weber family was also at fault, because no one made a serious move to challenge Franz's tactics. No one attempted to put the modulating mechanisms into effect, to question whether or not the family was spatially centering itself or temporally synchronizing itself in accord with the ideals by which it wanted to live. Nor did anyone raise the question whether guidelines currently in force were the best ones the family could follow. Indeed, Franz's blocking out and duration-setting maneuvers seem to have evolved from his concern that the family strategy of emotional cohesion threatened the targets he was seeking at interface with the Weber's interpersonal subsystem, by forcing him to stay "too close, too long." Yet he, too, failed to call the family's modulating mechanisms into effect for a discussion of the family model, particularly of its space-time—affect interface. Thus, linking, clocking, and their submechanisms—bridging, blocking out, sequencing, and duration setting—combined with the modulating mechanisms, centering and synchronizing, delineate the relationship of the Weber family strategy of emotional cohesion to the access structure of the Weber family system.

The Weber sequence thus demonstrates the importance of both themes and mechanisms to an understanding of family strategy. In the last part of Chapter Four we discussed the importance of themes in identifying strategies and relating their specific purposes to the primary targets of affect, power, and meaning, and—on rarer occasions—the targets of space, time, and energy. Now, we are stressing the importance of the access mechanisms and submechanisms in delineating strategies in terms of the functions of particular family structures. Themes stress the target aspects of a strategy, while mechanisms stress the access components: it is important to recognize both.

One of our research families, the DeSicas (Mr. and Mrs. DeSica and their three children, Rosa, Anthony, and Maria, aged twenty-two, twenty, and sixteen, respectively), lived a stormy existence in their six-room dwelling in an old working class neighborhood a few miles from the psychiatric facility where Rosa had been hospitalized as a diagnosed schizophrenic several times since her sixteenth birthday. Both hospital and family remained concerned about Rosa's occasional dramatic "outbursts," and yet at the time of our study these were much less frequent than her father's uproars. Mr. DeSica was a deeply emotional man whose caring sentiments matched the intensity of his explosive harangues. During the period covered by our research, Maria rather than Rosa was the chief target of her father's assaults. Mr. DeSica's periodic outbursts had a significant influence on a family strategy involving all the DeSicas, a strategy we identified as emotional crowding. As we shall see, this strategy was dependent upon the restrictive deployment of the family's bounding mechanism.

Although the family had emigrated from a small town in southern Italy almost fifteen years before, Mrs. DeSica spoke only rudimentary English. In addition, owing to the father's rapid speech pattern combined with a confusing mixture of Italian and English vocabulary, a person unable to speak Italian had extreme difficulty in communicating with either parent except through the English-speaking children, a circumstance which seemed to increase the father's distrustfulness. The fact that the family lived only several blocks away from the expanding black community, plus their all too real awareness that criminal acts were on the increase in the neighborhood, increased the DeSica family's already strong restrictive bounding tendencies. Mr. DeSica demarcated a stringent safety zone around his family, a zone that, for the two girls, did not extend much beyond the physical parameters of the household. As a male, Anthony was permitted freedoms his sisters were denied. He had access to the family car, friends outside the neighborhood, and no curfew. But Rosa had not been allowed to date, or even to be in the company of boys, from the time she reached puberty. Mr. De-Sica equated sex with evil and attempted at all costs to protect his daughters from seductive temptations. When Maria reached sixteen years of age and decided that she, like her sister at that age, wanted to quit high school, this resolution triggered some rather fearsome images in Mr. DeSica. He believed that Rosa's quitting school was a cause, perhaps *the* cause of her breakdown and subsequent hospitalizations. Indeed, interviews with family members revealed that Rosa's initial hospitalization six years earlier had climaxed a period of intense restriction and crowding. Now, the same destructive pattern was being repeated with the younger daughter, as is evident in the following observer's report.

> Maria came home in the afternoon with her married friend, Sally, who is pregnant, Sally's unemployed brother, and the brother's boy friend. The boys left a half hour later, but Sally stayed. Anthony wanted to eat before Mr. DeSica came home. Rosa said, "Oh, Daddy will be angry." Mrs. DeSica said they should eat now before he came home. Maria invited Sally to stay for supper. She said, "My father isn't home yet. Come and have something to eat." Minutes later Mr. DeSica did come home unexpectedly and found Sally eating. He greeted her but didn't say much. Anthony murmured, "Oh, oh, wait until he hears Maria wasn't in school today." After supper Maria and Sally left to sit down in front of the three-family house on the

stoop. Becoming increasingly agitated, Mr. DeSica went down to get Maria to come up. Unknown to him, Maria was at that time using the bathroom inside the apartment. She called to her mother for protection, but Mrs. DeSica indicated it was none of her business. She was going to stay out of it. Rosa became quite frightened and went to her room. She didn't come out the rest of the night. Mr. DeSica came back up and started to pace around the parlor like a raging tiger, talking rapidly to himself, his face puffed with anger, mumbling incoherently in Italian. Slipping past her outraged father, Maria went downstairs again to rejoin Sally. Her father went down after her and evidently scared the two girls because they both started running down the street. Mr. DeSica came back up. Then Maria returned upstairs, picked up her coat, and slammed the door very loudly on her way back down again. A little later, Mr. DeSica called Maria's friend Berty's house to see if she was there. She wasn't. "Tell her she can't come back," Anthony suggested. "Lock her out of the house. That'll get her home." The shouting got really loud when Maria returned. Maria yelled, "You embarrass my friends and you embarrass me." She then started to blame him for Rosa's hospitalization. Berty came over to find out what was going on. She said her mother was hysterical. This got Maria really angry because she felt her father was getting her friends into trouble. She continued to scream at her father, "Sally thought you were going to kill me and that you'd kill her, too." By this time, Mr. DeSica was quieting down. "Don't act so phony," Maria said. Anthony started criticizing Maria for hanging around with a married girl. "That has nothing to do with it," she said. "That has a lot to do with it," he argued back. Eventually, Mr. DeSica went to bed. Mrs. DeSica talked with Maria in the kitchen until Maria calmed down.

The family's broadly defined boundary restrictions are everywhere apparent in this rather dramatic sequence: in the generalized anxiety surounding the commonplace act of inviting a friend to dinner, in the compromising of loyalties as different members seek to protect themselves from the father's anger, in Mr. DeSica's violent border patrolling as he attempts to separate Maria from Sally (the symbolic representative for Mr. DeSica of sex and "dropping out" of the neighborhood culture), in Anthony's secondary border patrolling and unconditional alliance with his father, and ultimately in Anthony's betrayal of his sister and her freedom of movement. The resultant bounding that takes place restrains the movement of traffic both into and out of the family, insulating the interior family space and closing it off from its exterior surroundings. A strategy of restrictive bounding, a form of spatial constraint, need not be disabling, and yet the DeSicas' variant of this strategy clearly proved disastrous to family harmony. The primary reason is that, while Maria was restrained from leaving the family space, she was simultaneously subjected to an oppressive linking strategy dominated by spatial and emotional crowding. This strategy was implemented by a combination of three tactics: double standard containment (restricting the girls alone from access to the outside), oppression (bombarding and counter bombarding with high amounts of energy), and constraint (labeling violations of containment as morally reprehensible). The cumulative effect of these tactics was to channel the girls toward targets they did not entirely want while blocking them out from crossing over to targets they did want. Within the dimension of affect, the DeSicas' crowding amounted to emotional invasion. Within that of power, it meant virtual imprisonment. Within the meaning dimension, it required absolute conformity. Maria's only recourse, other than giving in, was to bombard the other members back, thus continuing the strategy and escalating its intensity.

In our experience, few family strategies are more potentially destructive than those leading to the simultaneous restriction and crowding of members. The pressures placed on such members are very great indeed, because they are not only oppressed but also prevented from escaping oppression. No doubt sequences containing some elements of simultaneous restriction and crowding occur in all families. For such sequences to stabilize into a strategic pattern, however, simultaneous restriction and crowding maneuvers must be consistently employed.

Thus the emotional crowding of the DeSica daughters was all the more insidious and frightening because the other members of the family were caught up in strategic maneuvers that prevented the possibility of any protective buffering taking place. No one suggested that father and daughter had come too close and therefore ought voluntarily to back off a little from each other. When one family member attaches himself destructively to another, and buffering attempts are either totally absent (as in the DeSica episode) or rendered ineffective, blocking-out maneuvers, even though they are based on coercion, are obviously preferable to no protective response whatsoever. Thus, Maria shouted back and leveled her own accusations at her father, crowding him in return to force him to retreat. With no one to help her, however, her blocking out became total. She rejected her father completely, not recognizing that he truly cared about her safety and future. The scene is ugly, but not as destructive as her being completely overrun by her father's crowding. From what we were able to discern during our month of study, Rosa had never been able to block out her father so successfully. Indeed, Maria's dramatic and accusatory blocking out of her father was both designed by her and accepted at least in part by other family members as a preferable strategic alternative to a repetition of Rosa's unfocused outbursts and subsequent hospitalization.

As the foregoing narrative helps to demonstrate, identification of the linking submechanisms of bridging, buffering, channeling, and blocking out is vitally important for an understanding of family process. Again and again it is these submechanisms that seem to enable one to describe the primary structures of those actions that regulate the gaining and denying of access to goals within the three target dimensions. If suitable bridging strategies have not evolved in a family, learning, communication, and the sense of belonging all suffer. Where appropriate buffering strategies fail to exist, individual rights to protection, privacy, and selfhood fall heavily under threat. Channeling and blocking-out strategies are frequently among the most harmful of family operations. In systems overly dominated by channeling and blocking out operations, a lack of trust among members invariably exists, usually because the vested interests of one member or group of members take precedence over those of another. Under such circumstances, the family may turn into an armed camp, with various coalitions pitted against each other, or it may suffer painful paralysis, causing the entire system to come to a halt.

Nevertheless, it is misleading to think that all bridging and buffering strategies are "good," and all channeling and blocking out "bad." As we noted in our discussion of the DeSica episode, blocking-out maneuvers must be employed if individuals are to be protected from harm when buffering fails. Channeling can perform a similarly beneficial function. When bridging moves fail to produce a necessary effect, such as the picking up of mess, channeling strategies can be employed with great success. Indeed, too much bridging and buffering may actually impede self-development, autonomy, and an individual sense of responsibility. Rescue strategies, which demand an excessive amount of bridging and/or buffering actions toward a specific member, may serve to extend and reinforce a mother's alcoholism or a son's slow learning ability and thus prohibit the growth and development of an entire family system. Similarly, in many conflict-avoidance and intimacy-avoidance strategies, a third party (usually a child or mutual friend) will be invited to bridge two family members together to create the appearance of mutuality, affection, and togetherness, when these sentiments are not separately experienced by either of the original parties. The child who is conceived to hold a shaky marriage together is a too frequent example of destructive third-party bridging. Another classic disabling bridging strategy requires a child to manifest some kind of medical symptom or else draw attention to himself as a "problem child" whenever his parents appear on the verge of emotional conflict. All of these examples present a misapplication of voluntary linking maneuvers.

Throughout this and the preceding three chapters we have been emphasizing the access aspects of family process by attempting to describe the variables of space, time, and energy as explicitly as possible. In our discussion of strategies we have extended this concern and focused our attention on the linking mechanism of the spatial dimension. We are aware that we have given but cursory attention to one temporal mechanism and none whatsoever to the mechanisms of the energy dimension. In our research and clinical work, we have begun to isolate strategies associated primarily with temporal and energic maneuvers, but we, like the field of family therapy in general, are far behind in documenting and cataloging time and energy strategies. The general reason for this lag seems to be that time and energy are more difficult concepts to master than space. Spatial variables seem to be more easily reproduced, both in the office or laboratory and in the retelling of naturalistic processes.

Time and energy seem much more ephemeral, much more difficult to describe in words or to reproduce in simulated examples. Initially, space, time, and energy were all dealt with as implicit variables in family research, because observers were occupied primarily with target issues and outcomes of family interactions. We have reversed this emphasis somewhat in our presentation in the hope that our theory will give new impetus to the investigation of strategic access issues. We recognize that the specific mechanisms we have been able to identify in this and the previous three chapters may not all be of equal importance in producing characteristic family outcomes or in delineating each system's substantive or thematic properties. Perhaps only when a detailed and inclusive cataloguing of strategies, in which energy variables are given special attention, has been completed, we will be able to document conclusively which mechanisms and submechanisms are more important than others. When such a strategic catalogue is completed, a new level of understanding and achievement will be available to those in the field of family process.

Chapter 9

Family Types:
Structural Arrangement

In this and the following chapter we shall be concerned with the fourth component of our theory, the three major types of family systems, which we designate as closed, open, and random. These stereotypic systems differ in both their structural arrangements and strategic styles. *The three basic types are based on three different homeostatic models. Each is a variant of the generalized concept of family as a semipermeable system.*

All family systems are in a sense semipermeable systems. They are adaptive information-processing systems that are structurally "open." Unlike mechanical systems, a family system regularly engages in interchanges with the environment. These interchanges permit its viability, its continuity in the sense of reproductive ability, and its capacity to change or adapt to changing ecological circumstances. Family systems are semipermeable in still another way. They are constantly being called upon to respond to internal as well as external disturbances. Consequently, the internal structures of the family system are never permanent structures. As a family grows and matures, its structures are frequently challenged, torn down, and built up again. Thus, since structural change is an inherent function of the family's organic development, the three terms *closed, open,* and *random* are relative. We are not offering descriptions of the fixed structural characteristics of different kinds of systems. Rather we are designating three stereotypically different ways in which the semipermeable system of family can maintain itself and achieve its purposes, ways that may often be mixed in actual family practice.

Many theorists have made the mistake of thinking that there can be only one homeostatic ideal for all social systems, that is, steady state or harmonious equilibrium. Many family practitioners make the same mistake, attempting in their therapy to restore families to a state of tranquility that may never have existed and may not even now be desired by family members. In our own research and clinical experience, we have noted that different family systems espouse different equilibrium-disequilibrium ideals. The description of three basic types of family systems we have developed takes into account the distinctively different modal patterns through which families try to achieve their purposes and attain their goals. In our view each family type conceives of its purposes and goals differently from the other types. Each delineates a different homeostatic ideal and sets up a different distance-regulation plan for attaining that ideal.

The design question of foremost concern to a family's homeostatic ideals is the question of how the family maintains its boundaries. By "boundaries," of course, we don't simply mean the boundary between the family unit and its external environment. Rather, we mean all the interface rings that constitute the totality of family process interactions. Families that adopt the closed-type homeostatic ideal, define their boundaries in terms of the fixed constancy feedback patterns. They rely on such constancy loops in an effort to attain distance-regulation order at interface by establishing and preserving a harmonious set of mutually supported values, norms, and expectations. Strain and deviant traffic patterns are not permitted in such a closed-type boundary maintenance system, for they challenge its goal of steady state equilibrium. As we have already suggested, not all families adopt the closed-type homeostatic ideal.

Many choose either the open or random ideals and maintain their boundaries quite differently. Families that seek the random ideal define their boundaries in terms of variety loops rather than constancy loops. These variety loops are employed to foster maximal distance regulation freedom at interface by establishing a pluralistic set of values and expectations. Structural strain and deviant, exploratory traffic patterns are not only permitted but encouraged as well, for disequilibrium is the random homeostatic ideal. Families that adopt an open homeostatic ideal opt for a mixture of equilibrium and disequilibrium. Open family boundaries are defined in terms of a combination of constancy and variety loop patterns, employed to maximize the potential for a joint negotiation of distance-regulation issues at interface. Structural strain and deviant traffic patterns are permitted but restrained, lest the prevailing open-boundary maintenance system become either too rigid or too anarchic.

We believe that all interactional behavior in family systems, even behavior dominated by unconscious or subconscious elements, is purposive, goal-seeking behavior. In Chapter Four we proposed that the goals of family interactions are usually to be found within the target dimensions and occasionally in targets associated with the access dimensions. Now in this and the following chapter we are proposing that a family's style of distance regulation, our construct for linking interactions among the access and target dimensions, is governed by the system's homeostatic ideal.

The substantive differences among the three family stereotypes and their homeostatic ideals lie in the way each type organizes and uses its mechanisms. It is in the mechanisms that the internal linkage of parts underlying purposive, goal-seeking behavior is structurally delineated. Each type of family system implements its own criteria for the ways in which its access dimension mechanisms are to be employed. For example, the criterion variables for the space dimension can be defined as *fixed, movable,* and *dispersed.* Thus, space in the closed system is designated as *fixed;* in the open system, as *movable;* and in the random system, as *dispersed.* The criterion variables for the dimension of time are *regular, variable,* and *irregular.* For the dimension of energy, the criterion variables are *steady, flexible,* and *fluctuating.* In essence what we are proposing is that each type's patterns for the ways in which its mechanisms are to be used remain within certain limits and that these limits are demarcated by the system's criterion variables. This means that distance regulation in each of the access dimensions is controlled by a family's criterion variables. Indeed, in a metaphoric sense, the criterion variables are the basic distance-regulation alternatives a family has available to it in setting its traffic control thermostat for each access dimension.

A family's type determines its characteristic response to everyday events. Each system selects its own reference frame through which both external and internal events can be processed and ultimately through which change can legitimately occur. This is another way of saying that the three system types employ feedback loops in support of their homeostatic ideals. What we are primarily interested in is the process whereby events or stimuli are sampled by the system and matched against its internal criterion states as a means of controlling relations, that is, a means of regulating distances in each of the access and target dimensions. Throughout the rest of this chapter, and in Chapter Ten, we show how each of the three basic system types employs the access mechanisms to effect its characteristic purposes. We also show how in its operation of the mechanisms each stereotype's criterion variables carry out its system design. The following section presents a summary of the distinguishing features and substantive differences of each type of family system.

In the closed family system, stable structures (fixed space, regular time, and steady energy) are relied upon as reference points for order and change. In the open family system, order and change are expected to result from the interaction of relatively stable evolving family structures (movable space, variable time, and flexible energy). In the random system, unstable structures (dispersed space, irregular time, and fluctuating energy) are experimented with as reference points for order and change.

Closed-Type Family

Space in the closed-type family is fixed space. Bounding, the major social space mechanism for regulating incoming and outgoing traffic, is carried out by those designated as authorities by the family in such a way that the family's discrete space, distinct and apart from the larger community space, is created. Locked doors, careful scrutiny of strangers in the neighborhood, parental control over the media, supervised excursions, and unlisted telephones are all features of a closed-type family. Closed bounding goals include the preservation of territoriality, self-protection, privacy, and, in some families, secretiveness. Perimeter traffic control is never relinquished to outsiders or even to anyone within the family not specifically assigned bounding responsibilities.

Linking, the major social space mechanism for regulating the distance among members within the family space, is governed by those in authority, usually by one or both parents in the closed-type family. Individual members' traffic is prescribed. All are channeled in directions selected by those in authority and blocked out from targets deemed inappropriate. Bridging and buffering requests are judged for their appropriateness. If such requests are deemed inappropriate for a given situation, bridging and buffering will not be provided. Members who adhere to the directions and movement patterns prescribed for traffic within the family are rewarded, and those who deviate from such patterns are punished. Linking strategies are the cross products of traditional family unity, propriety, and fairness to individuals, somewhat in that order. In sum, each member is expected to gain access to designated targets through prescribed channels and only through prescribed channels.

Centering, the social space mechanism for designing and implementing a model of the family's spatial shape is also controlled by those designated as authorities. All members, however, even the authorities, are required to bring their flow of traffic into conformity with the closed family design of how each should live. The closed family uses icons and symbols in its space to spread and deepen members' allegiance to the credos that constitute the basis for a family's closed centering strategies. Formal teaching, including the use of moral slogans, homilies, and proverbs is a popular feature of the closed centering style, especially as members of the older generation seek to convey and confer their values on the next.

Time in the closed-type family is regular time. Orienting, the major mechanism for regulating family members' traffic in the time sphere, remains fairly constant for the closed family. Closed families tend to orient primarily to the past or to the future. The purpose of a closed past orientation is to preserve or restore something that was—to go back to something that was better than the present. The purpose of a closed future orientation is to attain or achieve something that has not been accomplished in the past or the present. The closed family's orienting strategy is to ward off and rule out as unwanted deviations those experiences which do not facilitate preservation and restoration of the past or attainment and achievement in the future, or, in more marginal circumstances, those experiences which do not directly facilitate the family's survival in the present.

Clocking, the major temporal mechanism for regulating the sequence, frequency, duration, and pace of immediately experienced family events, is executed with little variation in the closed family. Time limits are set according to the clock. There is a metaphorical "family clock" to which all "individual clocks" are expected to conform. Deviation from schedules is viewed as disruptive and is punishable. Important family events, such as getting up in the morning, mealtimes, and going to bed, tend to take place at the same time every day. Schedules for maintenance chores, field trips, appointments, and other activities determine each member's comings and goings as a train or airline schedule governs departure and arrival times. Even "free periods," in which members may do as they wish, may be rigidly scheduled. That events occur on time, and tasks get done on time, is a matter of urgency and necessity for the closed family. By means of their clocking strategies, then, closed families attempt to control events rather than be controlled by them.

Synchronizing, the major temporal mechanism for developing and implementing a family life plan, is carried out in the closed family by a program that is virtually permanent and unalterable. This program, which is developed by family designated authorities, serves as a fairly detailed blueprint of how all members are to clock and orient their movements in pursuit of the closed family's lifeplan targets. In general, the closed family tries to be certain of where it is going and when it will get there. It tries to plan for the future, because it feels that the best way to gain access to appropriate targets is to maintain a consistent and regular temporal rhythm, one in which temporal continuity is emphasized because the future is systematically brought into the present. Deviation from such regularity, it contends, inevitably leads to loss of or deflection from targets.

Energy in the closed-type family is steady energy. Fueling, the major mechanism for regulating the acquiring of energy, is carried out by prescription in the closed family. The closed family tells its members when, where, and how they may acquire energy. It establishes certain activities as refueling events and forbids others. For instance, members may be required to go to church on Sunday morning, permitted to see a movie that afternoon, but not allowed to go out in the evening. Members who follow such directives tend to return to the same prescribed sources of energy again and again. New or different sources are either not allowed or not found. Nevertheless, closed systems are not necessarily low-energy systems. A closed-type family can experience a high rate of fueling as long as it locates, taps, and charges off potentially rich sources of energy.

Investing is the major mechanism for regulating family energy expenditures. The closed family gives shape to its energy investments by means of family-wide discipline—a set of disciplinary measures to which the entire family is subject. Indeed, investing strategies in the closed family are such that discipline becomes a high art, for members are expected to expend energy directly toward specific targets without deviating away from them toward others. Waste and irresponsibility are decried. In the extreme they are regarded as crimes against the system, because, without discipline in energy expenditures, the closed family's predesigned advance toward its targets would not be possible. Though such strategies are not necessarily evolved as a response to hard times, the fact remains that the closed family is naturally equipped for survival. If its discipline is strong, its ability to endure can be remarkable.

Mobilizing, the major mechanism for developing and implementing guidelines for regulating the flow of energy in families, is carried out in accord with the closed family's traditional principles, rules, and customs. Family authorities in the closed family develop a budget for detailing the pattern of energy flow in the family. This budget prescribes how family members are to obtain and use their energies. Individual deviation from this budget is not tolerated. As a result, the closed family is less likely than the other two stereotypes to experience either overabundance or a serious depletion of energy in its routine day-to-day affairs. It is confronted with a considerably more serious crisis, however, when one or more members find their energic needs unmet or even aggravated by the family's mobilizing guidelines. How does the closed system resolve such serious energy crises? A frequent reaction is suppression of the individual. A less frequent resolution is successful rebellion. A third alternative, one which occurs quite frequently in mature closed families, is serious schism. A fourth is compromise by means of a rare alteration of the energy budget.

CLOSED-TYPE FAMILY SKETCH: "They're back," calls out Maureen, the McKenzies' eleven-year-old daughter, from the window at which she has been watching for the family DeSoto. Immediately, the other children start gathering in the kitchen, breaking off their other activities. "Hey, how about some hands on these bags?" Father calls up the stairs. John, Stephen, and Kevin, the McKenzies' three oldest children at ages fourteen, thirteen, and twelve, hop down the stairs and accompany their father to the car where they pick up the family's grocery bags from out of the trunk. Each boy makes several trips with his bags up to the kitchen, where Maureen supervises their unpacking and Patty and Tina, the Mc-Kenzie "babies" help out by putting canned goods in pantries and cabinets, wherever they can reach. Bryan McKenzie, the ten-year-old, also helps with the unpacking until he notices a pack of Hershey bars in one of the bags. He tears off one bar, smacks his lips, and tosses the bar into the air. "Hey, you can't eat that now," Maureen shouts. "I know that," he replies. "I was just thinking how good it was gonna taste." He puts the bar back in the bag with the rest and resumes helping with the unpacking. When the last bag is picked up from the car, Mr. McKenzie locks up the trunk and says, "We'll be back in ten minutes." "Where are you and Ma going?" John asks. "That's none of your business," Father replies. "I bet it's a treat," Kevin says. "You'll all find out soon enough," Mother adds. By the time the parents return with an angel food cake and some ice cream some ten minutes later, all the groceries are put away and the bags folded up neatly for subsequent use as waste basket liners. Mother slices the cake and Father scoops out the ice cream in quantities appropriate to the age of each of the children, who stand in line for the goodies. "You all did a very good job with the groceries," he says.

The senior McKenzies and their seven children live together in a six-room, four-bedroom apartment in a low-income housing project. The parents occupy the only bedroom with any architecturally built-in privacy, a privacy obtained solely by virtue of its being farthest from family gathering places and the flow of foot traffic. What privacy does exist is a credit to simple ingenuity, organization, and respect for boundaries. A second bedroom is occupied by the girls (Maureen, Patty, and Tina), a third by three boys (Stephen, Kevin, and Bryan) and the fourth by John, Jr., the eldest son. John's room doubles as storage space for large items such as bicycles (kept beneath his bed) and other objects displaced from more crowded rooms. Painstaking organization is the McKenzie's key to survival in inadequate physical surroundings, to reasonably peaceful coexistence as whites in a predominantly black housing project, and to successful access to the health, recreational, and educational reources of the community at large.

In every realm of life, the McKenzies work together like the parts of a simple and well-oiled machine. In addition to developing routines for physically maintaining the small apartment, the McKenzies manage to encourage athletic and academic achievements, which have resulted in some of the older children gaining recognition at school. In general, the family achieves maximal efficiency and productivity by ascertaining that each knows the parts he or she is to play, and can be depended upon to perform them accordingly. The entire McKenzie family believes firmly that the rights of individual members can be guaranteed only if the whole family's interests come first, if each individual is willing at all times to sacrifice personal interests for the collective balance.

John is the family's one source of imbalance, the only member who challenges the family's predilection for strict adherance to official policies. His interest in rock music and monster comic books is condemned by Mr. McKenzie, the member who is most rigidly observant of a system whose boundaries he helps to defend. John's deviations are viewed by his father as assaults on the carefully bounded family meaning sphere, especially since, in the family's traditional view of hierarchic authority, John has important example-setting responsibilities. As the eldest son, he also has certain rights and prerogatives, but these can only be exercised after he has satisfied the stronger claims of those above him in the authority structure, particularly the claims of his father. He fails to do so on occasion—actually, on rare occasion—but in the McKenzie household slight deviations may be subject to punishment.

John's younger brothers are more adept at deviating slightly and getting away with it. Stephen, a conformist to the family's established meanings, occasionally tests the family's time regulations with impunity because his outstanding academic achievements gain him an unofficial freedom from certain family restrictions. Kevin, an outstanding local basketball player, is also a good student. He is perhaps the most directly outspoken of the children, but seems to know better than John when and who to debate and challenge. Unfortunately, John lacks his brothers' academic achievements to buttress his position in the family. Meanwhile his avocations, including an interest in drawing cartoons, are put down by Mr. McKenzie, who worries that his eldest is being diverted from the straight and narrow road to achievement and future success.

Though discipline is often emphasized to the older children in particular, it is rigorously enforced throughout the family. The younger children, for instance, do not earn the right to a door key until they are judged responsible enough not to lose it. Failure to carry out responsibilities at any level can result in a loss of privileges. All of the children's comings and goings are closely screened and monitored. Children's friends, when they come to call, stop at the door, but do not enter. In general, the children tend to visit rather than be visited. The outsider feels the family's metaphoric system boundaries as walls of solid reality. Detailed proofs of trustworthiness are required before the McKenzies allow anyone into their inner circle of interpersonal relations. Adult visitors are few in number. They are screened through a series of phases as the conditions for entry, participation, and dismissal are negotiated.

The senior McKenzies are unquestionably the actual as well as the nominal heads of their household. They take unabashed pride in the fact that they run a tight ship, because its requisite discipline helps secure the family's island of safety in a sea of neighborhood violence and unrest. The parents also hope and believe that family discipline is a training ground for achievement at school and eventual financial betterment for their children. At the slightest provocation, or mere hint of interest, Mr. McKenzie will wax pontifical on these and other family matters. Mrs. McKenzie is more reserved, especially with strangers, but together they have built strong fortresses in defense of their physical and conceptual spaces. The children are better acquainted with their parents as a couple, or as spokesmen for the parental system, than with either one as an individual. What the parents usually share about their private lives is revealed not for the purpose of attaining stronger intimacy, but rather as a lesson in service of some family ideal or rule of order. In intelligence, aesthetic sensibilities, keenness of judgment, and social poise, Mrs. McKenzie would seem to be her husband's superior, but such is not what they choose to say to the world or to their children, and their differences are restricted to their private domain. The children seem to know when the fictional power features of their parental system are to be upheld and under what circumstances they can be ignored. However, all are aware that the fact that Father's superiority is a myth not to be shared with outsiders. Despite some uneasiness about this myth, the McKenzies feel secure in the knowledge that they can take care of their own.

Members' access to intimacy is regulated with the same discipline that is implemented in other spheres of their existence. Strong emotions are rarely expressed in public. Affection has a place in this family, but there is also an appropriate time for its expression. At the proper time and in the proper place, bids for affection are granted. Out-of-phase seeking of affection is at best discouraged, and, at worst, put down or punished. Overly invested demands for nurturance, closeness, or affection are strongly counteracted. The McKenzies' central message to members might be expressed as follows: "Process your most intense emotional needs indirectly, through faith in the family's meanings and goals. We do not have time for whiners or malcontents. Our efforts must be effectively distributed. So be strong and self-sufficient."

Open-Type Family

Space in the open-type family is movable space. Individual members' bounding movements are regulated by a process of group consensus, which tends to extend the family territory into the larger community space and/or to bring the exterior culture into the family space. Individuals are allowed to regulate the direction and destination of their incoming and outgoing traffic as long as they do not cause discomfort to other members or violate the consensus of the group. Numerous guests, frequent visits with friends, unlocked doors, open windows, individual or group explorations of the community and its resources, and a freedom of informational exchange with only rare censorship of the media are all open bounding features. In general, open bounding fosters the desire for beneficial interchange with members of the community, since guests are not only welcome but made to feel important for the contributions they make to the family.

Closeness is encouraged, but temporary distancing is permitted to relieve undo discomfort from too much closeness in the linking operations of the open family. Each member is free to establish his own movements toward other members or toward targets, as long as he stays within the guidelines established by family consensus. Force and coercion may be employed, but only as a last resort. Implicit in all open-linking strategies is the conviction that relationships between people are not fixed by fate, tradition, or prescriptions of any kind. Rather, open strategies reflect a belief that a family's goals are and should be subject to change, variation, and negotiation. Experimentation, within limits set by the group, is encouraged. In its linking strategies, the open family attempts to affirm both collective cohesion and individual freedom. Freedom of choice is encouraged but qualified lest it turn into license. Each member is encouraged to feel a personal responsibility toward each of the other members as individuals, and toward the family group as a whole.

The open family develops, maintains, and projects a standard that requires a consensus for organizing the total space in which the family lives. No design can become a family centering design until each member has consented to its adoption. Once consent is granted, all members are individually responsible for arranging their lives within the guidelines of the design that has been agreed upon. Opposition is aired and conflicts confronted at gatherings of family members, a process that can result in modification of the design as well as modification of individual behavior. The centering strategies of the open style are often operational strategies of review and modification. Espousal is an important feature of these strategies, but so, too, are challenge and disavowal. Alteration is the characteristic result.

Time in the open-type family is variable time. The open-type family develops and maintains a set of modifiable attitudes, toward past, present, future, and nontemporal events, usually by referring to and emphasizing the present, including events at the past-present and present-future time interfaces. Since the open family lives in a rhythmic style that is variable, it tends to be in-constant in orientational set. Members are reasonably free to shift from present to past or from present to future in their temporal orientations, provided they do not seriously challenge the open family's broad temporal mandate to focus on relevance and utility in the present. For the open family, all time roads lead to the present, the other orientations being vehicles for reinforcing, enhancing, and enriching the present rather than being destinations in, of, or for themselves.

In the open-type family, the sequence, frequency, duration, and pace of clocking operations may be organized to conform generally to specific temporal notations, but either events or preset temporal time limits may be altered. "Individual clocks" may run ahead or behind, faster or slower than the "family clock," but only within a range of comfort permitted by the family. Members are not permitted to make unwarranted deviations. Schedules are employed as general guidelines rather than as blueprints for regulating the sequence, frequency, duration, and pace of events. Clocks and watches are not as important in the open family as they are in the closed. Members are much freer to determine when, in what order, for how long, and at what speed they will do things. Thus they are able to "keep one eye on the clock and one eye on what they are doing," knowing that the family clock can be adjusted to accommodate individual tardiness. Of course, members must also be ready to make their own individual clocking adjustments when the family clock is running slightly ahead or slightly behind its normal schedule.

Like the closed family, the open family develops a program

for synchronizing members' clocking and orienting movements in pursuit of lifetime family goals. Unlike the closed program, however, the open life plan is nearly always modifiable. It is developed by a process of consensus and can be changed by consensus. The open-family time plan requires that members be responsive to each other's temporal movements and attempt to accommodate them. Such responsiveness necessitates a code of temporal variability, one that permits alteration of both individual and group time traffic patterns. Thus the open family's life plan is evolutionary rather than predetermined. Both its life style and its values will evolve in the course of time. This does not mean that open families don't have specific visions or plans for the future at any one time, for they do: but such plans are alterable.

Energy in the open-type family is flexible energy. In an open family, members acquire energy in a variety of ways permissible to family consensus. The open family finds closed-type fueling strategies too limiting and confining for its taste. It demands more variety and seeks out multiple sources of energy. It is interested in tapping energy sources that are new and/or different from those it normally taps. The open family does not give its members unlimited freedom, however. They are not to cause undue discomfort to other members by their individual charging strategies. A teenager, for instance, who "turns on" to loud rock music may be required by family consensus to lower the volume or cease playing the stereo altogether when Grandpa is around.

The open family gives shape to its energy investments by its capacity to be elastic. Members may range extensively in their search for targets, incurring the risk of spreading themselves thin by making loose, plural attachments. Elasticity may thus produce energy depletion. Yet, this very capacity may enable members to shift, detach, and realign energy investments more easily when the unit calls for it. Thus, elasticity is also the basis for energy recovery. In other words, investment strategies in the open family are such that members are able to capitalize on two divergent trends, the tendency toward dispersion and the tendency toward concentration.

In the open family, members develop and implement their mobilizing model by consensus. Since it is not capable of demanding instant response from its members by enforcement of perfect discipline or summons of automatic loyalty, the open family's mobilizing operations suffer from a certain degree of day-to-day inefficiency. In a sense, the open family invites what it would regard as minor crises in daily living. It may not like them, but it prefers them to the individually constraining strategies of the closed system. This systemic sanction of routine crisis can result in frequent expansion and contraction of energy reserves, and periods of at least temporary disequilibrium can follow. During such periods, the open family attempts to reach a new consensus about its mobilizing strategies, a consensus accommodating an energy resolution that is satisfactory to all family members. The route to such a revised consensus is open discussion.

OPEN-TYPE FAMILY SKETCH: "What would you like for dinner?" Mrs. Cloud asks her nine-year-old daughter. "Steak or. . . . ?" "Cereal," replies Susanna who has recently decided to be a vegetarian. "Okay," replies Mrs. Cloud. "What about you, Pamela?" Mrs. Cloud asks Susanna's friend who is staying for supper. "Steak or something else?" "Steak," says Pamela. Susanna grimaces. "A little bit of steak and a big bowl of cereal," Pamela adds. Susanna smiles. During dinner, Mr. Cloud looks across the table and says, "Peter, I'm afraid I've got a bone to pick with you." "What's that?" "The mess from your mice is getting out of hand. I almost broke my neck in the hallway outside your room this afternoon. When we agreed to let you keep those mice it was on the condition that you clean their cages." "I do clean them," Peter counters, "once a week." "Well, it's not enough," Father says. "Their excrement's piling up on the floor." "That's because they're getting out of their cages," Peter replies. "Because you've got too many mice," says Father. "No, because you won't give me the money to buy new cages." "Wait a minute," interjects Mrs. Cloud. "Dad's right, Peter. Something's got to be done about the mess. But Peter's got a point too, Dad. Those cages are falling apart." "I'm glad somebody believes me," Peter remarks. "We can't afford new cages," says Father. "Well, what about the two of you getting together to repair the ones that are in there now? That might solve both your problems," says Mother. "On one condition," agrees

Father. "You agree to clean them twice a week." "Agreed," says Peter.

The Clouds live on the first floor of a family-owned two-story frame house. Their flat, renovated by architect Oscar Cloud, consists of a large open public living room space (achieved by knocking down several walls), a large parents' bedroom, and two small children's bedrooms with a double bunk in each. The large, unobstructed public space of the flat is symbolic of the Clouds' family process. Friends and guests are frequently brought home by both parents and children. People may drop in or telephone at virtually any time of the day or evening without feeling uncomfortable. The parents' bedroom often becomes an extension of the family's public and semipublic space, partly because of its size and partly because members want to use it in that way. The television set is in there, as is Oscar's drafting table, so that the room draws in not only children and guests, but, on rarer occasions, business associates.

The Clouds, both individually and as a group, enjoy visiting with friends. At any point in the day, the four Clouds could be doing different things in different parts of town: Oscar meeting with a client, Muriel working on a terminal hospital ward, twelve-year-old Peter printing some photographs in a darkroom, and nine-year-old Susanna dressing up in costumes at a friend's. Partly as a strategy to bring themselves and their various jobs, hobbies, and activities together, the Clouds have purchased a farm jointly with another professional family, whose parents and children they consider part of their own "extended family." The idea is that the farm become something of a gathering place on weekends and holidays for both households.

Events frequently take place at the last minute, or close to it, in the Cloud household. Oscar's work pattern is one of taking it somewhat easy on a project and then launching a big, all-night push as his deadline nears. Muriel is also frequently behind schedule, whether she is cooking dinner, meeting her ride to work in the morning, or buying gifts for birthdays and Christmas. Yet somehow all these tasks are eventually done before it is too late. Muriel's tardiness is not due to laziness or lack of energy. Rather, it comes about because she has so much to do. There often don't seem to be enough hours in the day for her to satisfy all her duties as therapist, wife, friend, and mother. Yet, surprisingly, both Oscar and Muriel seem to invite interruption. They seem to experience little or no resistance to distraction from a task, even a task with an immediate deadline, and readily deviate from it in order to respond to the needs or enjoyment of another person.

Decisions, too, seem to be made at or near the last minute. They may be made earlier but go uneffected, so that the possibility of altering or reversing them is left open. On one occasion, for instance, whether Mr. Cloud is going to accompany the rest of the family on a holiday trip to see the grandparents is not firmly decided until an hour or two before the plane leaves. Recruiting someone to take care of the house and what's inside is also left until moments before the family's departure. Basically, none of the Clouds likes to get locked into a decision he or she no longer has any investment in implementing. They prefer instead to make their choices as the occasion arises, without allowing any theory or ideology to confine their gut-level, empirical responses.

A corollary to this type of decision-making practice is that everyone is permitted to say what he or she thinks or feels about a particular subject. Such openness of discussion helps guarantee that too many promises don't go unkept. For example, when the parents had located a farm without a barn and were thinking of making an offer on it, Susanna broke into tears and accused the Cloud parents of violating their promise to her because they had told her she could have a horse at the farm. As a result, the Clouds continued looking until they eventually found a suitable farm with a barn. As this incident suggests, any member of the family can influence the family's decisions by persuading the other members of the correctness or necessity of a particular course of action. Thus, though the parents are the heads of the Cloud household, there is no permanent or static power hierarchy. Instead, each member has an egalitarian right to challenge and be heard within the family.

The Cloud apartment is filled with a number of plants and animals. A dog, two cats, a bowl of goldfish, several hamsters, some thirty mice, and a python snake are all part of the family scene. The plants belong to Muriel, who also finds herself feeding and taking care of many of the animals. There is thus a large variety of living things within the Cloud household, providing Muriel and Susanna at least with a strong sense of nurturing. Both respond affectionately to animals and feel it their mission to provide a home for them. Indeed, it is Susanna's love of animals that has prompted her to try out the life style of a vegetarian. Peter, who owns the mice and snake, deals with them in a more managerial fashion. He considers selling his surplus mice at a profit and trades one snake in for another more exotic one. With the exception of his favorites, Peter feeds the other mice to the python to keep him alive—one every other week. This feeding, as one might suspect, creates some tension in the household. Nevertheless, the family attempts to support and reward both children's ways of relating to animals, and each is permitted and encouraged to develop further his or her particular outlook.

The Clouds' approach to the target of identity is that any topic is suitable for discussion in the household, and family conversations range from a debate on men's and women's rights and obligations to a discussion of the Anglo-Saxon origins of curses and swear words. Everyone is encouraged to present his own point of view, though he must be willing to have that view subjected to criticism and at times ridicule, at least from Oscar. For the Clouds there is no such thing as an absolute answer to the problems of the day or of the family. There are, however, certain points of view that members generally hold to be true, one being that the happiness of family members is more important than their individual achievements.

Perhaps nowhere does the Cloud family system push its openness further than in its approach to the target of nurturance and intimacy. As a general rule, all requests for either joining or separating are viewed as legitimate. Peter, for instance, is free to determine when he will accompany the family to the farm and when he will stay in town with his friends. Such a procedure produces conflicts, but the Clouds are not afraid of conflict. The Cloud parents make very little attempt to prohibit their children from hearing them fight. The reason seems to be that they view their fights as an important part of the decision-making process. Though feelings get hurt in such fights, the Clouds believe that negative feelings must be aired if more constructive arrangements are to result. In short, they contend that a family must be free to fight if it is also to be free to love.

Random-Type Family

Space in the random-type family is dispersed space. Each person develops his own bounding patterns in establishing and defending his own and his family's territory. There may be as many territorial guidelines as there are members of the family, for the random family's territorial pattern is an aggregate of individual styles, including their effect on each other. Any member's bounding pattern may be challenged for any reason by any other member. Such challenges need not be resolved. Features of family life that one might normally expect to find inside a family's space occur outside a random household as well. Arguments and embracings might occur in the street as well as the living room or bedroom. Items usually found outside, such as printing presses, motorcycles, other people's children, and test tubes or other experimental apparatus, might be kept inside a random family's space. In general, the random family's bounding operations are aterritorial. Rather than impose limits on exit or entry, random strategies deemphasize the territorial defense of the family. Indeed, they have a tendency to extend entry and exit prerogatives broadly, not only to members, but to guests and strangers as well.

Individuals regulate their own linking movements within the interior of a random family space. When invasions, evasions, obstructions or other linking conflicts occur, it is the responsibility of the individuals involved to mediate their disagreement. Since individuals may or may not be willing to mediate, conflicts may or may not be resolved. Members gain closer voluntary contact with other members and with objects on the basis of interest and desire. Similarly, members voluntarily separate from one another or from objects when they feel their freedom of movement impeded or their interests no longer shared. Random linking strategies are efforts to allow people to gather together and withdraw from one another without the usual constraints on individual movements. In a random family, members maintain relations with one another and with targets strictly on the basis of personal choice. Thus random linking strategies, by definition, necessarily take on a paradoxical cast, particularly when one member's linking choices interfere or obstruct another member's. In such a situation, one member may have to lose his freedom in order that the other can exercise his.

In the random family, each individual develops, maintains, and disseminates a centering design for organizing the family's space, including how traffic should flow within and across family borders. Each decides for himself whether the traffic or the design should be changed. Icons and symbols tend to be eclectic. A photograph of Einstein may stand next to a sculpture of Jesus or Buddha, which itself is placed on top of a record album by the Rolling Stones. "Do your own thing," is perhaps the most important random family slogan. Membership in the random family is nonobligatory membership, a fact that pushes members' freedom of choice and action to a dramatic extreme. The asserted justification for a random family's utopianism is a conviction that if a family centers itself in some nonvoluntary or coercive way, it is not centered genuinely or properly.

Time in the random-type family is irregular time. The family selects and alters its attitudes toward past, present, future, and nontime events by emphasizing any or all of the four time spheres. Claims for the preservation of the past, attainment in the future, enjoyment or utility in the present, and exploration of nontime are all of potentially equal ethical weight. Other members need not share one member's sets or place a similar value on one's time associated artifacts. Under the impress of an irregular rhythmic style, the random family displays its orienting strategies apparently without discrimination. Indeed, it fosters potentially absolute temporal fluidity, switching and allowing its members to switch orientational sets, largely at will. Thus, in comparison with the other family types the random type has no orientational preference if only because it, by definition, lives in an unstatic consciousness of its temporal space. Like all families, the random lives in the present and must come to terms with it. Like the others, it has a special relationship to the moment. Unlike the other types, the random-type family does not come *to* the present orientational set, temporal map in hand; it comes *out* of it, spontaneously.

The sequence, frequency, duration, and pace of clocking events in the random family are regulated by the desires of each member. There is no "family clock," only an aggregate of "individual clocks," which may be in or out of phase with each other. Actual clocks are of little consequence to the truly random family. Indeed, the family may not even have a clock, and, if it does have one, its members are free to ignore it. Events in such a household can occur with little or no regularity. Some people may sleep while others are awake. The main meal of the day can take place at any point in time—morning, noon, or night—for any one member. There is no dominant ethic of making adjustments for each other as there is in the open family. Rather, it is expected that each member will try to find and establish the daily rhythm that suits him best. The pure random-type family executes a credo of "doing what one wants to do when one wants to do it."

In the random-type family, members develop for themselves a synchronizing plan, often a dream, of the way in which each wants to clock and orient himself in pursuit of his hopes and desires. The random life plan is certainly not predetermined, as it is in the closed family, nor is it evolutionary as it is in the open family. Rather, it is spontaneous. If there is a plan, the plan is that events should happen of their own accord. The program generated by such spontaneity is often a discontinuous program. Events and projects need not be completed. Rather, they can be discarded, never to be resumed or further developed. The temporal goal for the random family is the goal of multiactuality. The assumption is that there are many ways to spend one's time. Each person, therefore, ought to discover and pursue those activities which give him or her the most satisfaction.

Energy in the random-type family is fluctuating energy. Random family members may engage in fueling operations in whatever way they want. Singly or cumulatively, they may seek out all potential sources of energy. The random family places no official limits either on the means of acquiring energy or on sources through which energy may be acquired. Thus, strategies for fueling are by official sanction a function of the interplay of the creative imaginations of individual members. We would suggest that random families tend to be high-energy families, if only because a main characteristic of these families is their institutionalization of behavioral flux in seeking access to potentially unlimited energy sources.

Random family investments take a rather pluralistic form as each member makes his own idiosyncratic energy investments. Random investments in general are dominated by a strong spontaneous strategic quality. Members attach, detach, commit, and shift their energies at will. As a result, the random family's energy investments are in a perennial state of flux, and constantly changing. Yesterday's commitments are today's detachments and vice versa. Tomorrow could be different again. In this way, the random family gives its members the experience of continuously varying energy investments. The random family has a knack for spontaneously generating effects, for locating energy very quickly, for readily expending it in the direction of a particular target and diverting it just as readily, for bringing things to life even in otherwise desert-like spaces, though not necessarily for long.

Members of the random-type family create and carry out personal models of how they want to mobilize their energy. The random family's mobilizing strategies tend to generate more frequent crises of energy in routine living than either of the other two types. Routine crisis is inherent in this type's way of life. How, under such circumstances, does the random system resolve its serious crises of energy? Frequently, it doesn't. There is a strong tendency among random family members to fly apart. Another possibility is that a serious crisis may not be perceived as "serious," or even perhaps as a "crisis," in the random family, but as a continuation of day-to-day energy disruptions. In such a situation, the effects of the crisis will go unchecked. Often, however, one member will try to impose his own mobilizing model on the collective to hold it together. Though such coercive leadership runs contrary to most random family values, it can also be accepted, at least temporarily, as the best solution of the moment.

RANDOM-TYPE FAMILY SKETCH: "The bathroom door handle is off again," shouts Maria Canwin. "Teddy, will you fix it?" she calls to her nine-year-old son. "I'll do it," her husband Herbert volunteers. "That's what you said last week," retorts Mrs. Canwin. "I'm sorry, dear, I put it on the repair list, but I can't seem to find the list," he replies. Now Teddy, who, in spite of his young age, is more skillful than his father in most mechanical matters, starts looking at the door handle. Meanwhile, a huge toolbox stands as a monument of promise, blocking the doorway to Mr. Canwin's study. Melissa, recently turned thirteen, perches statuesquely on the toolbox. Dancing in gracefully slowed movements, she sings in falsetto to an unseen audience, laughing in uncensored self-admiration. Moments later, Maria Canwin answers the telephone. She lodges the receiver loosely between her ear and shoulder so she can continue stirring her dinner pots on the stove. Ringlets of smoke from the burning haddock in the oven play around her nose, but she fails to notice it. Waving a glass of wine in her free hand, she is deep in a fiery conversation, punctuated by raucous laughter. An old college chum, phoning on a layover from the airport has just been stampeded into coming over. "We'll save dinner for you," Maria says, hanging up. "No you won't. You've burned the fish again," Herbert remarks, snorting under his breath. A shrieking Teddy, leaping from the stairs to a chair and onto his father's back in an impossible acrobatic sequence shouts, "I heard that, skunk-head." Enter Melissa, trying to peel her brother off her father's back. "Get off, jerk." She also tries simultaneously to pry her parents apart from a cluttered and obviously too energetic embrace. "Leave him alone, Mom. I want him now. You can have him later." Meanwhile Teddy shouts, "Put up your dukes, Herby!" "Stop it." roars Maria, suddenly overcome with the chaos. Sound and motion come to an instant stop. The three onlookers check in with each other: does she mean it? "One of you three children can set the table. We're having a guest."

Believing that they were entering a new phase of their life together, the Canwins decided to leave a fashionable neighborhood and buy an old house in a decidedly less affluent neighborhood. Over a period of months, the four Canwins met with an architect friend who was redesigning the house. Like many Canwin decisions, this one had both its beautiful and its stormy moments. Though the family supported each person's right to have his or her selfish needs represented in the architectural design, there were bitter disagreements over what would be sacrificed when the Canwin budget limited individual freedom. Melissa's animal kennel, a fireman's pole between Teddy's third floor room and the ground floor, and Herbert's greenhouse in the bedroom hallway all had to give way, but not without threats, tears, seemingly irreconcilable polarizations, and quite a bit of fun. The architectural result of these stormy deliberations is a house tailored to the predilections of a random collective. It is a house dominated by a completely open common living space with the view from the entrance covering four different levels. It is also a house accented with private spaces that have been designed to accommodate the interests of its occupants. Thus, Teddy's room has a lock on the door to permit him his withdrawals, shelf space for his mechanical investigations, and a rope to the balcony that he can climb. Melissa's room has large wall spaces for her to tape up cutouts and pictures and it lets in a great deal of sunlight so that she can grow her own plants.

The Canwins' decision-making process reflects the family's belief in the viability of diverse meanings and images. Oftener than not in their deliberations, family-unit meanings give way or accommodate themselves to individual ones. Nevertheless, as their planning for a new house demonstrates, an amalgamation of meanings and images does take place. In a sense, the eventually agreed-upon architecture of the house is a structural embodiment of the Canwin family-unit credo that each individual's lifestyle and meanings ought to be permitted as free a reign as is emotionally and financially possible. While in progress, however, the Canwins' decision-making process seldom approaches such structural coherence. Negotiations in the meaning sphere are almost always dominated by a strong sense of ambiguity concerning whose meanings and points of view will actually be put into effect. As often as not, solutions to Canwin family problems seem to come spontaneously out of nowhere. When such fortuitous solutions are not found, highly charged emotional impasses can result.

The Canwin household is likely to be as cluttered with objects as it is with people. The hallway is typically strewn with clothes, yesterday's or last month's, forcing people to pick their way, as through a gentle minefield. Either the Canwins do not see the disarray or they are too preoccupied and cannot take the time to tidy up routinely. Mainly they do not seem to notice. The study contains papers, books, unopened letters, garden and carpentry tools, a movie projector, several dead plants, and other seemingly unconnected items, some of which are swept by the wind into messy confusion every time the children pass through the room on their way to the backyard.

Life in the Canwin household is sparked by projects, planned and spontaneous, mostly spontaneous. In spite of their preference for spontaneity, the Canwins are ceremonially romantic about holidays and traditional events, which are rarely celebrated in the same way from one year to another. This past Halloween eve, for instance, the Canwins drove to their house in the country after the children finished trick-or-treating in the neighborhood. On the way, they stopped to visit a quiet graveyard along a dark country road where, with the aid of candles and flashlights, they inspected gravestones in search of one that touched some inward light. The family completed its game at the farm around a fire in a darkened room, where each person told a story whose central character was the person whose name appeared on a gravestone.

The individual Canwins frequently disperse to different private corners of the house, immersed in totally unshared activities which reflect four completely different tastes and styles. Although everyone endorses, at least in spirit, the idea of being together at table, it doesn't work out that way, even when all are in the household together. An air of deep uncertainty prevails around mealtime. Melissa's tendency toward social clubbiness exerts an aggressive drag upon Teddy's irrepressible attachment to *Star Trek*, a science fiction television series that everyone agrees he has a right to view even though it frequently overlaps with mealtime. Herbert Canwin openly opposes the high degree of autonomy enjoyed by the nine-year-old-boy. He shares Melissa's penchant for social sharing at mealtime, but also shares with his wife the idea that Teddy's investment in scientific subjects ought to be supported. Maria Canwin, more often than not the family's ideological defender of personal freedoms, vacillates in her stand but usually enforces the priority of Teddy's right to independence over the family desire for togetherness. However, no set rule is established. One night the other members may grant Teddy his television program and the next evening demand he come to the table.

The Canwins' mealtime dilemma is a prime example of the

contradictions inherent in their random-type lifestyle. Herbert, Maria, Melissa, and Teddy all individually decry the fact that mealtimes do not provide a greater opportunity for emotional sharing and closeness. To set aside a specific time of day for their evening meal and to require each individual member to be present is not a strategy the Canwins care to impose, for it would imperil each person's right to be elsewhere, to be doing what he wants to do when he wants to do it. The upshot of this and other similar dilemmas is that the Canwins find themselves unable to formalize contexts in which emotional sharing and closeness will definitely take place. Closeness and intimacy do occur, but they occur spontaneously. As the Canwin family sketch presented earlier makes clear, emotional exchanges are not only unplanned but also unpredictable in both intensity and range. Teddy is free to display his aggressive affection for Mr. Canwin by shouting epithets and jumping on Herbert's back while Melissa is free to compete openly with her mother for Herbert's physical attention. Likewise, Maria is free to call a halt to the whole accelerated scene when it begins to overwhelm her, even though moments before she, too, was enjoying the whimsy of the scene.

Another example of Canwin contradictions lies in the area of spatial and emotional privacy. Herbert Canwin often complains about the lack of adult privacy. He feels oppressed by the television set, which gives him an impression of having feet of its own, appearing wherever he wants to be either alone by himself or with his wife. To combat such crowding he purchased a second-hand, nonportable TV for the basement, where it was immediately stationed. One week later, however, this nonportable model was perched precariously on a wobbly stool in the dining area, obstructing traffic. Meanwhile the portable set also continues to make its way around the house, violating his privacy.

The Canwins handle property in much the same way they handle other power issues—erratically. The children meet and play with their friends in the parents' supposedly private bedroom. They also feel free to pick up and use any material item in the house. Yet Herbert's tools, wherever he can find them, are supposed to be private property. Moreover, no one is ever completely sure about which tools he will designate as "his" and which he will not.

Melissa begins her day in her mother's closet, looking for something to wear to school. Maria Canwin doesn't object, for she has a dread of property and proprietorship. "Ownership of things is like imprisonment," she maintains. In addition, Melissa and Maria, who cannot keep a pair of socks together in their bureaus, wear those belonging to Herbert, who can. Such violations amuse Herbert, but appall his son, whose private room is off limits to everyone, including his parents. This appreciation of his own privacy doesn't deter Teddy from making enormous contraptions out of snowtires, encyclopedias, antique chairs, and pieces of junk gathered from the streets, and then placing them in positions where they dominate the basement and make it inaccessible to everyone else.

The ways in which the Canwin establishment regulates access to the power dimension are in some ways the least predictable of all their dimensional interactions. Herbert, and, to a lesser extent, Teddy at times make efforts to regulate access to power and wield control in a closed-style fashion. In fact, Mr. Canwin acknowledges a personal preference for a more traditional arrangement in which the parents exercise control, but usually accedes to the family's preference for a random-type regulation of the power dimensions, particularly in the interpersonal sphere. His occasional authoritarian harangues cause considerable confusion and uncertainty both to himself and to other family members.

The flow of energies in the Canwin home is dynamically erratic. Quiet times do, of course, occur, but silence is almost always breakable. Someone reading a book or thinking almost never objects to an escalation of noise and/or energy. During the family's high-energy periods, the Canwins appear to be, in the phrase of one of their friends, "connoisseurs of chaos." At such times too much seems to happen too fast, since no one member of the family has the surplus energy needed to counteract the momentum propelling them all forward into unknown events with increasing speed. At such times members either rein in their energies after some minor disaster or else slip into exhaustion after experiencing a creative high.

Chapter 10

※※※※※※※※※※※※※※※※

Family Types: Purposes, Flaws, and Ideals

In the previous chapter we have compared the three basic types of family systems in an examination of their differing homeostatic ideals, their individual criterion variables, the substantive differences in certain mechanisms, and their different modes of empirical organization. We have suggested by means of these various levels of comparison that closed-, open-, and random-type family processes have different primary goals, or what we prefer to call core purposes. In this chapter, we discuss what the core purposes of each structural type of family are, together with their more specific target ideals. We also delineate the flaws inherent in each typal design and suggest the degrees of disability through which each may fail. Finally, we take a look at some enabling and disabling strategies associated with each typal variant.

In our discussion of the closed-type system, we emphasized the operational obligation of members to conform to the distance regulations established by those designated with authority in the family. Implicit in this type of structural arrangement is the notion

143

that tradition (whether ethnic, religious, or ideological) is the ultimate authority to which all family members must bow. The closed-type family believes that an ideal of what is right and good and true and beautiful can be established and, once established, adhered to. In a sense, the primary function of the mechanisms in the closed-type family is to interpret, protect, and maintain the family's traditions for its members. Yet, tradition is not an end in itself as much as it is a means devoted to the end of a stable family system. *Stability within and across all six dimensions of family process is the core purpose of the closed-type family.* Such stability requires discipline, a discipline of adhering to the verities of the family's tradition, for, without such discipline, the closed-type family's traditional center could not hold together, but would fly apart.

The open-type family does not share the closed system's belief in tradition or its goal of stability. We emphasized throughout our descriptions that members' traffic is regulated by consent in the open-type family. The open family is perpetually faced with the task of seeking a consensus of opinions and feelings through which the entire family can be governed. *The purpose of this open-style process is to create a system that is adaptive to the needs of both individual and family system.* The premise is that no tradition can know those needs as well as family members themselves. Therefore, each decision reached in the family requires its members' consent.

In our descriptions of the random-type family, we have emphasized each individual's prerogatives to act as he or she wishes. The random family wants its members to exercise their freedoms, unfettered either by consent or tradition. Only in this way, according to the random ethic, can a family help an individual to find himself and be true to that self. *The core purpose of random family system process can best be summed up as free exploration.* Unlike the closed-type family, the random system offers no universal answers except that each must intuit what is right and wrong, good and bad, or ugly and beautiful for himself. The family's job is to facilitate and reward individual intuition, a kind of unstructured understanding that is not primarily logical or rational.

Each family type uses its core purpose as a guide to regulating distances within each of the target dimensions. In a very real sense, each family's core purpose functions as a modifier of its primary targets. For instance, the primary meaning dimension target of identity remains the same for all families, and yet each family type defines this meaning target differently. Let us now summarize each type's target ideals, dimension by dimension.

Affect Ideals

The closed-type family strives after an intimacy and nurturance which is stable. Affections are characterized by earnestness and sincerity rather than passion. It is expected and natural that members share good feelings with one another. Loyalties based on blood ties are usually honored above those to friends. Affections are deeply rooted in each member's strong and enduring sense of belonging. Feelings of tenderness predominate. Even in times of conflict or separation, fidelity is maintained. Members' relations with one another are fastidious and sensible. The emotional, or affect, mandate is to *care deeply, but be composed*. In the closed system, sentiment is preferred to the vivacity of open-type or the fervor of random-type affections. Ecstasy is viewed as a fullness of pleasure within the fidelity of relationship. Durability, fidelity and sincerity are the closed system's ideals in the affect dimension.

Members of an open-type family seek an intimacy and nurturance that is adaptive. Emotions are more overtly expressed than they are in the closed system. Members are encouraged to reveal their honest feelings and thoughts to each other. Feelings of all kinds are permissible, as long as they are true ones. Members may communicate a greater intensity as well as a larger range of emotion than can those in a closed system. In addition, emotions may be more readily tapped. If a member is not showing his or her feelings, others are free to ask him to do so. Whereas the closed system relies on proven affections, the open-type family seeks out new emotional experiences. Its emotional mandate is to *share and not withhold* whatever is being felt. Ecstasy is felt to be a profoundly authentic experience, an exchange of truly and deeply felt emotions. In sum, responsiveness, authenticity, and the legitimacy of emotional latitude are the open system's major affect ideals.

The random-type family pursues an exploratory nurturance and intimacy. Emotions wander and are characterized by passion. They can be trenchant, profound, caustic, electric, tender, romantic, or hysterical. In short, members' emotions are unlimited. Random family affections are penetrating and penetrable, rapt and quick. Intense emotional moments, which spring unplanned from nowhere, are preferred to planned or habitual experiences. Random systems have a flair for the absurd. Caprice, novelty, and humor are common. The random affect mandate is to *raise experience to levels of originality and inspiration.* Ecstasy is defined as rapture, a state actively to be sought along with whimsicality and spontaneity as the primary ideals of random affect regulations.

POWER IDEALS: The closed-type family strives for an efficacy which is stable. Toward this end, power is vertically organized. Rules are extensive and clear. What feels like coercion to the open- or random-type systems feels like a natural necessity in the closed system. Members are diligently prepared to grapple with tasks of ever increasing difficulty. They are not so much urged to achieve perfection as they are to do their best and to strive for it. Competence is assumed; mastery is attempted, but can be attained only by sound preparation. There is a reliance on and a faith in the law. Obedience does not mean submission, but apprenticeship to something bigger than the self. In the ideal closed system, opposition is rare, for it obstructs the goal of true devotion and freedom. *Persevere and you shall prevail* is the power mandate of the closed system. Authority, discipline, and preparation dominate the pathway to a stable efficacy for the closed system. The typical member of a closed system chooses to observe and conform and in so doing acquires his autonomy from above.

The open-type family seeks for its members an efficacy that is adaptive. Toward this end, the open system's power regulations are marked by laterality. Members are encouraged to exercise their talents. From early on members have the opportunity to develop a proficiency in acquiring and manipulating the tools of their culture. Universal participation in the decision-making process insures that all members are heard and their needs and desires taken into account. There is a faith in the basic goodness and wisdom of the members, and the members rely on these values more than on the rules of behavior they evolve. *Persuade rather than coerce* is the mandate of the open system's power dimension as the unit tries to reconcile differences between its autonomous individuals and its shared management of the collective. Individuals are free to determine their own destinies, for mastery over self is highly valued. Members' right to autonomy is ideally balanced by their skill in negotiating with one another, even in situations of significant conflict. Opposition is an integral part of the decision-making dialectic. The ideal open-type community is affirmed rather than imperiled by disagreement and dispute, for opposition is understood as a necessary step along the way to family resolution. Synthesis, along with allowance and cooperation are the key power ideals of the open system.

The random-type family pursues an exploratory efficacy. Toward this end it adopts total laterality in its power regulations. Individual choice is permitted free reign. There is a relaxation of rules and an informal congeniality of relationship. All forms of experimentation are legitimate, for members of a random system have faith in the efficacy of creative anarchy. Any hint of coercion, impinging on the individual's right to control his own destiny, is forbidden. The ideal random way to alter another's behavior is to inspire him or her to choose a better course of action. Positions of authority are interchangeable and are determined by charisma and personal capability. Competitions may be present, but typical members of a random system do not set themselves against one another. They are interested instead in developing a nonrivalrous individuality. In contrast to the parsimonious and disciplined preparation of the closed system, the ideal random system is exuberant and extravagant in paying tribute to potentiality. Talent is lavishly celebrated and subsidized, because the assumption is that, once talent is unleashed, it will flourish and flower. The random system's power mandate is to *discover your potential.* Opposition need not be resolved, for the random type family believes in a multiformity of purpose. Interchangeability, free choice, and challenge rather than unity are the random system's power ideals.

MEANING IDEALS: The closed-type family strives to maintain a stable identity. It insists that assertions and points of view be substantiated by evidence, either theoretical or factual. Careful observation of distinctions is both demanded and carried out in members' discourse. The entire reasoning process is refined to a high art of discrimination, clarity, and precision. Evaluations and judgments of worth are made from a vantage point supplied by a traditional ideological system. Closed-system beliefs and images afford members a great deal of certainty about the world and their place in it, for they tend to be tangible, extensive, internally consistent with one another, and unanimously adhered to among family members. The closed system's primary mode of communication is formal. Its style of expression is reserved, distinct, concise, and exact. Creativity is recognized as the systematic application of accrued knowledge toward the goal of discovery. The closed system's meaning mandate is to *be integrated*. Certainty, unity, and clarity are its ideals.

The open-type family seeks to develop an adaptive identity. Its reasoning processes are rational. The open system is dominated by a desire to hear and consider different points of view. It prefers dialectical argument to ideological unanimity, for it believes in the necessity of rational dialogue, of meeting and leveling with each other face to face to uncover the existence of important contradictory and conflicting evidence, so that as complete as possible a view of reality will be obtained. Its beliefs are subject to doubt and often modified and qualified to preserve and elaborate the spirit of truth held within them. In this way, the ideal open-type family insures that its meanings will continue to be revelant to members' ongoing lives. In addition, the open system canvasses its interior and exterior worlds for new images and meanings to assimilate into its own, thereby creating a new imagistic synthesis in which similarity and affinity, rather than uniformity, are sought. The primary mode of communication is informal. Members' expressions are straightforward, salient, and demonstrative. Creativity is exemplified by empirical pursuits in which disparate details are assimilated, and the end result is serendipitous discovery. The open system's meaning mandate is to *be authentic*. Relevance, affinity, and tolerance are its ideals.

The random-type family pursues an exploratory identity. Within its walls, exception is the norm. All points of view are possible and are presumed to be supported by evidence of some kind.

Even if contradicted by the facts, assertions are valued as long as they reveal some metaphoric truth. The reasoning process is dominated by personal intuition and inspiration. Stale legalisms quickly wither and die. On the contrary, original and inventive concepts receive an enthusiastic response, for there is a genuine excitement and hunger for new ideas in the random-type family. Paradox and ambiguity are not only permitted, but they are preferred as suitable vehicles for representing the perplexity and diversity of life. In this way, the random system gains perspective through absurdity. There is a novelty in members' modes of communication. Their expressions may be concise or straightforward, but they may also be pregnant, inventive, symbolic, elliptical, or original. Creativity is recognized as an inspired and imaginative rendering of reality. The random system's mandate is to *be creative*. Ambiguity, diversity, and originality are its ideals.

Having completed this survey of target ideals, we can understand more fully how the three basic types of family systems we have been describing represent three different styles of distance regulation. As we have seen from discussions in this and the preceding chapter, each typal style consists of two major elements: its criterion variables, which represent applications of its homeostatic ideal to the access dimensions of space, time, and energy; and its definition of the primary target goals, which are applications of its core purpose to the subject of targets. The chart in Figure 3 illustrates in more specific detail the relationship between a family's typal style and its access and target dimensions.

A system's typal style informs its members how to carry out distance regulations throughout the six dimensions of family process. For instance, the closed type family prefers to establish fixed spaces in its approach to the spatial issue of closeness and distance. This means that it picks a point on the closeness-distance scale and establishes that point as the most appropriate distance for members to maintain in their interactions with each other in one particular behavioral context. Ideally, such fixed regulations of family space will enable the family to realize its core purpose of stability through tradition and its target goals of fidelity, discipline, and integrity, to name but three. To draw upon another example, a ran-

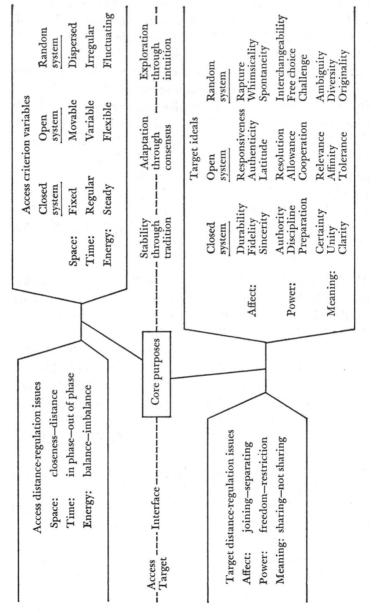

FIGURE 3. Three distance-regulation styles.

dom-type family opts for fluctuating energy in its approach to the energic distance-regulation issue of balance-imbalance. The system's energy will thus fluctuate between the two states as members pursue the random core purpose of exploration through intuition. The target goals sought by this means might include spontaneity, interchangeability, and originality. Likewise the open-type family's variable time organization enables it to pursue its core purpose of adaptation through consensus and its target ideals, including responsiveness, allowance, and relevance.

Flawed Versions of Types

Unfortunately, not all families attain their ideals. Many approach them, but some fall far short, regardless of their typal propensity. As a result, when we look at families, we see many flawed, as well as ideal, versions of each type. For each theoretically pure or ideal variety of any of the three types, there is a corresponding theoretically impure or flawed variety. These flawed systems evolve out of a family's failure to consummate its typal design, either because it fails to attain its target ideals or because the criterion variables it evolves are inadequate for regulating access to those ideals.

The emergence of a flawed typal variety is in our minds symptomatic of a family experiencing serious crisis. The flawed varieties generally support a *crisis chain* that features five linked eventualities: (1) *Each type's probable direction of error,* the self-maximizing tendencies of the system carried to self-destructive extremes; (2) its *homeostatic impasse,* the standard pattern of impasse into which the system lapses when it cannot find the means to abort or reverse its self-destroying tendencies; (3) its *probable errors of substantiation,* the perversion or inversion of the system's goals; (4) its *propensity for ritual sacrifice,* the form that tyranny takes as competition between the individual and the system escalates into unreconcilable conflict; (5) the *emergence of runaway,* that is, unchecked movement of the system in a direction opposite to the probable direction of error, a condition based on the successful institutionalization of rebellion, sometimes violent rebellion. With the exception of "runaway," each of these linked eventualities, listed in order of occurrence, is a potential source of a subsequent, more serious level of crisis disability in families and other social systems. Thus, family tyranny can be observed to develop out of a context of means-and-goal perversion, which can grow out of an impasse, which follows a system's probable direction of error. Runaway processes can originate at or between any of these levels as a reversal of the direction of error. As a result, a family in runaway can look and act momentarily like one of the other basic system types. The paragraphs that follow summarize what the flawed versions of each type experience at each link in their crisis chain.

Following its probable direction of error, the first link in its crisis chain, the flawed closed-type family becomes a system of insular purity, sealed off from the outside world. It seeks to forestall all evolution and change, to remain the same despite the onrush of time. Its traditional standards become isolated and parochial. The flawed closed-type family offers its members no escape or relief from absolute obedience to these standards, even though loneliness, frustration, or lack of interest result. Members of a flawed closed system tend to be overly inbred, undifferentiated, and poorly equipped for life in the heterogeneous community at large.

When the closed system reaches its own form of homeostatic impasse, interaction sequences are denoted by feedback patterns of absolute constancy. The result is a deadening routinization of movement. Members experience the feeling of being "stuck in a rut" without knowing how to get out. Their allegiance to specific disabling strategies requires their own self-deprivation.

Once the closed system's probable errors of substantiation have emerged, interchanges of affection may deteriorate to hollow echoes of true exchanges as members become slaves to a conformity of expression, both bored and boring in their stereotypic range of emotional responses. Fidelity and sincerity are perverted into artless unperjurability and fanatical obsequiousness. In the power dimension, the authority of tradition can be distorted in a flawed closed system to a point at which designated persons acquire unchallengeable prerogatives and powers over the affairs of the others. In such an authoritarian situation, discipline can be transformed into restraint, inhibition, or prohibition, while preparation, a valued precursor to competence, can become an end in itself. In the meaning dimension, dogmatism and conformity dominate meaning dimension interactions. Even creativity and originality may be punished as unwarranted deviations from established norms.

If the self-maximizing tendencies of the closed system move in accordance with probable errors of substantiation, the smaller entity is virtually always sacrificed to the benefit of the larger system. Compromises in human individuality are inevitable, for tyranny in the flawed closed system logically falls from top to bottom, suppressing the individuals underneath who are required to be obedient and accept their punishment.

In runaway, opposition takes the form of rebellion against tradition and authority in the flawed closed-type family. In one form of rebellion, individuals direct violence against the system and its authorities. In another, individual violence is turned inward, against the self. Closed-type runaways are often generated by either the absurdity or unenforceability of the traditional authorities' demands. Such demands tend to legitimate and reinforce individual members' rebellions, for they reveal those designated in authority as unwise holders of a traditional office who ought to be either replaced or rendered ineffective. During the periods in which these runaway processes prevail, the closed system may occasionally appear like a flawed open- or random-type system as patterns of interaction become dominated by public disagreement and turbulence.

The flawed open system, following its probable direction of error, undergoes serious schism. The opening of its interior to outside influences can either disconnect members or make them dependent on outsiders. A confusion of insiders and outsiders, and of their roles and prerogatives, frequently occurs. Another consequence is an interior move toward conflict and separation. The core purpose of adaptation through consensus begins to hang like a millstone around the neck of a flawed open system. Eternal wrangling and disagreements that never get resolved prevent the adoption of system-wide standards. In response, the system tends to extend its perimeter boundaries ever further, either as an exercise in pseudo-containment to prevent any outright splitting off of members and factions, or as a means of obscuring conflicts and thereby prolonging them by the introduction of external ideas, forces, and events.

The open family's homeostatic impasse is dominated by a curious amalgam of constancy and variety feedback patterns. The attempt to harness simultaneously the benefits of both closed and random patterns results not in resolution but in ambiguity, incongruity, and internal contradiction. The system transmits to its members simultaneous signals of a contradictory nature, placing them in a sort of typal double bind, so that they are damned if they go either way.

When a flawed variety's probable errors of substantiation emerge, purposes and ideals break down and become perverted. In the affect dimension, the quest for emotional authenticity is satisfied either by a burlesque of exuberance or else by dispassionate resignation. Interchanges tend to consist of either meaningless flattery or quibbling toward no foreseeable end. Authority and power are compromised by a combination of halfway measures and intransigent opposition as the system's strengths become its weaknesses. The desire for synthesis results in a middle way, which goes nowhere. In the realm of meaning, there is a breakdown in the rationale both for maintaining the family's icons, symbols, and other statements of meaning and for deciding which new values ought to be adopted from the exterior culture. The family's purposes dissipate. Communications become extraneous, impertinent, and perpetually trivial. In the process, tolerance leads to indeterminancy, quick identifications replace reflection, and, as meanings are spread more and more thin, truth becomes indeterminate; or, worse, all values become equal.

At the fourth stage in the flawed open system's crisis chain, either the smaller or the larger system entities may be sacrificed to facilitate the survival of the other. The unforeseen and, certainly, the unintended consequence of latitude, allowance, and tolerance is a form of tyranny in which individuals resist the system while the family group as a whole pressures individuals to give up their autonomy. Each thus holds the other in an intransigent death grip, proclaiming its own sovereignty and ritually sacrificing that of the other.

In the runaway stage of open-type crisis, a schism that has been ignored or denied becomes manifest in outright rebellion based on a complete disqualification of the consensus gathering process. In runaway, the open-type family no longer tries to do anything together. Ultimately, members either withdraw emotionally with their talk becoming an empty shadow of action, or physically leave, or splinter the whole into separate units by separations and divorces of one kind or another. A more corrosive kind of tyranny can also evolve, the family in effect telling its dissidents "to get the hell out," while the dissidents try to explode the system from within. The tyranny of such runaway is the mindless destruction of both the family and its individual members.

The random-type family's probable direction of error is to become truly chaotic. Members experience shifting images, jarred rhythms, and unregulated entries and exits. Life becomes careless, scattered, and incomplete. Members fail to attain satisfactory relationships. The people and their movements neither mesh nor serve as counterpoint to one another. Instead, other members are experienced as totally independent entities, making no vital connections with one another, each getting in the other's way. Interactions are marked by spasms of hostility. For many members frequent and furious fights are the only alternative to systemic alienation.

The homeostatic impasse of the flawed random type is characterized by an absolute preference for the unstructured variety feedback loops. Nothing is allowed to remain constant, not even successfully functioning strategies. Attempts to maintain some kind of stability are, if need be, forcibly thwarted. The resulting irony is that a system devoted to encouraging variety prohibits one behavioral variety, namely constancy, from ever taking root.

As a consequence of a flawed random system's perversion of goals, high levels of turbulence and contradiction occur in interactions. Pathways to the ideal of rapture are littered with one disaster after another in the affect dimension. Emotions exceed ecstasy, overflowing into intoxication or unrestrained furor. Most often people are stranded with whatever feelings they do have unrecognized and unvalidated. Epigrammatic nonsense, pointless buffoonery, extravagent pathos, and driven humor become the nearest approximations of spontaneity and whimsicality. Power relations are sabotaged by the erratic laws of caprice and unrestrained volition. A pervading lack of discipline and an unwillingness to cooperate make system efficacy not merely impossible, but also irrelevant. In the meaning sphere, irrelevence itself becomes institutionalized as the pathways to purpose and identity are cluttered with extravagant contradiction and egregious nonsense. In the resulting confusion, the acts and ideas of the flawed random system become incomprehensible and its members run the risk of losing their grasp on all meaning.

The flawed random system's self-maximizing tendency is such that some larger entity of the system will be sacrificed to the survival of individuals. Individuals have the power to push the system beyond its endurance, to demolish it, or simply to declare it dead and disband it. Relations among the members themselves are governed by an adherence to a "survival of the fittest" philosophy. The individual who has trouble learning how to become self-supporting is ritually sacrificed in the flawed random type family. Where there are no restraints on the freedom of choice and movement, the person in pain cannot compel the attention and support of the others. He or she is viewed as a drag on the system rather than a victim of its practices. The result is that the victim is left to fend for himself, to wither and die, at least metaphorically, for no other member need respond or even recognize the victim's pain, unless he desires to do so.

Runaway occurs in the flawed random system when different individual members try to extend their own brand of order over the entire family system. Intense competition and tyranny can result as various members try to save the system as a whole from the disorganized propensities of the other members. Individuals can get squashed in the ensuing conflict, for physical strength is the frequent and final arbiter of disputes. The runaway breakdown of the flawed random system characteristically continues until members' opposition ceases and a new authoritarian closed-type system is established, either because one family member attains supremacy or because an outside agency, such as a court, is introduced and family members submit, at least temporarily, to its authority. If neither of these potential resolutions proves possible, the flawed random type continues in runaway until it is emotionally if not physically torn apart.

Mixed Types

The three typal designs we have identified do not in themselves constitute a typology for classifying all families. To propose that there are only three kinds of families would be simplistic at best. What we are proposing is that the distance-regulation processes of all family systems are governed by the homeostatic ideals and strategic core purposes of the closed, open, and random family designs. These designs, though not a typology in themselves, are a foundation on which a more detailed typology of family systems might be built. Although, for purposes of clarity, the family processes we have described in this chapter have been uniformly closed, open, or random, such "pure" typal manifestations do not represent the norm in our experience. The consistently closed, open, or random family is much more stereotypical than typical.

Families in the real world frequently have to be classified as mixtures of type. A family that is predominately open in its affections may be rather closed in the way it makes its decisions or possibly even random in its pursuit of meaning. Some degree of mixture across typal lines is to be expected. After all, the core purposes of stability through tradition, adaptation through consent, and exploration through intuition are all highly valued themes in Western civilization. Each may give shape to different forms of distance-regulation organization within the same family. Sometimes, differing distance-regulation patterns will coexist side by side, each with its own sphere of influence. At other times, split core purposes can generate intense competition and conflict over how traffic in a particular dimension or subsystem ought to be regulated. Different typal tendencies may dominate a family's processes during different periods of its life cycle. Thus, a closed-type family may experience a great deal of stress when its offspring become teenagers, so much stress that the system decides to change form by developing a preponderance of open-type strategies. Such a decision may result in the formation of an open-type system, or it may produce a curious hybrid, such as a family with closed-system goals and open-system means for attaining those goals. Whether temporary or permanent, such means-goals hybrids are important examples of mixtures of type.

The prevalence of type mixtures in real life requires an elaboration of our presentation of three basic process styles. The distinction between stereotype and mixed type might be described as that between theme and variation: it is that between core purposes and their application at different family system interfaces. Because each theme has its variations, a family analyst wishing to classify a family's type must examine many different interface patterns before he can feel sure of his findings. Such interface analysis, though it must be done carefully, does not require an endless examination of interface variables. Family strategies tend to repeat themselves, both at the same interface and at other interfaces. It is our experience that, while families vary their processes, their application of one typal style will usually dominate other styles, an outgrowth perhaps of the necessity to establish a priority of purpose ideals. Thus, though it exhibits a mixture of different distance-regulation tendencies, a family may still be classified as a predominantly closed-, open-, or random-type system.

Even though we have expanded our description of family types to include far more than just three stereotypic types of family systems, we are nevertheless able to classify different varieties of family within the same general type. We can make these intratypal distinctions by identifying the kind of traffic plan developed and implemented by the modulating mechanisms of each family. In this way we can focus on the important ways in which an anti-centric open family, whose general traffic flow is away from the family center, differs from a procentric, acentric, or ecentric open-type system. We can also identify similarities of experience between a prosynchronous closed type family, which spends most of its time together on the same time track, and a similarly prosynchronous random type family, despite their overall typal difference. Thus, with the intratypal distinctions made possible by the application of the *pro-, anti-, a-, and e-traffic plans,* discussed in Chapter Eight, our model of basic family types is further elaborated and qualified.

Though our typal designations are offered as a means of classifying families rather than individuals, they can also be applied to identify the distance-regulation style of each subsystem of family, including individuals. As a result, one is led to ask, "Can a person of one typal style be a member of a family primarily exhibiting another typal style?" Most assuredly, yes. Such difference is the source of much of the conflict occurring in families, namely, a struggle over which type of equilibrium, core purpose, and distance-regulation model is best for the family and each of its members. Typal variance between the individual and his family is generally allowed greatest leeway in the random family system, less leeway in the open system, and still less in the closed. This is particularly true of overt expressions of stylistic discrepancy. In the closed-type family, typal variance tends either to be latent or to be consciously withheld. In the open system, variance is permissible but held in check, lest typal discrepancies grow too large between one member and the others. In the random system, typal variance is not only permitted, but expected. Indeed, did it not occur, the random-type family might feel it had failed to provide a true multiplicity of options for its members.

Functions of Typal Design

The typal design of a family is its detailed blueprint for operationalizing its homeostatic ideal and core purpose by regulating traffic in both the access and target dimensions. Each system's design, regardless of type or mixture of type, performs three important family process functions. It serves as a distance-regulation comparator, a pathways indicator, and an opposition regulator. Let us examine each of these functions in turn.

On a moment-to-moment operational level, a family's typal design functions as a *distance-regulation comparator,* informing family members what distance regulations to observe. It provides parameters governing when, where, how, and why to move. The parameter-testing aspects of any event are sampled by the family organism and compared with the internal criteria of its typal design. On the basis of this relationship between event and design, judgments are made about the value of ongoing events and, on rarer occasions, the appropriateness of the typal design itself seeking to regulate the flow of such events. For example, a co-worker may be introduced by the father of a closed type family to his wife and children. The co-worker moves spontaneously as if to embrace the wife. Immediately his move triggers images of physical oppression which members of the closed type family compare to their sense of what constitutes an appropriate greeting. Mother responds by physically withdrawing, a response dictated by the family's typal design fulfilling a distance-regulation comparator function.

Second, a family's typal design functions as a *pathways in-dicator*—its master traffic manual for moving spatially within and across dimensional fields toward target goals. As we have seen, the closed-, open-, and random-type systems have distinctively different traffic patterns for gaining access to their goals. The stylistically different strategic pathways that the closed, open, and random family types might take toward their goals are schematized in Figure 4.

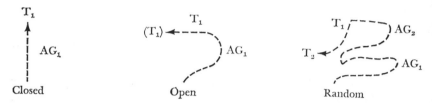

FIGURE 4. Strategic pathways by type.

The closed family style tends to define its targets and move in a straight and direct path toward attaining them. Detours and deviations are characteristically rechanneled back into line. The open family style is to keep its goals clearly in sight, but to sanction detour and deviation. Its general tendency is to redefine its basic goals: for example, in the figure T_1 becomes (T_1)'. The random family style is to let traffic go where it will. Erratic and unpredictable pathways are the frequent result. Detours may dominate. Unlike the open system, which maintains and/or redefines its goals, the random family may replace or lose sight of its original targets, but discover other targets, such as T_2 in the figure.

Third, the typal design functions as an *opposition regulator*. Every system must make provision for responding to deviations from its typal design. In accord with the parameters of accessibility established by the criterion variables of each family type, the closed-type family controls opposition and the open-type family encloses opposition, whereas the random-type family opposes control. Each system's response to opposition is linked to its core purpose as well. The closed system develops strategies to control opposition by way of preserving stability through tradition. The open system develops strategies to enclose opposition, that is, both to encourage and constrain it, in order to facilitate the family's goal of adaptation through consent. However, the random system opposes control (except insofar as it is controlled by opposition)' in order to realize its core purpose of exploration through intuition.

The way in which a family characteristically responds to opposition offers important empirical clues about a family's typal design. Though a complete and conclusive rendering of type requires an examination of all family interfaces, a system's mode of opposition provides a rather reliable vehicle for identifying, at least tentatively, a family's typal style. Conflicts generally heighten the visibility of the strategic pathway and of distance-regulation issues within families, as viewed by both member and observer. They make manifest a family's otherwise invisible homeostatic ideal, because a family's style of opposition control is a natural outgrowth of its preference for a particular kind of homeostasis. A system that emphasizes quite rigidly established constancy feedback loops simply will not permit many distance regulation or strategic pathway deviations, whereas a family that prefers the more flexible variety loops will permit all kinds of deviation. The subject of opposition control therefore relates theory with empirical reality and, as such, offers shortcut clues for identifying families.

Typal Biases

The model of family types we propose offers no single homeostatic process ideal for all families. Rather, it suggests that there are three ideals, each with its own plan for balancing the forces of equilibrium (relaxation), disequilibrium (tension), and the restoration of equilibrium (relaxation of tension). Regardless of type, all families have to contend with obstacles to their target strivings—that is, with intrusions on their typal design. Ultimately, they must remove such obstructions in order to preserve their typal design. Each time a system's chosen state of equilibrium-disequilibrium is restored, feelings of accomplishment can be experienced. The family's typal design is proven to be viable and the family itself is reaffirmed.

Though the three basic family types each attempts to implement a core purpose consistent with the values of Western civilization, they are likely to be valued differently by specific Western communities. Each ethnic, religious, and economic subculture will make its own judgments about which typal design represents a better or more viable form of family organization. In the American culture as a whole, it has been our experience that major institutions, such as schools, hospitals, agencies, and clinics, generally announce a preference for the open-type family, perhaps because the process style of the open system more closely approximates the democratic ideals of our nation as a whole than does either of the other two family types. In their day-to-day dealings with families, however, such institutions seem to exhibit an operational preference for the closed type family, perhaps because it seems to offer the most successful form of organization for maintaining the larger social order. In addition, closed system members offer the least amount of threat to institutions and institutional employees. The random-type family and its members are most often perceived as the most threatening system type, both to institutions and the social order they represent. Correspondingly, random-type families are perhaps the most distrustful of institutional intervention of any kind.

Many therapists, as well as many important systems thinkers, tend to equate movements toward randomness with undesirable chaos. However, we find the random design to be of great value. Variety feedback cycles can be destructive, but they can also "increase the survival potential of a given system" (Hoffman, 1971, p. 286) through the generation of mutations. In family systems, trends toward randomness can lead not only to chaos, but to the successful implantation of a new order of innovation and freedom for all family members. We believe that the randomness of creative random systems is an ordered randomness. The random meaning of order is, of course, a very special one, in which systematically structured disagreements, conflicts, and deviance take place, and in which novel, even whimsical, alternatives are permitted. It is incumbent upon family theorists, social planners, and agency practitioners to recognize this difference and acknowledge the viability of the random style, and to reconsider those theories, institutional programs, and social interventions that exhort the random family either to suppress its randomness or to give it up entirely. Indeed, we believe it incumbent on all professionals to discover and sustain a family's typal style based on the family's own interior criteria rather than attempt to impose a typal style upon it that is based on external criteria.

Strategies According to Type

The examination of a family's typal style ought normally to begin with the identification and classification of its strategies. They are the brick and mortar of a family's typal blueprint, the existential rendering of its stylistic propensities. Yet, it is not always easy to classify a single family strategy according to type, for any strategy may represent a mixture of typal styles. Given the difficulty of this task, one can understand why it is virtually impossible to classify a family's typal design on the basis of one or two sequences. Family members simply do not announce their targets as they go about their daily business, nor do they fully or clearly delineate their pathways for reaching their goals. When one has witnessed an accumulation of strategies, one's classifying task becomes much simpler. The more time one has to observe a family, the more confident one can feel about classifying its strategies, because in the course of time families define their goals and delineate their typal styles through their strategic interactions.

The ideal and flawed varieties of type further complicate the classification of strategies, for they require an observer to isolate a family's enabling and disabling strategies. The term *enabling* refers to those strategies which facilitate a family's pursuit of its target ideals, and *disabling* to the patterns associated with a system's failure to attain its targets. These brief definitions require that a distinction be made between single sequences and a family's larger strategic patterns. A sequence, that is, an act or series of acts occurring in a certain context, may be successful or unsuccessful in terms of whether the particular goal of the sequence is attained. A successful sequence does not necessarily represent an enabling strategy, however, for the target success of the sequence may run counter to the family's strategic target goals. Likewise, an unsuccessful sequence may not correspond to a disabling strategy, for the failure to attain a particular goal may on occasion actually facilitate rather than obstruct the family's overall target ideals. The burden of evaluation is on the observer, who must make these distinctions carefully, lest he confuse sequence effects with strategic effects or vice versa.

Extended observation is imperative to an observer in helping him decide in what ways a strategy is enabling or disabling to family process. In addition to distinguishing between the short-term effects of a sequence and the long-term effects of a family strategy, the observer may have to make a careful examination of a particular strategy's effects on the different subsystems of family or on different access-target interfaces. As a general rule, one cannot feel certain of the enabling and disabling effects of a strategy until he identifies its thematic context and measures the enabling and disabling aspects of a strategy in regard to this context. To show how this might be done, we present three basically successful series of family interactions and analyze the typal components of each sequence.

The closed-type Parker family, having just finished a Sunday game of badminton, sits down at a table in a nearby park to enjoy a picnic lunch prepared by Mother earlier. When Father and Betty go to retrieve the picnic items from the car, Mother assures Bob they will get back in time for his meeting with his friend Charley, Bob having reluctantly postponed the meeting for an hour to please his sister Betty, who was looking forward to the picnic.

The open-type Simpson family leaves the river enbankment, following the city's annual kite festival. Bob is going to help his friend Charley haul his kite back to Charley's garage. Betty's disappointment that he won't be home to play a game of Scrabble with the family during the evening is molified when Mother suggests that she, Betty, and Father stop off at the horse stables, only a couple of miles out of their way, before heading home.

One by one, the random-type Hines family leaves the house. Mother hops in the station wagon to go bird-watching. Betty takes off on her bicycle to join a friend studying pond life at the reservoir. Dad peddles to the office on his bicycle, and Bob walks next door to see if his friend Charley will hitch a ride with him to the festival at the river embankment.

On this particular Sunday, the Parker, Simpson, and Hines families experience spontaneous play, each in its own way. In the foregoing descriptions, each family is portrayed at the end of a series of successful play sequences. We shall now examine the way in which each family experiences play as a function of its type, and then the way in which each follows a strategic pathway representative of its type in order to get into a sequence of spontaneous play. Before we focus on these different methods, however, let us briefly consider certain aspects of play that need to be clarified. Both adults and children play as a means of perfecting their boundaries of identity. As such, play is a meaning phenomenon. Play is also a power phenomenon. Competition in the playing of different roles and the performance of different skills is an intrinsic derivative of play. Play is also richly affectual. It is a common vehicle which families use to structure themselves in a shared space as they imaginatively pursue the primary affect targets of nurturance and intimacy. In the following examples, we will stress the affectual components of play. Note in the sequences that all three families get into spontaneous play, although they have slightly different ways of defining "play" and of getting it underway. The basic strategic question we ask in these examples is, "How does each type's pursuit of the goal of spontaneous play strategically differ in style from the other two types?"

The Parkers drive through the park looking for a picnic site on their way back from Grandmother's. They change into their play clothes, find an appropriate site, and put up their badminton net. They play out a singles tournament in which Bob narrowly beats Dad in an exciting finale to become the family champion. Betty playfully suggests the men aren't really so good, that the women can beat them at doubles. "Like fish," says Bob, whacking a serve Mother can't return. Desiring to end the game quickly so he can meet his friend Charley on time, Bob goes all out in using his superior ability to beat the women. Father has to chuckle, "Bob, I never thought you were such a male chauvinist pig." Everyone laughs, even Bob. Betty calls for a rematch. Bob groans, "Can't we eat our lunch so I can get going?" Betty's face falls because she wants to continue playing. Mother suggests that while she and Betty get the lunch ready Bob and Dad might find a pay phone to call Charley and let him know that Bob will be coming home later than expected. After the picnic lunch is eaten, Father suggests one

final match in which all right-handed players transfer their racquets to their left hands and vice versa. A rather hilarious and
much more evenly matched game ensues as both men and women
stumble around desperately trying to hit the shuttlecock on the
strings of their racquets. At match point, Bob and his father let the
cock fall between them, each expecting the other would hit it. The
women let out a cheer. "Allow me to introduce myself," says Father,
offering to shake with his left hand. "I'm Mr. Alphonse." "And
I'm Mr. Gaston," says Bob, shaking with his left hand.

Distance is regulated in this closed system sequence so that
members' goals are successfully reached. The mechanisms of channeling and bridging are employed to keep Bob in the field so that
the family can pursue its goal of spontaneous play. Father's teasing
suggestion that Bob is a "male chauvinistic pig" and his invention
of the left handed match are gentle channeling directives to Bob
about how he should move. These interventions simultaneously
contain Bob's opposition and redirect him toward the common
family goal. Mother's pay phone suggestion helps serve as a bridge
for Bob to his peer social life. This maneuver also eliminates the
possibility that Bob's competing affect target of loyalty to Charley
will interfere with the more imminent goal of spontaneous play.
The Parker family's closed typal style is most evident in its choice
of an organized game like badminton to serve as the framework for
members' spontaneous play. The skillful improvisation members
exhibit all takes place within this framework. The emotions members show, even Bob's oppositional emotions and Betty's momentary
disappointment, all take place within the parameters of polity and
appropriateness. They, too, are framed in and structured.

The Simpsons arrive at the riverbank in time to see hundreds of kites of many different sizes and shapes soaring above
them. "Now, isn't this better than sitting around your old reservoir?" Bob asks Betty. "I don't just sit around the reservoir,"
Betty explains. "I study the frogs." "Of course you do, dear," says
Mother. "Bob's just trying to get you to enjoy this as much." Mr.
Simpson locates some of the more interesting kites in the sky and
starts pointing them out to his family. He launches into a half
technical, half comic mythological spiel about what keeps a kite in
the air. Mother and the kids laugh enthusiastically. For much of

the rest of the afternoon, Father and Betty go off in one direction, and Bob and his mother in another. After walking around for awhile, Betty and her father stop to watch a team of aeronautical engineers trying to launch a giant sized kite. One of the engineers offers Betty a ride on the kite. "Can I, Daddy?" she asks. He agrees and helps the men hold the guidelines of the kite, which rises a couple feet from the ground before coming back down. Betty is all smiles as she hops off. Mother and Bob meanwhile have located Charley, who, together with two friends, is having trouble getting his kite into the air. Mother, Bob, and the friends work on the problem with him, taking turns running with the kite strings in their hands to get it to stay up in the air. Father and Betty catch up with them just as they get the kite safely in the air. Standing next to a concession stand, Mister Simpson buys some Coke and beer, which he and Betty carry over to the group flying Charley's kite. Relaxing on the grass, family and friends toast the kite and share with each other stories of their afternoon's experiences.

The strategic pathway the Simpsons choose in successfully gaining access to spontaneous play is not straight and direct. Members' distance regulations evolve from an interaction of target ideals and context rather than from a predesigned plan. Betty's residual discontent, which she brings with her to the river from earlier transactions, is channeled but in a much more open-ended way than it would have been in a closed-type family. Taking their lead from Mr. Simpson, the family fuels up with new energy at the festival. To facilitate this fueling, the Simpsons separate into two groups and follow their own interests. Their splitting is in effect a combination bridging and buffering maneuver. Characteristic of the open system, Bob and Betty, the residual combatants, put some distance between each other (buffering) while they individually gain access (bridging) to a variety of spontaneous play experiences which also happen to satisfy their separate individual interests. All four members make a connection with people and events outside the family, whose open bounding style facilitates such access with little or no strain. This is especially true of Betty's interaction with the engineers, a situation which contains potential risks to both daughter and kite, but the possibility of risk is not even mentioned, as it might well be in a closed system climate. Finally, the Simpsons' strategy culminates in a gathering of all family members together with some outsiders, a convergent bridge that completes their experience of spontaneous play, appropriately reached through a succession of episodes alternately emphasizing the difference, separation, reconciliation, and agreement of family members.

Mr. and Mrs. Hines head for the trunk to find a suitable costume to wear. Father puts on a feathery hat and an old corset and starts belting out, "I'm a Red Hot Mamma," affecting a manner imitative of Sophie Tucker, drawing the laughs and appreciation of other family members. "Wait a minute, wait a minute," shouts Mother. "None of you seems to realize this is serious." Throwing a black cape over her head and shoulders, she whispers dramatically. "To be or not to be. Hasn't someone asked that question before?" Though he has come downstairs with the rest of the family, Bob doesn't join in the costume play. Instead, he sits down and plays "Jingle Bells" on the piano. "Come on, Bob, try one of these things on," calls Mother. "Don't bug me, Mom. I'm concentrating," says Bob as he continues playing one Christmas carol after another. Betty swipes the black cape out of her mother's hands and turns it over so the red satin inside is now on the outside, covering her head. "I'm Little Red Riding Hood," she says, "On my way to Grandmother's house." Father changes to a deep baritone voice and says, "Well, I'm the big bad wolf, and I'm gonna eat grandmother up." He grabs Mother in a mock fierce way around the throat. She screams and pretends to faint. "Now, little Red Riding Hood, I'm gonna gobble you up," Father says, turning to Betty. Betty laughs at first, but then, when the wolf lunges for her, she screams and dodges him, yelling in her brother's direction, "Help! Help! Where's the woodsman?" Bob punches out some very loud, very dramatic chords then turns around announcing, "Faster than a speeding bullet, I jump over tall buildings in a single bound." He jumps on his father's back and rides him to the ground. Dad pretends to gasp his last breath. "You're too much for me, Superman." The women cheer and sing, "Who's Afraid of the Big Bad Wolf?" When they finish the chorus, Bob says, "Well, I think that finishes our visit to Grandmother's house." The rest of the family laughs in agreement.

The Hines family also attains its goal of spontaneous play.

The key distance-regulation issue grows out of Bob's relationship to the shared activity of the rest of the family. Though he does not completely hold out or withdraw from the others, he rejects his mother's attempts to channel him. His initial piano playing creates a dissonant counterpoint to the others' charade, a counterpoint which threatens to compete with and make more difficult the spontaneous play of the others. Ultimately, however, he answers their bridging request and joins himself to the play of the rest of the family. His entry as a combination Superman-woodsman extends and climaxes the madcap play of the family. It is as if, in inventing a play requiring four parts, the family channels its wayward member into a new jointly shared space. The channeling that takes place thus grows out of the dramatics of the play rather than the overt acts of family members. For the Hineses, spontaneous play is governed by few if any formal rules. Members may be not only silly, but also illogical, as long as their personal associations elaborate the whimsicality of the situation and fuel family energies. To be sure, there are vestiges of framework in their improvisation. Vaudeville, Shakespeare, the Brothers Grimm, and the Sunday comics all supply material for the entertainment, but the result is a totally individual melange, a creation of the Hines family.

If we look back further, to the beginnings of this Sunday, we can see even more clearly the strategic pathways the three families follow.

The Parker family has breakfast together at nine o'clock every Sunday morning. On this particular Sunday, Father reminds the family that Grandmother Parker is expecting them to visit her after church. Betty, who has spent most of the week studying very hard for her exams at school and has scored the best marks of her academic career, approaches her mother a few minutes later to explain that she was hoping to have some free time today. Mother replies, "Grandmother is expecting all of us." "What about later?" Betty asks. Her mother says, "Well, maybe we can stop off at the park on the way home." She goes to the bedroom to get Father's opinion. He at first says, "No, there won't be time." But when he hears how hard Betty has been applying herself all week, he says, "Okay, we'll try and head back early. Maybe we could even have a picnic if you don't mind packing a lunch." Mother starts getting sandwiches ready. She tells the children to bring a change of clothes along so they won't get their good clothing dirty. "Can we play badminton?" Betty asks. "I don't see why not," Mother says. "As long as I get back in time to meet Charley," Bob adds. "Well then, I think you'd both better help me with the lunch," Mother says.

At Sunday breakfast, Mr. Simpson reminds his family that Grandmother Simpson wants to know if the family is going to visit her today. Betty and Bob complain that they had to give up last Sunday to visit their grandmother and were both looking forward to having this Sunday free from obligation. Mother suggests that she call Granny, and, as a means of softening the blow, promise her a visit from the family sometime the following Sunday. Everyone agrees. "Well, then, what shall we do today?" Father asks. "I'd like to go to the reservoir," Betty says. "And watch the frogs and gold-fish, I suppose?" asks Bob. "Yes, if you must know," Betty replies. "Well, I have a much better idea," says Bob. "Today's the annual kite festival down by the river. There'll be hundreds and hundreds of kites there." "I'll never forget last year's festival," says Father. "Your friend Charley just couldn't get his kite to stay in the air. As hard as he tried, it kept coming down." Betty says, "Well, I don't think it's such a good idea." "Why not?" asks Mother. "Because, I think mine is a better idea," she replies. "Well, dear," Mother says, "I think the reservoir would be fun, but the kite festival only happens once a year, whereas we can go to the reservoir next Sunday." "No, we can't," Betty answers, "because we're going to Granny's." "Well, then the Sunday after next," replies Mother. "All right, if you promise," says Betty. Father and Mother both promise.

Just as Mrs. Hines is about to leave the house to go bird-watching, Mr. Hines comes downstairs and tells her she can't go, that his mother is expecting the family to visit her this afternoon. "Now wait a minute," Mrs. Hines says, "I'm not going to your mother's today." "Neither am I," says Bob. An argument ensues. Bob reminds his father that they were supposed to go to the ball game. Betty announces she is going to the pond with a friend. Mother says to her husband, "I thought you were going to repair the back stairs and then meet a colleague at the office. Father smiles and says, "I forgot. The three of you will have to go by yourselves." This remark prompts Mother to protest loudly. Betty goes downstairs to the basement to look for her nature identification book. She comes across an old trunk, opens it, and finds her mother's collection of old play costumes. She calls to her family and invites them down to the basement where she models an old bustle dress and dances to their applause.

Each family's use of its centering and synchronizing mechanisms in these three early morning sequences reveals its homeostatic ideal and typal core purpose. In the first sequence, Betty's private interests are honored, but have to be processed through the closed-type Parker family's decision-making hierarchy. The family moves along a strategic pathway directly to the target goal of visiting grandmother and only then to the alternative goal of spontaneous play. Obligation and filial loyalty are placed first, ahead of pleasure, which is put on the schedule as a reward for academic achievement. There is little or no parameter testing of the closed system's criterion variables. No one really opposes the visit to Grandmother's or the fact that it is given a higher priority than an afternoon of play.

In the Simpson family, more opposition is allowed as a means of developing a response that is adaptive to the family's recreational needs as well as its obligations to Grandmother. Thus, its response is linked to its open-system core purpose as well as its homeostatic ideal. In deciding to visit Grandmother next week and go to the kite festival today, the family employs a combination of constancy and variety feedback loops to maintain equilibrium. The Simpsons move along their strategic pathway to postpone the family's primary target obligation in favor of a temporally more important alternate goal.

In the Hineses' random system, the imminent target of going to Grandmother's is casually dropped from consideration altogether. Hostility to the visit permeates the atmosphere, although members don't seem overly threatened by opposition. Members' responses illustrate the random system's homeostatic variety ideal and its core purpose of exploration. As it progresses along its perpetually varying strategic pathway, the family substitutes the alternate goal of spontaneous play for the original system target of paying Grandmother a visit. In addition, the alternate goal temporarily supplants the various target pathways projected by each individual family member for the day.

As the Sunday experiences of the three families in the examples suggest, certain strategic preconditions must be met before goals can be successfully attained. The first precondition is that members have an actual systems awareness of the family goal being sought and share the view that it is worth seeking. The second precondition is that members be properly cued by the system on what is expected of them in a particular sequence. In other words, they must understand the system's distance-regulation requirements and accommodate their traffic accordingly. The modulating mechanisms are vital to this process, because it is by their application that the distance regulation of members' traffic is mediated, and the development and implementation of strategic pathways attained.

If a system's application of its modulating mechanisms is disrupted or flawed, unsuccessful sequences frequently develop as a consequence. Unsuccessful sequences accompany the emergence of discrepancies between the official design purposes of the modulating mechanisms and their actual manifestations. These discrepancies nearly always occur simultaneously with problems in communication. The concept of metacommunications, a favorite subject of communication systems analysts, helps to illuminate this process. Metacommunications are communications about communications. They can be overt or covert, verbal or nonverbal, the nonverbal and covert being expressed by gestures, body movements, or other unspoken forms of communication.

A system encounters problems whenever marked differences appear between its overt and covert metacommunications. The most destructive discrepancies occur when the discordant covert metacommunications obstruct the implementation of strategies associated with a family's modulating mechanisms. Successful sequences require that there be no major discrepancy between the model put forth by the modulating mechanism and its actual manifestation.

Covert metacommunicational discrepancies abound in situations in which a direct and overt recognition of phenomenological reality is forbidden. (Here, we are delineating an important interface between the modulating mechanisms of the three access dimensions and the meaning dimension.) If, in the closed-type Parker family, Betty's need for some recreation had gone unrecognized or, if recognized, had been handled in a way inappropriate to the typal style of the family, metacommunicational discrepancies could have been generated and a crisis chain set in motion. Similarly, in the Simpson family, if the irresolution of the sibling conflict had been allowed to continue to a point at which its prolongation would have interfered with members' gaining access to their system goal of spontaneous play, an open-system crisis chain could have been set in motion. Or, if the conflict had been suppressed in a closed system manner foreign to the Simpson family's typal style, metacommunicational discrepancies could have been stimulated, again leading to a crisis chain. In a random family like the Hineses, opposition is often so acceptable that it seems almost to go unrecognized. If members had responded to Bob's holding out in the way that closed- or open-type family members would have the family's random style would have been violated. Similarly, to have adopted a maneuver that would have coerced him, rather than drawing his voluntary participation, might have doomed the Hineses' sequence to an unsuccessful conclusion and sparked a crisis chain of events.

In each of the three Sunday experiences, then, the key ingredient—indeed, the key difference between successful and unsuccessful sequences in general—is the way in which opposition is regulated. To produce a successful sequence, a family system must appropriately recognize its opposition and then handle it in a way consistent with its style either for resolving or dissolving competing interests and goals. When a family fails to do so, its strategic pathways and distance-regulation patterns are found to produce disabling family strategies.

Disabling strategies are institutionalized distance-regulation patterns encompassing many different individual sequences. Although there may be no correspondence between a single unsuccessful sequence and a disabling strategy (or, indeed, between one successful sequence and an enabling strategy), there is usually a great degree of overlap between an unsuccessful sequence and a disabling strategy. The sequential pattern of traffic may be identical or nearly identical to the distance-regulation pattern of a family strategy. This is particularly true of disabling strategies in which family members get "stuck" into reenacting the same basic parts over and over again regardless of context or sequence.

Many descriptions of family process that appear in the literature are descriptions of what we call family strategies. Since virtually all of that literature is concerned with pathologic family behavior, its authors have been identifying disabling family strategies, without designating them as such. In general, disabling strategies can be recognized by the destructive effects they have on the family system. Such effects result from either a poor choice of family targets, a poor implementation of strategic pathways to attain these target goals, or a combination of the two. Lyman Wynne's reporting of *pseudomutuality* (1958), for instance, emphasizes a goals impairment related to intimacy and nurturance in the affect dimension, while R. D. Laing's notes on mystification (1969) stress a goals impairment in the meaning dimension of family process. Gregory Bateson and co-workers' *double-bind* (1956) and Jay Haley's *serial-disqualification* (1959) concepts, in comparison, are concerned primarily with access impairment. Their emphasis is not on meaning targets as much as it is on the transmission of meaning, or what we might call the strategic pathways to meaning and identity.

We believe it imperative that family diagnosticians using these or other approaches recognize that there are different types of families, each with its own core purpose and homeostatic ideal. Before asserting system disablement, diagnosticians should know what type of family they are observing, whether it is functioning in crisis or at rest, and, if in crisis, at what stage of the crisis chain it is experiencing most difficulty. It is also necessary to know whether disablement is occurring in the probable direction of error of the family's type or in the reverse of its type's probable direction of error, that is, in runaway. If such observations are not made, an enabling open or random system strategy may appear disabled to someone oriented exclusively to closed system methods and values; or, similarly, a closed system strategy might appear "sick" to practitioners with dominant open or random type propensities.

The reason for identifying each family's type is perhaps obvious. Those practitioners who, in dealing with families of one type, try to lead or coerce them into accepting goals of another type or who regard the style of interaction of a particular type as bizarre or pathological will generally not meet with great success. If they do succeed, the results are at the expense of those they presumably serve. In our view, then, it is imperative that anyone intervening in a family crisis must take into account and respect the homeostatic ideal and core purpose of the family in difficulty: if a family wants to change its typal design, the therapist should help it develop and implement a new style of interaction; but if the family wants to maintain its type, the therapist must respect such desires.

Thus far the primary focus of our discussion of strategies has been on strategies of maintenance, those strategies in which members attempt to facilitate the family's core purpose and its homeostatic ideals by preserving a style of distance regulation consistent with the family type. Periodically, however, another kind of strategy, in which family members generate stress of some kind to strengthen the bonds between one another, evolves. Fights, blowups, and eruptions are the frequent by-products of such stress strategies. We believe it important for both therapists and researchers to realize that, in most families, stress is a natural occurrence, as natural as maintenance or repair. The presence of stress does not in and of itself suggest disablement. In particular, the open- and random-type families may have a greater tolerance or preference for stress than a closed-type therapist or observer. Stress strategies, like all strategies, are purposive. Not only the stress itself but a natural recovery from stress is generally intended. In order to create either the stress or the recovery from stress, a family may select strategies that correspond to its particular type or strategies that are alien to its core purpose and homeostatic ideal. For instance, a closed system may employ a strategy of periodic eruption as a within-type design and unscheduled chaos as a form of stress which falls outside the boundaries of its core purpose and homeostatic ideal.

Most stress strategies have a limited period of duration. A few, however, develop a momentum so overpowering that they begin to dominate a family's processes. For example, a family system may intentionally generate a specific amount of stress for a specific length of time only to have one of the family subsystems prolong and/or amplify such stress to facilitate its own subsystem ends. This subsequent and unforeseen amplification complicates the original strategy and forestalls the intended recovery, creating a system wide crisis. Recovery must then be accomplished by the system through the development of a repair strategy. All families experience some degree of crisis and disablement in their life-cycle history. When they occur, a family's modulating mechanisms become even more important than they do normally, because these mechanisms bear primary responsibility for observing and solving distance regulation problems. Serious disablement and prolonged crisis often result because the modulating mechanisms have become inoperative. When these mechanisms cease to function, or when they function in a way that amplifies disablement, strategies of repair are not likely to be developed or implemented.

In developing strategies of repair, a family has two basic choices. It can generate repair strategies consistent with its typal design (renovation strategies), or it can adopt strategies associated with other typal designs (change strategies). A family that chooses to implement renovation strategies in response to crisis attempts to maintain its core purpose and homeostatic ideal. It does not basically alter its definition of targets or the strategic pathway it has designed for attaining them. Instead, it attempts to improve its actual operations, to bring them into conformity with system ideals, lest the gap between the real and the ideal grow so wide that it prove the undoing of the system. In strategies of change, however, the family seeks new goals and/or new pathways to targets. Such strategies are based on a homeostatic ideal and core purpose that are different from those which the family has heretofore been attempting to implement. This choice, to adhere to family type or to depart from it, is one of the most difficult for a family to make. Even though the different subsystems of a family share a concern about family disablement and crisis, they may differ on the kinds of repair they think should be made. Members who favor strategies of change can and do compete with members who prefer strategies of renovation. This repair conflict, another form of a basic typal conflict, if left unresolved, may prove as disabling to a system as the original crisis of impairment.

Chapter 11

Individuals in the Family: Four Player Parts

Where is the individual in all of this complicated interaction? What is his role, his function? What part does he play in the family? Throughout the previous chapters, in our treatment of the first four components of our descriptive theory, we have focused on the family as a whole system. In this chapter on the fifth and final component, we shall examine the individual as actor, interactor, and effector in the family system. We shall describe a system of four player parts, which we suggest is a convenient means for describing and analyzing interpersonal processes, especially within families.

The study of family has undergone a substantial development since its inception in the early 1950s, when growing concern with how the "family" affects its offspring began to be expressed. Most personality theories—the dominant one being psychoanalytic theory—have been preoccupied with the individual family member as the focal unit of experience. Focusing on the transactional effects of parent and child (frequently mother and son, or father and daughter) extended the theoretical interest of the personality theories to a two-person field. Later, as a consequence of the applications of small group theory from the social sciences, and of systems theory from the biological and engineering sciences, the family group came to be approached as an interacting system of three players, father, mother, and the "index patient."

Once the unit of focal concern was extended to analyses of three players, some of the field's richest concepts emerged. For example, Nathan Ackerman (1966, p. 80) suggested a three-player model consisting of persecutor, victim, and healer. Many other family therapists have relied on some form of a three-player paradigm in their search for interactional and small group constructs to guide them in their work with family constellations. Yet families can have as many as ten or more members. Does this number require a larger transactional model? If so, would it be functional? Beyond the number three the permutations and combinations of interacting human systems seem to many to be unmanageable—hard to juggle if not impossible to encompass, either conceptually or emotionally. Virginia Satir, one of the most sensitive and skillful of practitioners, suggested to us that she usually cannot deal successfully with more than one person or at best two at a time when working therapeutically in a live family system (private communication, 1971). Thus, up to now the theory of family interactions has been checked by the limits of analytic complexity and therapeutic practicality as functions of human capacity.

Because we are primarily students of family, our interest in the individual is a special one. It is not focused on his internal personality organization, but on his overt behavior, that is, on his actions as a player in the family system. To locate his overt behavior, we must look at his face-to-face exchanges with others. In other words, we must examine the individual's behavior at interface with the behavior of other individuals within the family. In the context of family process, the individual is continually responding to two forces which are often at variance with one another, the forces of inner directedness and outer directedness. The stress generated by this variance is fundamental to the development of both self-consciousness and system-consciousness, the one aspect of development stressing the experience of *self in relation*

to others, and the other the *relation of others to self.* While not denying the existence of individual personality system issues, we seek to
emphasize the individual as an actor in relation to other actors in
the social field, whether such interactions take place at the interfaces of the interpersonal and the personal, the family-unit and
the personal, or the exterior world and the personal subsystems.
Each of these interfaces provides the individual with a psychopolitical arena of judgment, choice, decision, and action.

We use the term "psychopolitics" to denote that thematic
area of family process in which family members try simultaneously
to cope with the institutional requirements of the family's unit and
interpersonal subsystems and the individual's right to be himself.
The term *psychopolitics* itself—*psycho* representing the interior
person and *politics* representing observable family interactions—is
an expression of our concern for connecting analyses of family
system matters with personal system goals and behaviors. In short,
our goal is to identify the ways in which the family affects the
individual, and the individual, the family.

In explicating an individual's psychopolitics, one has to be
aware of the simultaneous presence of three feedback loops at all
the interfaces of the individual system and the larger system. In
addition to the systems-conscious feedback system that we have been
describing in this book, the individual also has a self-conscious feedback system and an unconscious feedback system. Each of these
feedback systems provides the individual with information about
different aspects of his inner states in the course of his interface
interaction with the rest of the family system. Consequently, as an
actor in a social field, the individual may locate his participation at
a level of unconsciousness, self-consciousness, or system-consciousness. His acts, nevertheless, are "social acts." Consequently, the
individual's internal feedback system can affect and even alter
family process, especially in those situations in which the individual's psychopolitical decision is at variance with the system's expectations or demands, including the demands made by his own
system-consciousness. Although the distinction cannot always easily
be made, it is important to identify the internal feedback loop on
which an individual's action or move is primarily based—the unconscious, self-conscious, or system-conscious loop. In calling at-

tention to this multiple-feedback process, we realize that we are further complicating an already complex conceptual field. Unfortunately, such complications must be recognized, for they represent important aspects of all the interactions between individuals and the social systems in which they live.

It is our belief that each individual seeks and negotiates for a place in the family system, in order that his personality may be affirmed by the family in ways that are compatible with his own needs and, optimally, with the goals of the family establishment. With this goal in mind, the individual family member consciously develops personal strategies in response to his family's strategies. These strategies are intended to provide him a place within the family in which he can use the space, time, and energy available to him in order to gain access to the targets of intimacy, nurturance, efficacy, and identity he is seeking. Every individual asks and tries to answer, at least for himself, a battery of fundamental questions about his family. Do I have a place here? What is my place? Is it a good place? Is support given or withheld? What are other members like? What is their style? What is my style? Am I alike or different from the rest of my family? If different, dare I show my difference? What alternatives to my family are there for me? Do I have a place somewhere else? One's answers to these questions are the bases for his psychopolitical maneuvers toward other family members. In effect, each individual must decide whether he wants to live in ways that are approved or disapproved by his family, because every family action triggers an individual reaction, and every individual action triggers a family reaction. The lives and processes of individual and family are inextricably bound. As a result, one can gain no real understanding of an individual action or a strategy unless one can also identify those family actions that have stimulated it and those that have occurred in response.

Family observers frequently make the mistake of thinking that family power or love or ideology can be located in one single person and that this one person can employ it for the benefit or detriment of the others. Such mistaken observations are founded on the premise that a certain member can become dominant over the others. All students of family have witnessed such dominance, but we would assert that its existence is due not only to the strategic moves of the "dominant" party, but also to the strategic moves of the family as a whole, including the moves of the "submissive" parties. Even the pathogenic mother, the focus of so much literature on disturbed families, does not wield her power in a vacuum, but with the compliance of a family system made up of members who allow and may even encourage her to exercise such authority. The reality of such individual-family phenomena suggest two rather basic interface questions. How do individual family members, occupying the same social space, work out in observable interactions their psychopolitics toward each other and toward the family as a whole? From the opposite perspective, how do members' separate individual behaviors and strategies reveal their private psychopolitical views, both of themselves and of the family? Our four-player model delineates a conceptual framework in which these and other interactional questions may be coherently addressed.

We contend that members of a family (indeed, members in any social system) have four basic parts to play: *mover, follower, opposer,* and *bystander.* Our premise is that any social action initiated by one member of a family stimulates a reaction from the other members. The initiator of such an action is the mover of the action. The responders are co-movers. They may exercise one of three logical options: following—agreeing with the action taken by the mover; opposing—challenging the action of the mover; or bystanding—witnessing the mover's action but acknowledging neither agreement nor disagreement with it. Any two or more people meeting for the first time have the same basic options at their disposal in the genesis of roles they evolve in relation to each other. Even when there are only two persons present, there are four parts ready to be played, and if the relationship is to continue, all four parts most certainly will be played. This potential for parts remains the same whether the social system consists of two, three, four, seven, nineteen, or two thousand members.

If there are only four parts to be played, how do we justify the claim that our interactional system of analysis applies to contexts in which there are more than four participants? The answer is that any one part can be played by any number of participating players. Consequently, within a sequence any number of people may be playing the various co-moving parts. For instance, there may be three followers, one opposer, and four bystanders of a mover's move. Is it then possible that we might categorize highly individual members into strategic parts that are too broadly defined? We will not do so if we are careful to differentiate among those playing the same part. For example, if there are three followers, each may emphasize something different from the others. Follower A may say to a mover, "Yes, I am with you, sink or swim, because I love you." Follower B may announce, "Regarding this value I believe the same as you." Follower C may suggest, "Anyone who doesn't restrict my freedom has my support." Thus, they each follow the mover's lead, but within different spheres—A in affect, B in meaning, C in power. Though each plays the same part, we can distinguish them from each other by understanding the direction and destination of their separate following strategies. More precisely, the separate players within each part are differentiated by discovering (1) in what order or sequence they act, (2) in what situations and contexts, (3) with what flexibility, (4) in what combinations, (5) according to which meanings and images, (6) with which particular system strategies (including both enabling and disabling strategies), (7) in which access spheres, and (8) toward what targets. Patterns of sequence develop in every family as individual family members tend to play a part or combination of parts more than others. Sometimes a person is associated with a particular part in all six access and target spheres. More often, however, a person characteristically plays one part in one sphere and a different part in another sphere. For instance, a family may be so organized that mother is a mover in its power sphere, in which she experiences father's opposition, whereas in the meaning sphere Father more often exercises the mover option while Mother stands by and their son plays the follower.

If we envision the spatial organization of the four-player model, the four basic strategic parts encompass all potential moves individuals may make in an interactional system. Together they enable us to perceive, understand, and conceptualize the various patterns of behavior in human systems. Spatially, the mover is often at the center of things. His act of moving defines the space in which an action takes place. The act of following is associated with a validation of the action initiated by the mover. Characteristically, a follower moves in support of the center of action, or else promotes the supportive moves of other members. The opposer either obstructs the action of the mover, or pulls away from it. Persons playing the bystander part tend to place themselves on the periphery of an action field. From that position the bystander has three options: to remain in position as bystander, to move into the action as an opposer or a follower, or to leave the field in order to act as a mover in a new action sequence, to which the other players may or may not respond. As long as the initial action continues and a player maintains his position as a mover, follower, or opposer, he cannot leave the field. Only the bystander can leave the field. The rest of this chapter presents a more detailed analysis of the four player parts and the functions of each role in family interactions.

Mover

The mover is the player who initiates an action, the one who initially seeks to gain access to a target within the affect, power, or meaning dimensions. He establishes the context, thematic and actual, for the others' responses. In order to understand a particular move, an observer needs to identify the strategy the mover employs. He must also consider the strategic options available to the mover at the time he makes his move. Without a wide range of alternatives, movers can get locked into reenacting the same basic strategies again and again. For example, a family that affords its young son little or no attention, except when it perceives him to be "bad," eliminates an entire range of potential mover options. As this example suggests, the power of the mover part is subject to the co-movers' responses. Because of his family's unresponsiveness to his more positive moves, the "bad little boy" has very few resources for securing power and affection except by negatively defined means. In this way, of course, he may accumulate a great deal of power by disrupting family rhythms. He might even destroy family property and physically intimidate some of its members.

Family analysts tend to measure the psychological wealth of a family's social system by evaluating the richness of its thematic content and the complexity of its social strategies. We believe the mover is of primary importance in determining the richness of a family's thematic content, and that the three co-moving parts are crucial in determining the complexity of a system's strategic processes. Thematic richness is dependent upon the breadth and depth of a family's subtargets. Which of these subtargets materialize in family interactions is largely a function of the direction in which a mover proposes to lead. He is, after all, the one who initially defines the destination or target to be sought within any sequence. A system's co-movers influence the significance of the mover's initiating actions for a system, because they determine who will and who will not be allowed to play the prime moving part. In some social and family systems, the most potentially creative members are either denied access to the part or rendered impotent when permitted to play.

In our own clinical experience, for example, the members of one family systematically anticipated and pre-empted the mover inputs of one member as part of a collective scapegoating conspiracy. In another family, the mother's imagistic need to exalt her boy child led her to disregard and treat as irrelevant the initiating efforts of her brighter girl child; indeed, this neglect was supported by other family members to a point at which no one was consciously aware of any duplicity. In a third family, members systematically prohibited their "ugly child's" moves to act as a spokesman for the family to outsiders.

Opposer

Initially, the opposer is a reactor. His movement is made in response to the mover's action. He creates a challenge to the mover by blocking the mover's direction or intended destination. Inherent in the opposer part is the power to redefine the context established by the mover. For instance, a mover may start a sequence, in which he is basically concerned with affect, by putting an arm around another family member, and the co-mover might respond with opposition on the basis of a power or meaning issue. Thus, a move intended to convey the sentiment, "I am very fond of you" can be greeted by the challenge, "Why must you always be so controlling?" Such opposition can be an invitation to other players to

declare themselves on the side of the opposer. In this way an opposer can halt or redirect the action initiated by a mover. Within
the limits of his part, the opposer has a large number of options.
He may be global or specific in his challenges to the mover. He
may redirect and teach, or he may assault and maim. The opposer
may become an ignored dissenter, or he may become a tyrant who
constantly resists change in the status quo by systematically reject-
ing other members' mover initiatives without ever daring to play
the part of mover himself; or he may redirect the family and its
members into more fruitful directions than those suggested by
its movers.

Sometimes, whether he likes it or not, a person may find
himself consistently relegated to the role of opposer. Such a person
is frequently isolated, rejected, and in general made a victim by his
family's strategic processes. Some forms of schizophrenia, dumb-
ness, and radical-political suicide, not to mention timidity, may result from such unfortunate and unimaginative responses to this
part. Ideally, the opposer should have an important function in
any socially creative process. He helps to set limits on the energies
and directions of the mover, thus protecting a system from developing into a potentially tyrannical one by imposing checks and bal-
ances. By criticizing and dissenting, he can enter into a useful dialectic with the mover for the purpose of developing strategies that
are more productive for the family as a whole. Indeed, if such a
dialectic between mover and opposer parts works well, each family's member's right to assert himself as self without fear of re-
crimination and victimization is encouraged. Such a dialectic cannot work well, however, if the person playing the opposer remains
in that position so long that internal psychic and motivational con-
taminants begin to pollute his psychopolitics so much that he is no
longer able to distinguish truly viable reciprocal points of view from
outright obstruction by the mover. In such instances the opposer is
likely to become either oppressor or oppressed, or perhaps both.

Follower

The follower moves to support either the mover or the opposer. He is the prototypic ally and joiner. As long as he remains

in the part of follower, he has no potential for initiating his own movement, though he does have potential for shifting his alliance from mover to opposer. The follower can retain his independence by shifting his allegiance or he can lose virtually all autonomy by fixing his support so irrevocably on either the mover or the opposer that he cannot move in any other direction except as he is directed to do so by the person he follows. Another maneuver the follower has at his disposal is to maintain an allegiance with both mover and opposer simultaneously, either by professing separate allegiance privately to each, or by following mover and opposer for separate reasons: for example, he might support what the mover says while affirming the opposer's dedication to his ideals. Such a strategy can relieve the follower of the dilemma of having to follow one and oppose the other. This concern not to alienate either mover or opposer, if strong enough, can drive the follower into communicational double-speak, into affirming support simultaneously for two or more incompatible positions. Double-speak strategies can be employed by the follower to preserve his control over system affairs in certain important dimensions, especially the affect dimension, because double speaking allows him to remain close to all members, even when they are warring among themselves.

Inherent in the follower part is the capacity to empower others by granting them support. In the strategies of shifting allegiance and dual allegiance, the follower retains some of this capacity in order to enhance and strengthen his own position. When he does make clear allegiances to someone, however, the follower can confirm the other's perceptions of himself, encourage his growth, even beyond the limits that person has previously set for himself, and in large part determine which family members' target destinations will dominate. It is no wonder that followers are actively sought by both mover and opposer. Much of their personal affirmation lies in the hands of followers.

One family system in which such affirmation is highly prized and the appearance of opposers greatly feared is that dominated by processes of "pseudo-mutuality" (Wynne and others, 1958)'. The fear of opposers within such a system is so great that members would rather follow with little or no energy than announce their true interests and risk opposition. Unfortunately, such a system offers its members very little true affirmation. Jay Haley (1959) has observed that families which produce schizophrenic offspring experience a pattern of communication dominated by disqualification. Such families manifest an incapacity to maintain stable coalitions. In their interactions, each member disqualifies the other person for his point of view, even when a particular point is raised in support of the other's position. Players are even willing to disqualify their own previous statements in order to avoid alliance with another member. In such families, no one is allowed to play a consistent follower role. As soon as he tries, he is disqualified. As Haley has conceived it, disqualification is largely a feature of verbal communication. What is important for us is that he has described an unalterable pattern in which families fail to stabilize the follower part, and as a result, are unable to resolve frequent mover-opposer conflicts.

We believe that a system in which the mover and opposer parts do not in principle have access to a follower's support will soon be in difficulty. In one of our research families the father was invariably an ally of the mother, even when she was oppressive and brutalizing to their son. Their inflexible interactional pattern prohibited the child from ever turning to his father for support when he was being tyrannized. Meanwhile his mother was never held accountable for her behavior. Such a pattern often continues because the follower fears either that an opposer will gain an upper hand or that a mover will turn his anger on the follower for not following appropriately. Sometimes, there is an additional fear of shattering a tacit social contract between mover and follower. In most instances, such contracts start to generate truly malevolent effects only when a third party gets caught up in their process. In at least four of the more disabled families studied in our research, a tacit contract existed between husband and wife in which faithful following by the husband was based on a decision to protect the emotional fragility of his wife, a situation much like that described by Theodore Lidz and his colleagues (1957) in their work on "marital skew." The eventual disability occurring as a result in some of the children of these couples did not evolve out of evil intentions but rather out of a pattern of following that had become rigidly established because of an overriding concern for the health of the parental mate.

Bystander

The person acting as bystander in a sequence stays out of the direct action. He makes no alliances with either the mover, the opposer, or the follower, at least no alliances as pertaining to their three way interaction. (He can and often does, however, make private, bilateral alliances to maintain the security of his bystanding position.) From his vantage point outside an interaction, the bystander watches. This is his primary action—to be a witness to family events, initially keeping what he thinks about them to himself. The bystander's witnessing is itself a force exerted on and felt by the more active participants of an interaction. If a member of their family is watching but not saying anything, the interacting players can begin to feel uneasy because they do not know the bystander's psychopolitics. To overcome such uneasiness, the mover, follower, and opposer may each confront the bystander to force him to divulge what he thinks. They may try to recruit him to be their follower, especially if they feel he privately shares their perceptions: or they may try to block the bystander out if they feel his private views are in opposition to their own. The person playing the bystander part will sidestep all such attempts and continue to keep his psychopolitical views private as long as he desires to stay in the neutral bystander position, watching yet standing apart from family interactions. By preserving his neutrality, the person acting as bystander keeps his options open, often until he can make up his mind what to do. In standing apart, at least temporarily, he gains more options than persons selecting the other three parts. In addition to being able to move into an interaction as a follower or opposer, he can exercise three options not available to persons playing the other three parts.

First, he can leave the field—turn his back on family members' interactions—and enter into some other activity as a mover initiating an action in another social field. Upon leaving, he becomes an absent bystander. That is, he physically leaves, but an afterimage of his watching remains behind. The mover, follower, and opposer may be left uneasy, wondering what the now absent bystander thought about their actions, or they may feel free to continue as they were without any physical witness to bother them. In general, the bystander can comfort those he watches by helping them feel they are known and valued, or he can oppress them with the knowledge that they are known and not valued. When the person playing the bystander part leaves a social field, the other participants may feel betrayed; or they may feel liberated from an obligation to act within the confines of a morality based on a foundation of certain recognized family or subsystem credos and rules as represented by the person playing the bystander part. Children of all ages are familiar with the experience of doing something their family defines as illicit and having a parent drop in and watch them. An incredible amount of tension can be felt despite the fact that child and parent don't directly seem to interact. Much of that tension can be relieved by the parent's departure.

The second option open to the bystander is to remain where he is, continuing to witness the interaction of the others. He can remain silent, he can articulate his views to participants in private, or he can express his perceptions in public in such a way that he moves neither closer to any of the participants nor farther away from them. How can he do this? Does not his mere articulation, whether in public or in private, conclude his bystander part and pull him into the interaction as an opposer or follower? Not necessarily. Probably all of us have encountered at some time a person who announces his response, usually a following response, to separate warring individuals in private, but then asks them to understand that he cannot say the same thing in public, either because of love for or dependence on the other person or faction. The individual who adopts such a dual role of private follower and public bystander may have a variety of motives or intentions. He may want to accrue political gain for himself with each of the participants, or he may sincerely want to help resolve the conflict, but sense that his public entrance will only exacerbate it. Whatever his motives, such a bystander seeks to preserve his freedom to stand apart.

The case of a bystander's public articulation can be even

more complex. Let us suppose a mover pulls a chair out from underneath someone about to sit down. An opposer might attack him saying, "That wasn't a very funny thing to do." The mover might defend his action by stating, "It was a funny thing to do." "Very funny," the follower might pipe in. When pressed for his opinion, the bystander might say, "Man certainly has an extraordinary sense of humor." This response may throw everyone off balance since it does not express a clear position on the question, though the mover and follower may soon assert the bystander agrees with them because of his reference to a "sense of humor." The opposer in such a situation may also feel he has a follower, interpreting the bystander's comment as an ironic remark. Under such circumstances the debate could go on with each person remaining within the limits of his part, for the bystander has exercised a sophisticated spatial strategy of entering the field momentarily as a mover in order to preserve his option to retreat subsequently to his position as a neutral apart from the conflict. The situation is not exactly the same as before, however, for, in assuming the cloak of mover temporarily, the bystander has modified the thematic context by introducing the idea of mankind's sense of humor.

The person who articulates his bystanding position in this way runs some risk. In announcing a position, he can relinquish some of the mystique and power potential of his silence. In order to minimize such loss of power, the bystander may either develop a particular style of articulation or articulate the thematic context in such a way that he continues to maintain his neutrality toward the participants and their action, a principle seemingly understood by a number of family therapists. An onlooker's silence and a therapist's "hmmmmm" are both examples of neutral articulation. The field consequences of such steadfast strategies, whether articulated or not, are generally to diffuse the conflict by complicating the participants' projections of the bystander's position. A second effect may be to empower the collective by suggesting that its members can resolve their differences without the intervention of "outsiders" such as the bystander. This is an effect particularly sought after by family therapists who are in the process of terminating treatment. A third effect may be to empower either the mover or opposer alone by reaffirming the existing power balance, an effect often achieved by neutral, uninvolved bystanding.

A third option available to the bystander is an actual shift from the periphery closer to the action. His purpose may be and often is to mediate the conflict among the participants, or it may be to preserve and even increase his power to affect the action by standing apart. For example, if in response to the conflict about whether pulling out chairs from underneath people was funny or stupid the bystander had said, "No, you are all wrong. It is a dangerous thing to do. You can really hurt somebody so don't ever do it again, even if it does look funny," he would have been exercising this third option to move in closer to the action. The bystander who moves in does not have a foolproof strategy, however. Even more than the bystander who articulates a position but remains on the periphery, the bystander who moves directly into the action runs a risk of being drawn into a conflict and of having to relinquish the bystander position for that of a follower or opposer. Though a particular family member may lose much of his individual power in such an interaction, the system as a whole need not be adversely affected. In fact, some family systems in effect hold up the ideal of there being no personified bystanders at all, only equal participants. For others, enmeshing the bystander may be an ideal way of breaking down the disabling but fixed pattern of a nonparticipating member.

Not all persons playing the bystander part do so voluntarily. Some are condemned to watch and witness because they are forbidden to enter family interactions in any other capacity. Such individual family members are relegated to the bystander role, perhaps partly because they themselves prefer the role but also partly by the ways in which individual traffic is regulated in their families. They are given no encouragement, training, or confidence for playing the other three interactional parts. As a result, they repeatedly find themselves in positions that are at best marginal to the social fields defined by other family members. Like individuals relegated to the social intraspace of the family, members who are confined to a marginal bystander part may experience intense isolation. They may not be free either on a personal or interpersonal subsystem level to exercise the options inherent in the bystander part. System regulations may demand that a reluctant bystander be rendered isolated and impotent whatever he tries to do—leave, stay, or move closer to the actions of other family members. The terrible dilemma facing such a condemned bystander is that he may see everything that happens in the family, but have no one with whom he can communicate his observations.

Though one or more family members may actually play the bystander part in an interactional sequence, all family members continuously participate in bystander activity. In watching, listening, and being conscious of themselves and others, they exercise a bystanding capacity to perceive what is going on in and around them. Thus, even though members act in a sequence as movers, opposers, or followers, they carry out a bystander function as well. This secondary function deserves special attention because it can affect the interactions in a social field without anyone in the field actually playing a visible bystander part. As a result, in observing interactional sequences one ought to distinguish between those operations growing out of an individual's normal bystanding capacity regardless of role and those deriving from his playing of the bystander part.

Anyone playing the bystander part has the threefold task of representing four major aspects of a family's meaning dimension, sensitizing system members' attention (that is, their bystanding capacity) to those aspects, and thereby initiating participating members' assessment of their own behavior. The four sets of meanings are (1) images of the outside or exterior culture, (2) the family's corporate image, (3) images of the interpersonal subsystem, and (4) members' individual image hierarchies.

A bystander may represent all four sets of meanings, or he may select one or more aspects. In his first function of representing images from the exterior culture, the bystander presents what he thinks the world has to communicate to his family about a particular issue. The family or corporate bystander represents and conveys images and meanings which members have generated about themselves as a unit. Included in such representations are the meanings of the world as they are accepted by the family unit. The interpersonal bystander represents and conveys meanings and images gathered from the world and the family that are practical and useful for members' unique relationships with one another within the family. The personal bystander represents and communicates those images that are privately useful and meaningful to each person alone. As an internalized function, it constitutes the bystander's or the receiver's felt relationship between his inner realities and his external ordering of things. A person playing the personal bystander part expresses his private images and meanings to others in the interactional system—others who may or may not share these images.

The following example may help to illustrate the way in which bystanders represent these four areas. Let us suppose that in a family of four a decision has been made, despite some emotional sacrifice by members, to move to another city several hundred miles away so that Father can accept a high salaried job with the federal government. Several months after the move, the son, daughter and mother watch silently as father comes home late every night, very upset over his conflicts with his departmental superior. The other three listen as he complains about his boss, about how unreasonable he is, about his lack of concern for those impoverished citizens his department is supposed to be serving, and about how unpleasant the whole job has become because Father feels compelled to stand up to this man, to confront him and tell him when he is wrong. Night after night he informs the family of his experience on the job. His children and his wife respond with glances of caring and an odd question here and there, but basically sit silent. Finally, after months of unhappiness at work and uneasiness about what his family is thinking at home, Father asks his wife and children if they think he is right to stay on at his job and fight a dissenting battle on behalf of the poor. Very quickly, the son and daughter get into a conflict:

> *Son:* I think you should stay but stop dissenting so much. Play ball with your boss a little and he'll play ball with you.
> *Daughter:* I think you should hold to your guns and be honest, even if you get fired.

Son: If you get fired now, you'll never move higher. You'll never get into a position of influence where you can really do something worthwhile.

Daughter: It's more important to be honest than to have influence.

Son: Don't be ridiculous. If you want to accomplish things you have to swallow your pride and say yes a few times.

Daughter: That may be how the world runs, but this family happens to believe the world is wrong. Influence without integrity is not worth having.

Mother: Aren't you both forgetting something? If you think of our lives in this house, I think you'll both realize that integrity and influence go hand in hand. You can't have one without the other. We fail every time we aren't honest with each other about our feelings and beliefs. We only have influence with each other when we are honest with each other.

Daughter: Mother's right. She's absolutely right.

Son: Yeah, I guess so, but it's not how the world goes. The world is different from our family.

In the succeeding months Father stays on at his still unpleasant job, trying unsuccessfully to move his superiors. He comes home disgruntled night after night as the other three members watch him: his son continues to represent images of influence in the world, his daughter continues to represent the family or corporate image that integrity is more valuable than influence, his wife represents the interpersonal meaning that influence and integrity are inseparable, and each, of course, represents his own personal meanings as they are selected and incorporated from the above sets of images.

In addition to representing meanings and images, the bystander has the second and equally important function of generating and awakening in family participants a consciousness of the thematic concerns inherent in their interaction. Often he prompts this awareness by his very silence, other times by a gesture, and still other times by a word of explication. What another might go about doing mindlessly on his own, he has to think about with another person present and watching him act. If the first function of a bystander is to represent meanings and images in a social action field, the second or consciousness-stimulation function is a call to participants to reexamine the meanings they feel guide and justify their actions.

The third, or judgmental, function of the bystander is in essence a call to action. It goes beyond the arousal of awareness to ask the participants whether their actions are morally justifiable. Members may feel the impact of such questioning even if a bystander is silent, as long as he is alert and observant. In certain circumstances, however, the person playing the bystander part is enjoined to action in executing this bystander function. He must decide whether to continue in the safe option of not having to act or whether to give up his security and take a more active position within the action, so that he either opposes, follows, or initiates a new move. When a situation is disabling or unjust, the bystander's major dilemma is whether to act or not to act. Both are definitive actions and as such are subject to misjudgment. In the first instance of misjudgment, the bystander moves in when he should have stayed out. In the second, and, in our experience, more frequent type of misjudgment, the bystander stays out when he should have moved in. The onlookers who watch a violent crime take place, the prototypic bureaucrat who allows regulations to crush the hopes and lives of the people he is meant to serve, and the sibling who watches his brother or sister driven to distraction by his parents all choose to stay out when they might move in to alter the course of events.

The bystander's response can be crucial to the workings of any family system, whether it be closed, open, or random. By staying out and not intervening in families where the mover and follower have turned the opposer into a ritualized victim, the bystanding member may gain his own freedom and avoid being victimized, but he may virtually insure that the opposer never escapes victimization. By staying out, the person playing the bystander part allows the system to continue acting out unchecked a strategy destructive to one member by maintaining a morality which is not subject to challenge from within or scrutiny from without. An example from one of our research families illustrates such a pattern. While his grandfather, grandmother, mother, and aunt were engaged in conversation, Jason, a three-year-old boy, was attracted to a cigarette burning in a brightly colored ashtray set on the dining room table around which the four adults were seated. Though the adults plainly deciphered Jason's intent to handle the cigarette, they continued their conversation, and allowed him to approach the ashtray. No one moved or warned the young boy until after the inevitable happened, and he burned several fingers on the cigarette. Scooping up the crying child in his pain and hurt pride, they sent him away from the table without sympathy, and with no other ceremony than some derisive remarks about his chronic capacity for getting himself into trouble.

It is, of course, very easy for detached researchers to condemn bystanders who fail to move in to try to save or protect other members of their family from victimization. For a bystander to involve himself, however, can actually be quite risky. In many families the field of interaction may be so fraught with danger, either because of its vacuity, tyranny, or runaway chaos, that an onlooker with any perspective knows that to enter may result in certain engulfment without offering much potential either for the good of the participants or for personal escape. Bystanders in such highly disabled families often exercise their opinion to leave the action field whenever possible as a means of self-preservation.

Staying out when he should move in is not the only error the bystander can make. He may also move in, but in such a way that he renders a disservice to both the participants and himself. For example, in another of our research families the mother as bystander intervened in this destructive way. Fearful that her son might not "make it" in the world in the most effective way, she assumed the role of bystander at the edge of the family's space, where she fused her own personal images of the world with the experience actually available out there for her son. She consistently transmitted a distorted map of the exterior culture to her son, confusing him about the rules and relationships actually available to him at school, temple, and playground. As a result, he failed to find ways to deal with these institutions and with the people within them successfully. Moreover, most of his perceptions of his actual experiences in the world were confused. Significant in the development of this family's bystander actions was the role played by the father, a capable man who functioned with facility in the world of business and community affairs and who possessed a far less anxious and distorted view of the world than his wife. In order to reconcile his view of the world with the family's perimeter politics, he had to shut off his own bystanding capacities. In the family's player system, he was systematically forbidden to oppose his wife's attempts to interpret and manipulate matters for their son.

It is not always easy to perceive clearly when a person is playing the part of a true bystander or that of a pseudo-bystander. A *pseudo-bystander* is a co-mover who retreats to the periphery of the family space and overtly removes himself from the field of action. By taking this peripheral position, the co-mover appears to take on the role of bystander, detached from the action, when, in reality, he may be an opposer or follower employing a strategy of playing an active co-moving part from the edge of the field, half in and half out of the action. Thus, in the preceding example, the father who supported his wife's control of their son but seldom overtly revealed his support, was in fact a marginal follower. Similarly, an angry or rebellious son who rejects his family's meanings, but who spends most of his time on the edge of the family space, may represent marginal opposing rather than a neutral witnessing of ongoing interactions.

By introducing a neutral point of view, an important family meaning, or an image of the exterior culture, bystanders can help to ease and even to resolve polarized conflicts within their families. They can also enrich their family's life by introducing new meanings that add to the reservoir of aesthetic, intellectual, and cultural resources available to the family. Nevertheless, many families fail to train members to play the bystander part effectively. In families that all but eliminate the player's option to play the part of bystander, conflicts tend to become more polarized and members generally fail to resolve them satisfactorily. Also, if bystanding actions are ill-developed, critical consequences may develop. Each type of error—failure to act or misguided intervention—can contribute toward the ritualized sacrifice of a key family member and the unfortunate complicity of all other members.

Outside of the family, societies provide numerous opportunities for bystanders to help govern the internal affairs of a community. Priests, judges, historians, writers, and artists have all played this important part. In the past fifty years or so, members of the upper middle class have turned to another official bystander, the therapist, who, as a paid outsider and initially nonaligned neutral, helps embody the bystander part for individuals.

Though we are concerned primarily with the bystander part played by family members in this book much of our discussion about the operations and strategies of the part applies directly to the work of family therapists, who characteristically feel a need to stand back from the families they deal with in order to see clearly how they function as a system before attempting any therapeutic intervention. One key prerequisite governing any intervention the therapist eventually takes is that he be perceived as a neutral by all family members, that is, that he not be aligned with any person or group of persons within the family, but rather that he work to effect good for the entire family.

Ideally, one of the primary tasks of therapy ought to be the building or rebuilding of effective bystanding in systems where successful embodiments of both the part and function have broken down. What often happens, however, is that therapists make the same two kinds of errors as family members in the role of bystander: moving in when they should stay out and staying out when they should enter into an interaction.

Ideal Co-Mover

The ideal co-mover is not a fifth part. There are only four parts to be played, and none of them, in conception, is either ideal or nonideal. Rather, they are parts which may be played for good or ill. Opposing, following, and bystanding are the co-mover's range of options. Which option or options must he take to become an ideal co-mover? He may take any or all. He may even on occasion introduce a new move of his own, thus abandoning the co-mover part to become at least a temporary mover himself. This is not to suggest that a co-mover's options are either unfettered or simple. If he is to act as follower, he must decide whom or what he is to follow—the mover, the family system in which he and the mover are members, himself, or some third party. He must ask himself the same questions if he chooses opposing or bystanding options. However, regardless of the option or combination of options he chooses to take, the key question any co-mover must ask is, "What do I want to be the result of my co-moving response?"

The ideal co-mover will follow the mover when it is best for himself, the mover, the family, and other parties for him to follow. He will oppose when it is best for himself, the mover, the family, and other third parties for him to oppose. He will bystand when it is best for himself, the mover, the family, and other third parties for him to bystand. He will also initiate new moves when that is best for all concerned. Obviously, there are many times when the needs of the mover, the family, the self, and other parties are not compatible—when to serve one is unavoidably to disserve one or more of the others. When a co-mover chooses an option that benefits one of the participants—say, either the mover or himself—but in so doing harms one of the other participants—say, the family unit or a third party—he is, however pure his motivations, engaged in a strategic psycho- and sociopolitical move which is at least in part a disabling strategic move. Needless to say, there are many times when the "right" choice is a very difficult choice for the co-mover to make. The family whose members are free to perceive, choose, and execute "right" choices, choices which benefit all parties, including the family as a whole, is a very fortunate family indeed.

Manifest Mover

None of the four parts described in this chapter is by definition or function more powerful than the others in determining the direction and destination of family traffic. Depending on the players, the context, and the sequence of interaction, any of the four parts may be dominant in a strategic sequence. We probably all know of families in which certain key persons seem to bear responsibility and power for family interactions in such a way that they determine the kinds of decisions their families make, even decisions which seem to have been made collectively. By the end of a sequence or series of sequences, such a person in effect emerges as a family's *manifest mover*, its chief decision-maker and primary traffic regulator, at least for the sequence or series of sequences.

The manifest mover is not a fifth part; there are only four parts to be played. Designation of the manifest mover is determined by the way in which those four parts are played by family members. In many social systems, some members either wait to declare themselves until the person they have come to recognize most often as the manifest mover declares himself, or they willingly reverse their declaration of part, if need be, in order to bring themselves into conformity with his announced position. Prior to his declaration, the manifest mover may, as an individual strategy, play one or another of the four parts in order to gather all the data he feels he needs to make a proper decision. Eventually, however, he must make his move and declare himself, usually at some critical or well-timed point in a sequence. For such an individual manifest mover strategy to become a system strategy, the other players must either be dumb, play dumb, be in complete agreement, or lack the power and energy to oppose the acknowledged manifest mover.

Manifest moving strategies need not be "manipulative," at least not in the derogatory sense of that word. Some people dominate any social field they share with others. Their place and the aura of energy that surrounds it may be recognized as different somehow. Such charismatic individuals present problems for others in a social field. It may be comforting to follow such a person, but discouraging and inhibiting, too, for the charismatic manifest mover—even if he has the best of motives and intentions—runs the risk of becoming a tyrant who squashes others' freedom by permitting them no other option but to follow. Not all manifest movers are of a charismatic type. They may be covert as well as overt. Family systems in which the manifest mover openly declares himself are quite different from those in which the manifest mover's declarations remain obscure if not invisible to outside observation. The following dialogue helps to illustrate the way in which a manifest mover in the second type of system operates.

> *Father:* I think we should go to the theatre.
> *Son:* There's a good movie at the Majestic.
> *Father:* I say we go to the theatre.
> *Son:* I'd rather go to the movies.
> *Father:* What do you say, Mother?

> *Mother:* Either one is fine with me. We don't have to
> drive as far to see the film, but the theatre attracts a better class
> of people. You boys decide.
> *Father:* Well, I still think the theatre.
> *Son:* Yeah, I guess you're right. A movie just doesn't offer
> as much as a play.

The astute observer, by measuring and locating the direction of
system energy flow, recognizes that Mother is the manifest mover
in this scene. The key phrase, of course, is "better class of people."
Though this consideration is ostensibly granted the same weight as
that of "convenience" by Mother, the expression "better class of
people" causes her son to reverse his opposition and become a
follower of his father. Mother, while overtly stating, "You boys
decide," actually becomes the manifest mover and brings about a
system decision in line wth her own private beliefs. The reason she
is able to do so is because her family supports her beliefs, thus
allowing her manifest moving to remain subtle and largely covert.
As this sequence suggests, the manifest mover, whether overt or
covert, may never have to play the mover part within any particular sequence. Yet he is the player who ultimately functions as
the prime regulator of a system's access and target dimensions.

The Individual in Family Process

Our four-player model is an extremely simple one. To the
extent that it does indeed delineate the possible "moves" which
players can make in a social field, it constitutes a "working theory"
of social interaction in that it is based on actual transactional
events rather than on theories which are many levels of abstraction
or inference removed from observable reality. In addition to being
a system of analysis for understanding interpersonal behavior, our
four-player model may also serve as a basis for a social or field
view of personality theory. If it were to be employed for this purpose, however, it would be necessary first to explore both theoretically and empirically the interactions of the three individual system
levels of consciousness which we mentioned at the start of this
chapter—the unconscious, the self-conscious, and the system-con-

scious levels of experience—toward the end of predicting the effects
of these interactions on social and personality systems. In this discussion our purpose is to use the four-player model as a basis for
focusing on the individual in family process, so that we may consider individual acts systemically with special emphasis on their
importance as distance-regulation phenomena. In attempting this,
we ignore the "black box" of the unconscious, the central nervous
system, and other unseeable psychic considerations and concentrate
instead on that region of personal-interpersonal interface, at which
the individual functions in accord with his system-consciousness
level of experience.

In Chapter Two we stated that our conceptualizations of
abstract family process and concrete family strategies both begin
with the "act." This chapter makes clear that we think of the
individual not as an independent entity, but rather as a being
intimately interdependent with his environment and with other
individuals with whom he relates in a systemic manner. Concur-
rently, we think of the act in family process as a complex behavioral
event, within which the individual is "an active agent with degrees
of freedom, selectivity, or innovation mediating between external
influences and overt behavior" (Buckley, 1967, p. 95). Note
that, although we started this chapter considering the individual
and his acts, we placed him immediately into a social field in which
he plays a combination of four player parts in his transactions with
others, with objects, and with events.

Every individual act in a family or other social system is a
move to regulate distance and as such is goal directed. Generally,
the mover identifies the goal or target of an action while all players
together determine the means of gaining access to a target by the
moves they make in a sequence. This includes the bystander who
throughout permits the actions of the other players to take place
without his direct participation. Through both action and inaction,
the bystander serves as a check on the system's homeostatic and
substantive distance-regulation operations. The bystander function
is the ultimate carrier of error information into the interactional
field on the basis of which players regulate distances, making adjustments in their associations and dissociations as they regulate the
direction and extent of their traffic. Since all players carry the

bystander capacity within them and may take up the bystander part at any time, we identify the bystander *function*, rather than the *player* or *part*, as the carrier of error information.

As we noted in the preceding discussion a manifest mover can emerge from any of the player parts to affect the interaction in such a way as to determine the final outcome of a sequence. As a regulator of distance in the interactional field, the manifest mover often remains a silent and invisible force, whose work is executed by the composite interaction of all four player parts in conformity with a family's core purpose and homeostatic ideal. In a very real sense, *a system's typal design usually emerges as its manifest mover.* When a family's purposes and ideals are under stress, however, and either error information has been inaccurately received or distance regulation corrections have been improperly executed, both the manifest mover and the typal design are likely to be represented by individuals closely identified with one or more of the player parts. For example, an opposer may halt a system's desertion of its ideals and help return it to conformity with its typal design.

In Chapter Ten we showed how a family's typal design functions as a distance-regulation comparator and opposition regulator, telling members what distance regulations to follow on an act-to-act basis in interactional sequences. In the language of cybernetics, the comparator transmits an error signal which actuates the system's output effector, producing a response to some original stimulus. *In the framework of our general distance-regulation theory, the four-player interactional model is the family's output effector.* Each time an individual member acts, whether in accord with or in opposition to the demands of the family system comparator, he bases his move on the signals of one or more of his systems-conscious, self-conscious, or unconscious internal feedback loops—usually on all three, with one exerting a dominant influence on the behavioral act. Once committed, the individual's act becomes part of the family environment, where it provides a new input stimulus for all players in the field. Thus, feedback processes occur at various levels of experience for all players in the course of each act in an interactional sequence.

One of the more remarkable aspects of family process is the tendency of each individual to play particular parts in the same or similar interactional contexts. An individual's stereotypic player moves are derived from two major sources: (1) his personal preferences as influenced by his internal feedback system's signaling of private needs and impulses; (2) his family experience from which he learns what parts he is allowed or required to play in the family system. Much of the drama of family life can be traced to the strains resulting from the interplay of these simultaneous quests for autonomy and compliance.

Chapter 12

─────────────────────────────

Individuals in the Family: Strategic Player Interactions

In this chapter, we take a look at how our interactional player model operates in four different sets of family sequences. The first of these represents a successful sequence, the second an unsuccessful sequence; the third set of sequences is symptomatic of a cumulatively disabling strategy in which the bystander is rendered ineffective; the fourth set of sequences is symptomatic of a disabling strategy in which the bystander is systematically disqualified.

A half hour or so after dinner, members of the Howland family gravitate toward the living room. Each is occupied with his or her own activity, be it reading, knitting, playing solitaire, or watching television. Deborah Howland tosses down her cards and says, "God, I'm bored. Let's play some charades." *She is the mover. She initiates the action by starting the sequence. She also establishes the field and identifies the goal.* Mother and Father immediately respond. Mother replies, "Oh, that's a good idea!" Father gets up from his chair and says, "I'll get pencil and pad." *The parents' moves are the moves of followers. Their relationship to the action is that they support and continue it.* Fourteen-year-old Peter Howland says, "I hate charades. I'd rather watch TV." *He is the opposer. He refuses to support or continue the action.* Eight-year-old Charlie remarks, "That's not true. You're just jealous cause Deborah suggested it." *He is a bystander-opposer. He refuses to continue his brother's action, except from a position of interpretation typical of the bystander part.* Grandfather Howland peeks over his newspaper at this interaction and chuckles to himself. *He is the bystander. He stays out of the action, but remains in the field, observing what takes place.* Seeing Grandfather smile, Deborah says, "Okay . . . I mean Charles is right, Peter, but if that's the way you want it, feel free to watch TV." *Here she is the follower to the opposer. She supports her brother's right not to continue the action.* Also seeing Grandfather chuckle, Peter has a change of heart. "Oh hell," he says, "I'll play charades, too." *Peter here becomes a follower, a supporter of the action, freeing the family to start its game.*

In the foregoing everyday sort of occurrence, the cues are far from conclusive, but the scene does seem to feature members of an open-type family gaining access to the affect target of collective play. But for the "move" of Grandfather Howland, however, the family might have experienced an impasse or at least a delay in reaching its target. Within the context depicted, it seems reasonable to identify Grandfather's chuckle as the act of a manifest mover, transmitted through the bystander part to influence members in the direction prescribed by the family's open-type homeostatic ideal and core purpose. We are, of course, surmising that his chuckle is a powerful reminder, interpretable by the others, of this open type family's affect and power ideals. The concluding moves by Deborah and Peter seem to be consciously designed as expressions of these very ideals. Their systems-conscious feedback processing and psycho-political judgments appear quite visible, while their self-conscious feedback processes are nearly accessible. What the sequence primarily and directly shows, however, is that the four-player interaction functions as the Howland system's output effector in determining the outcome of a family interaction.

Having observed and analyzed a sequence in which the family effector function is successfully employed, let us now examine another after-dinner sequence in which the Howland's interactional system generates an unsuccessful sequence:

Mrs. Howland unwraps some picture frames she has purchased earlier in the day. She seems anxious and unsure of herself. *Mother makes a tentative power move.* She shows them to Mr. Howland who instantly expresses his distaste for them. "I wish you had consulted the rest of us," he says. "I wanted modern frames for those paintings." *Father moves as an opposer to the action.* Peter says, "It's all a waste of money. I don't even like the pictures." *He, too, is an opposer to Mother's action, but his perspective is different from that of his father.* Angrily, Mother turns on Peter. "Well, Peter you have no taste." *Mother and son start to get locked into a series of opposer-opposer moves as each follows an initial move and opposes the other's opposition.* "You have no right to talk about taste, does she, Dad?" Father doesn't answer. *He moves to the bystander position at the edge of the action.* "Listen, Buster, if it were up to you, we'd never spend any money fixing up the house. Everything would go to you and your damned camping equipment, which somehow you never manage to use more than once before it goes to rust in the back of the garage." *Mother puts Peter down, opposing his autonomy, just as earlier Father has put down her tentative move of autonomy.*

Deborah enters the room and says, "Hold on, hold on, you're both getting carried away. Can't we talk about this thing calmly?" "Not when she's accusing me of things I don't do," says Peter. "I'm sorry, I can't be calm about him telling me how to fix up *my* house," Mother retorts. "Look, you're both right," Deborah says, "but you're also both wrong." Neither Mother nor Peter is willing to admit to being wrong, however, and the argument escalates, forcing Deborah to leave the room shouting, "Go ahead. Argue 'til doomsday. I don't care." *Deborah's attempt to be an active bystander who is simultaneously a follower and an opposer to both her mother and brother fails.* As she passes her father on the way out of the room she taunts, "Why don't you try to do something? You're the one who started everything." *Though retreating, she remains an active bystander, suggesting a new move for her father.* The squabble between mother and son continues to escalate, and Father turns on the television set, remaining a silent witness to the interaction. *Though he is perhaps in the best position of all Howland family members to effect an intervention, Father winds up playing an ineffectual, passive bystander part, his silence in part continuing to express his opposition to Mrs. Howland on the issue of the picture frames.*

Autonomy is the power dimension theme in this family sequence. Significantly, none of the players in this sequence, with the possible exception of Mr. Howland, experiences an increase in personal freedom. Mrs. Howland's initial power move is never affirmed, nor is her anxiety about it relieved. Peter's right to challenge his mother is seriously impinged, and his right to buy his own goods threatened. Deborah's loss in the power sphere occurs as a consequence of their struggle, but this decline is more a failure to establish herself as an effective bystander and manifest mover than it is a decrease in her own individual autonomy. Mr. Howland may conceivably experience a small psychopolitical gain in that the others' losses may enhance his own sense of autonomy and protect it from encroachment by wife and perhaps even by son. As a family system member, however, he fails to help move the family toward an effective resolution of its conflict. In this respect, he is even more ineffective than his daughter, who at least manages to leave the unpleasant social field. The end result is that the interaction among the various parts played by family members creates a conflict-ridden feedback loop which obstructs their access to the autonomy goal of the power dimension.

Of all the component parts in our theory of family process, the four-player model brings us closest to the actual transactional events involved in family strategies. However it does not reveal the psychopolitics prevailing in a given interaction of family members. If applied to the interactional moves of a single brief sequence, our four player model can illuminate how family members play their parts but it cannot tell us why they play them as they do, including why they choose some moves rather than others. In the following example, we apply the four-player model to a broader family context, that is both current and historical, in order first to reflect the quality and complexity of psychopolitical moves adopted by many families, and second to show how past and present can be seen to merge whenever interactional moves rigidify or become stereotypic.

Although the four-player model is a valuable tool for describing and analyzing single family interactions, when it is applied to a large number of sequences in an historical context, it can also serve as an important clue to members' individual psychopolitics toward the family. When such psychopolitical information is obtained, either through interview or long and extensive observation, and the four-player model applied to that information, the family analyst has at his disposal what we feel is the best conceptual tool presently available for understanding the interpersonal dynamics of family process.

The Yost family (Eli and Elaine, each about seventy, their son Richard and his wife, Joan, both in their middle thirties, and Paul, twenty-eight years old) specifically undertook family analysis so that the positive emotions members held for one another could be expressed more freely and openly. All the Yosts shared a tremendous investment in creating such changes, even Mr. Yost, a man of renown in the larger community, who was recognized by all family members including himself as the chief roadblock to a more open, free-flowing affect style. Ironically, the Yosts had been able to effect a successful open-type style for regulating access to targets within the power and meaning spheres of their lives. The following sequence, featuring as it does a stereotypically disabled playing of parts, helps explain why they were unable to extend their open style into their affect relations as well:

In the middle of a therapy session, Richard, Paul, and Elaine Yost take turns explaining to Mr. Yost how they all feel emotionally short-changed by him, and thus why, after all these years, they are still angry with him. Richard's wife Joan, who is also present, listens to the others make their complaints. Eli Yost counters his accusers with a historical defense. His conditioning by a severe and orthodox mother, who trained him to restrain and never display his feelings to other people, prevents him from being more demonstrative. Yet, he reminds the others, he loved her. He doesn't feel deprived. Paul is unsympathetic. "I know, Eli, but I feel deprived," he says. "I'm unhappy at my work. My marriage has failed. I feel miserable most of the time." Mrs. Yost starts crying. "That's why these sessions are so difficult for me. Your unhappiness is just too much for me to bear, Paul." Paul turns on his

mother. "Christ! Your tears are a pain in the ass." Richard tries
to mediate between the two: "You're turning on each other because you two miss Eli the most." Joan says nothing. She stares
disgustedly at her mother-in-law. Father Yost sits gripping the arm
of his chair, staring unsympathetically at his distaught wife.

The moves of the Yost "players" are very characteristic in
this sequence. Elaine, Paul, and Richard collectively move against
Eli while Joan bystands. They are the movers in qualifiedly different ways, however, each having different psychopolitical bases.
Paul and Mother run neck and neck as initiators who "petition"
the withheld affections of Mr. Yost, with Richard running on the
same track but enough behind to enjoy a perspective the other two
lack. A move that is qualified by petitioning is one in which the
leading edge of an action is an appeal for support or continuance
of the act. It is a move inextricably interlaced with followership.
With the exceptions of moves by Eli and Joan Yost, movership in
the Yost family's affect relations are consistently tinged with such
petitioning, ranging from unburdening requests for emotional alliance to embarrassingly loaded appeals and irritating demands that
someone either move closer (that is, follow) or allow the initiator
to follow (that is, move closer).

It is clear that Father Yost has difficulty responding to the
others' requests for emotional nurturance and intimacy. His bystanding self-critique seems accurate, but gets in the way. Whether
meant to or not, it opposes the collective momentum of the others.
The other family members want him to follow their lead, not tell
them why he cannot. From their point of view, his self-critique is
merely another failure to answer their appeal, a failure which helps
trigger the conflict between Paul and his mother, the petitioners
who feel most deprived. Their conflict, as this later passage from
the same therapy session makes clear, works to sabotage the family's
announced strategy of making father more emotionally accessible.

Richard once again tries to encourage Eli to express his
feelings for Paul. "Paul needs you," he says. "Give him a sign.
Show him how you feel!" Eli says, "I know what you want, but I
want you to know how difficult it is for me to do it right, however
much I might want too." Richard replies, "You've got to be able
to." Following a nervous moment, which seems an eternity, Eli,

still sitting, stiffly opens his arms toward Paul and says, "I suppose this is what you mean." Then to his younger son, he says, "I do love you, Paul." Though visibly affected by his father's action, Paul makes no immediate response. Mr. Yost continues to hold open his arms. Everyone watches. Paul becomes tearful, and then, after a long pause, stands up and starts to cross the room to his father. Exploding with emotion, Elaine turns to her husband and says, "Eli, Eli, it's all so wonderful." Leaving her chair, she kneels down in front of her husband and reaches out with her arms to hug him, cluttering the pathways. Ignoring her, Eli continues to hold out his arms to his son Paul, whose passage is blocked by his mother's petitioning body. A now sobbing Paul walks around to the side of his father's chair where he kneels down and with some discomfort tries to lay his head on his father's lap. Awkwardly, Eli moves his arms to touch his weeping son on the shoulders. Moments later as the family considers what has just taken place, Elaine says enthusiastically, "It's wonderful." A very angry Joan says, "Shit." Paul remarks, "To be perfectly honest, I'm really disappointed." Eli says, "I feel I've disappointed you all. I'm not very good at this." Richard says, "It looks to me like Mom got in the way." Indeed, the family is struck by the "familiarity" of the scenario they have just played. It was, they gradually conclude, a densely epitomized condensation of many family sequences.

The inadequacy of the Yosts' collective efforts in both phases of this therapy session were perhaps doomed from the start. In each, family members could seemingly find no other way to effect the kind of intimacy they wanted except by a collective coercion of the father. The free flowing open intimacy members desired, by definition, could not be coerced but had to be voluntarily offered and accepted. Yet, how else could members turn their system around to get what they wanted in the way of emotional openness? This was the family's dilemma, a dilemma made even more serious by the fact that each member was skilled and practiced at resisting the will of the majority. If coercion was the strategy of the group against the father, cooption was the initial strategy of the mother toward her sons.

In the first part of the sequence, she attempted to take over and channel the momentum of the group for her own ends. More specifically, she tried to replace Paul as the primary victim and thus the sequence's center of focus. The others wouldn't let her, however. Joan and Paul both criticized and ridiculed her, forcing her to retreat from the center. In effect, they blocked her out, pushing her farther away from the shared family affect ideals. When a breakthrough with the father was finally achieved, she returned to the field by crossing over to him before anyone else could reach him. Her strategy here was one of preemption, of beating out the others to the common goal of greater intimacy with Mr. Yost. By preempting his attention, however, she robbed the otherwise tender moment of its meaning and fragile hope, giving it rather a bizarre and frustrating cast.

Resistance, coercion, cooption, ridicule, and preemption all worked together, sabotaging intimacy in the Yost sequence. All four tactics short-circuited the emotional exchange among family members. Power dimension considerations dominated the affect field, turning a quest for intimacy into intense competition. The fact that Mr. Yost was granted "great man" status by the public at large heightened members' feelings of deprivation as well as their competition with each other, for each could feel that the public got more out of Mr. Yost than he or she did. Though the Yosts present a unique example of a "great man's" family, deprivation and intense competition are bound to result whenever access to a precious family target becomes blocked.

In summary, the preceding sequence shows the individual Yost members playing the following parts in their highly disabling intimacy-sabotaging strategy: Father Yost is a bystander to moves made against him, an overt follower of collective demand for greater closeness, but a covert opposer to that demand. Mother Yost is an overt follower of collective moves against husband and a covert opposer of moves in which she is not the central concern. Joan is an opposer to Mrs. Yost, follower of Richard. Richard is the follower of the collective desire to increase family intimacy and bystanding-opposer to whatever or whoever obstructs such intimacy. Paul is a mover for greater intimacy with father; opposer to mother's covert moves.

Although we do not know exactly what parts individual Yost family members would prefer to play, we do know some of the historical background from which their stereotypic choice of parts was induced:

The Yosts are descended from several generations of New England Yankee stock. In describing the closed severity of his own childhood, something he did with pride rather than bitterness, Eli Yost recalled how his mother had kept his hair long and tied it with ribbons while clothing him in the girlish attire fashionable at the turn of the century among certain sections of the upper class. As a young boy, he was not allowed to question this practice, even though it continued much longer than for his peers. Mr. Yost also recalled how he was forbidden to look at a girl while riding in the family automobile. If he wavered, he was punished. The only physical intimacy he could recall his parents exchanging came during his own adolescence when his father put his hand on his mother's knee to comfort her at a time of crisis. As a result of his familial experience, Mr. Yost believed he developed a tremendous discipline for harnessing his energies to professional projects, an ability of which he was extremely proud.

Mrs. Yost grew up in an upper-class family with roots in New England. A college graduate, Elaine Yost became interested in the women's rights movement. When she became very depressed during the early years of her marriage, she entered psychoanalysis, still a rather new therapeutic practice at the time. Despite her social capabilities, intellectual competence, and political interests, all of which her family supported and helped develop, Elaine felt deprived and strongly dependent on other people. Emotionally fragile, she felt a craving for closeness. Even though her mother had been of great help to her in many other ways, Elaine felt she had been too occupied with her own social responsibilities to carry on a sustained, intimate relationship with her daughter. As a consequence Elaine was left with strong residual feelings of emotional disconnection. Elaine's relationship with her father was less well articulated. Her memory of it was dominated by the image of him spanking her, an image which, for her, conveys an aura of sexual closeness.

Mr. and Mrs. Yost both recall feeling very close to each other during the early years of their marriage. Their closeness wasn't fully satisfactory, however, for Eli could seemingly shut his emotions on and off whereas Elaine could not. Elaine soon became jealous of the time and energy her husband devoted to his work, even though she placed high value on what he was doing. She began to feel cast aside. Eli, on the other hand, had difficulty recognizing and acknowledging his wife's requests for continued and deeper closeness. He began to feel trapped by her needs. Believing they were not really legitimate, he devoted more of his energies and time to his profession. Elaine's response was to embarrass him, often in public, thus ridiculing his growing prominence. The friction between them became so great that he began to suspect that her periodic depressions were feigned as an appeal to his strong sense of duty, which would prohibit him from abandoning her under such circumstances.

Richard grew up with a nagging resentment toward his mother, stemming from a sense of his own emotional deprivation. This resentment was fueled by his father's attitudes and covert critical insinuations. While he was in his early twenties, however, Richard suddenly realized that his mother suffered from emotional problems and that these had prevented her from giving him the affectional nurturing he had desired as a child. Having recognized this situation, Richard lowered his expectations and along with them what he would demand of his mother. Their relationship improved greatly from that point onward, as Richard grew increasingly aware of how he might best relate to her. About this time, Richard also started to question the validity of his mother's assertions about his father's emotional unavailability. He began to seek ways to get closer to his father and in part succeeded.

Paul grew up with a feeling of strong bitterness toward his father, a feeling that had been fueled by his mother's highly visible sufferings and often voiced reproaches against Eli. At school Paul was perceived as a bright and sensitive boy, but something of a lost soul. By the time he was eleven years old, Paul had begun to worry about himself. Feeling he couldn't open himself to his family, he confided to his teachers that he had become frightened by "dirty thoughts," increasingly bizarre dreams, and wild fantasies. The school alerted Mrs. Yost, who in turn told Mr. Yost about the school's concern for Paul's well-being. Mr. Yost reacted with outrage at Paul's exposing to quasi-public scrutiny both himself and

Mr. Yost, who by this time had become something of a public figure. Mr. Yost's outrage was, in a sense, the outrage and shame he would have expected his own mother to express if he had ever revealed his own shameful or dirty thoughts to her. Rather than seeking help for Paul, Mr. Yost enrolled him in another private school. At the time, Paul was deeply hurt by being treated as a family disgrace in this way, and strong residual feelings of deprivation and discontent continued into the present. Even though he went to an Ivy League university and became a practicing professional himself, he never forgave his father for doing what he did, or his mother for not intervening more successfully on his behalf. In the following years, he lashed out at both with his resentment. Indeed, the incident had become virtually unredeemable for him.

Like Mrs. Yost, Richard's wife Joan grew up in an affluent liberal family, married, and became subservient and dependent on her husband, who, unlike his father, experienced a decade of professional frustration and failure before coming into some prominence. Partly in response to the women's liberation movement, Joan began in more recent years to hold out for her own self interests and to reject the subservient role she had played toward her husband, a role Mrs. Yost, by her own acts of dependency, reminded her of whenever they met.

Once one is acquainted with the histories of these individuals, the Yosts' attempts at making father more accessible take on greater poignancy. The failure to achieve a satisfactory emotional intimacy among members for any length of time was felt by all the Yosts to be a common disabling occurrence. As much as each individual wanted to create a closer emotional linking, something always got in the way. Mr. Yost's images of emotional and sexual propriety, Mrs. Yost's of abandonment, Paul's of revenge and hoped for redemption, Richard's of the unavailability of affection, and Joan's of unwanted subservience all reinforced the family's affect disability. Psychopolitically, each of the Yosts was compelled to act out parts consistent with his images, parts which taken together frustrated attempts to increase family intimacy. Richard was perhaps the one person currently free to undo the past and open up the future, since his early images of resentment toward his mother for her unavailability had been corrected by the ensuing nurturance he had been able to gain after he had made an important realization about his mother. This freedom enabled him to play a creative bystander part in the foregoing sequence, for he knew that until the blocked emotional link between Eli and Paul could be opened up, he could not hope to have his own emotive needs met within the family.

Despite the Yost's severe affect disablement, we find Richard's recognition of a disabling strategy an encouraging sign. Though the bystander function is often rendered ineffective in Yost interactions, it is not disqualified completely. This distinction may not seem significant at first, but we believe it can be of crucial importance to families. It means that the system has at least some check on its own worst tendencies. As long as a bystander is available, the family has the potential for recognizing its disabling strategies and of developing new strategies to replace them. Where no accurate bystanding is allowed, a highly disabled family is condemned to repeating its mistakes: if expression of the family's full range of distant-regulation information and imagery is disallowed, if imagery and information from outside are blocked, and if the capacity of mover, follower, and opposer to influence interactional behavior is interfered with from the bystander perspective, family disablement is not only inevitable, it is probably irreversible.

The Claritys, another of our research families, consistently misplayed the bystander part, obscuring the fact that family interactions tended either to produce or maintain a high level of access and target disablement among members. In this family, the bystander was almost never free to oppose. Three generations of Claritys lived together in the same urban household: the senior Claritys, a retired teacher and his wife; their sons Leo and Jim; Jim's wife Betty; and the married couple's three children. Leo, the Clarity's thirty-two-year-old son, had previously been hospitalized and diagnosed as a schizophrenic.

The Clarity family members' interactional positioning, according to our four player model, can be summarized as follows: Mrs. Clarity was the primary mover. Mr. Clarity was a silent bystander and tacit follower of Mrs. Clarity. Jim was a mover away from the house, a passive bystander within. Betty was an infrequent and ineffectual opposer. Leo was a conflicted follower/opposer of parents. Priscilla, Greg, and Todd (the children) were bystanders and followers of their grandmother.

As the almost sole mover in family sequences, Mrs. Clarity engaged in a rather eccentric style of linking with other family members. In one sequence, her grandson Gregg was plainly imitating in play a barking dog, but Mrs. Clarity insisted on labeling his role as that of a cat. In another sequence, when the child had clearly asked for his bottle of milk, Mrs. Clarity kept inquiring, "Is it *tea* you want?" until the child bent under the insistent pressure, and said yes. In still another sequence, Mrs. Clarity proclaimed that Leo should no longer be allowed to eat his dinner in his bedroom. Moments later, however, she delivered his dessert to him. When Leo showed interest one afternoon in accompanying Mr. and Mrs. Clarity to the store, Mrs. Clarity asked him repeatedly if he were going with them, suggesting that perhaps he should not. On another afternoon, she asked her grandchildren if they would like to go shopping with her, and then, upon hearing them say yes, told them that unfortunately they couldn't, that they would have to go with their own mother next time she went shopping. As can be seen from these examples, many of Mrs. Clarity's communications were grounded in irrationality. Yet no one in the family challenged her right to dominate the family's linking operations.

The Clarity family's disabling strategies were dominated by two principal features, an undermining of logic (apparent in the scenes cited above) and an indulging of incompetence. No one in the family seemed to expect that orders and requirements need be carried out. For example, though Mrs. Clarity was an indifferent homemaker and housekeeper, Mr. Clarity indulged his wife's inadequacy by never interfering in her sphere of activity. The Clarity children followed suit, never questioning her slovenly housekeeping and frequently unattractive meals. Meanwhile, Mrs. Clarity indulged her son Leo's ineffectualness by never expecting him to do anything, not even to help decorate his own room. The result of such systematic indulgence was that family members gradually became more incompetent. They experienced general feelings of impotence, of being unable to tackle quite simple tasks. For instance, when an electric blackout occurred and a broken candle was lit, none of the family could figure out how to fix it. Instead, they watched it drip its wax on top of the dining room table. On another occasion, when some razor blades were missing and the grandparents feared the young children might be playing with them, no one bothered to make so much as a brief search.

We believe the family's indulgence of incompetence represented an attempt on the part of family members to redeem some undefined loss. Mr. Clarity's noninstrumental bystanding of his wife's activities seems to have been his way of atoning for both the lack of emotional closeness in their marriage and her unspecified sense of loss, caused by an austere and unfulfilling childhood. The sons followed Mr. Clarity's passive bystanding pattern. They seemed to be able to deny both their mother's irrationality and their own incompetence. Like him, they managed scrupulously to avoid the painful skeletons located in Mrs. Clarity's psychic closet. Jim, the one potentially effective bystander, stayed completely aloof from the rest of the family, allowing the others to maintain their patterns of indulgence intact. Mrs. Clarity for her part seemed to have been indulging Leo in an effort to compensate for the fact that he had never found a place in her heart. Ironically, the practice of indulgence and noninterference increased everyone's sense of loss in the family. By disqualifying the system's bystander function through a pattern of internal denial, members lost the options of renovation and change. Since only minor and tangential criticism was permitted, the Clarity family was condemned to continue its disablement.

When the bystander part is creatively played, it in effect says to the family, "Thou shalt see!" In the Clarity family and in other highly disabled families, the bystanders say by their presence, "Thou shalt not see!" or "Thou shalt not see what must not be seen!" If all strategies are begun with good intentions, why, when a strategy becomes disabling, does a bystander ever back off into a posture of absolute noninterference? The reason is that active interference and accurate recognitions of events can produce significant interpersonal risks for all family players. The energies of the family become invested in strategic means as well as strategic ends. To oppose such energies or to open up the possibility of opposing them, as an accurately recognizing bystander often does, is to risk exposing one's own hitherto unthreatened interests and position inside the family. Thus, if Jim is to expose his mother's domestic incompetence, he must be willing to expose his own lackluster work achievements.

In the Yost family, members failed to recognize that Father Yost could probably never be the openly emotive person they wanted him to be, in part perhaps so they could lay the onus for emotional failure on him rather than on themselves. By not recognizing his limitations more accurately, however, they also sacrificed what emotional exchange they could get from him. As these examples suggest, to remain the silent and aloof bystander is not without its own risks. All players in the family system share a responsibility for what happens in a family. When something goes wrong, even if only one member is victimized and disabled, everyone is affected. Guilt, shame, failure, and feelings of isolation can accrue to a bystander who either fails to recognize the disabling features of his family's strategies or fails to intervene and negotiate for a better, more enabling strategy.

The bystander function encompasses several specific perceptual and conceptual activities. First, the bystander must perceive an interaction: that is, he must gain an impression on some level of consciousness. Perception leads to contemplation (or reconnaissance), followed by some determination. The bystander makes a judgment that is actually an identification, an insight that goes beyond noticing and contemplation. Identification culminates in understanding or comprehending. It is an acknowledgment—not an approval or endorsement, but the recognition of a situation for what it is. Identification usually requires an interpretation (a definition or explanation of a state of affairs), and finally a comment or judgment, either inferred or expressed. In this final "disclosure" lies the ultimate power of the observer as commentator to affect the other players in a system.

When the bystander is allowed to perform most or all of these activities of identification, an accurate rendering of reality is available to family members. When the bystander function is disqualified, however, family interactions are condemned to suffer from perceptual and conceptual nonidentification and/or misidentification. In interactions dominated by processes of nonidentification, no rendering of reality is made. Instead, members refuse to recognize that a certain activity is taking place. In still more pronounced instances of nonidentification, the presence of one or more members in the social field may not even be acknowledged, producing a style of interaction in which A may be permitted to talk to B about C in C's presence without recognizing either that C is present or that he has a right to enter the conversation. In interactions dominated by processes of misidentification, only a slanted or inaccurate rendering of reality is permitted. In such circumstances, a family may identify the hesitant or passive moves of a member or outsider as aggressive or dangerous to family survival. Correspondingly, real threats may be perceived as inconsequential.

The inevitable result of both nonidentification and misidentification processes is that the social field of family process experiences a serious perceptual distortion that can only be maintained through the systematic denials of all family members. When the specific office or actions of the bystander part are improperly executed on an extensive and continuing basis, strategies of repair are difficult if not impossible to develop. In such a situation, the toll of continuing disabling effects can become very great indeed.

Chapter 13

Distance-Regulation Model

In the prceding chapters, we have presented the various components of a comprehensive and unified model of family process. We have proposed in essence that the family system is made up of five major interrelated parts, each part a system itself consisting of interrelated subparts. To summarize, we have identified these major components as (1) the subsystems of family and their interfaces, (2) the access dimensions and mechanisms of family process, (3) the target dimensions, (4) the three family process types, and (5) the interactional system of four player parts. In this chapter we intend to show how the five major components relate to one another and to the system as a whole, by coordinating them within a distance-regulation model of family process.

In the Preface, we made the assertion, "we shall understand families when we understand how they manage the commonplace." Is such a complex theory as the one we are expounding absolutely necessary to an understanding of family? We believe it is. First of all, let us remind ourselves that the commonplace, though ordinary, is not simple. Even everyday family events require each system member to make myriads of assessments and judgments. Although crisis and conflict raise both the pressure and the stakes of family events, they do not, as a general rule, significantly alter the complexity of the basic range of component part interactions. Indeed, such continuing complexity is probably to be expected, because the human animal is a highly complicated organism, more complicated in fact, than the most sophisticated information processing computer machinery he has thus far been able to devise. It is for the purpose of identifying and comprehending this complexity of variables, in commonplace events as well as in crises, that we have formulated our theory of family process.

Let us reiterate our basic approach: a belief that the family, like other social systems, is primarily an information-processing system and that the information it processes is distance regulational in nature. Throughout our presentation we have contended that families seek to attain their goals by continuously informing their members what constitutes a proper or optimal distance in establishing relationships among themselves or between themselves and specific events. Although our distance-regulation model is theoretical in nature, it is buttressed by intensive empirical observations of families in their natural settings and by our identification and analysis of strategies prevalent there as well as in the therapy room. The distance-regulation feedback model we present in this chapter integrates abstract, theoretical representations of family process with empirical analyses of felt reality. What we are attempting to provide is a logically complete and empirically verifiable model of family process.

Now that we have described the five basic components of our theory of family process, let us demonstrate how an understanding of their workings might be applied to the commonplace, to an everyday interactional sequence, such as that introduced in the Preface.

A small child stands outside his parents' bedroom door on Saturday morning. He knocks on the door. Both parents hear it. Mother says, "Come in." The boy enters and goes directly toward the bed where he hugs his still half asleep father, who groggily hugs him in return.

Even in this superficially simple sequence every component

is in operation. The knock on the door establishes that the child wants something, that he wants to gain access to some target. Thus, the dimensions are present. Furthermore, the signal of the knock demonstrates the existence of a boundary that can be named. Assuming that the knock on the door is not a totally unprecedented event, we would suggest that it takes place at the interface between the personal subsystem and the interpersonal subsystem of the family. In another household the door might not have been closed or the knock necessary. The fact that the door is closed and the knock seemingly necessary suggests that the child has absorbed what his family's typal model for regulating distances permits and does not permit at this interface. If we further assume from their history together that members know what each others' spatial prerogatives are, we are also made aware that the access mechanisms are in operation. The parents know that what the child is seeking is access to affect through physical and emotional linking. In response to the child's knock, the parents must make decisions affecting the system's interpersonal bounding, early morning clocking, and energy-investing mechanisms. In short, they must make a co-moving response to their child's move. Each interactional player's rudimentary bystander function is also at work, deciding what moves to make or permit in accord with his or her own individual psycho-politics.

Once again, we need to assert that in the complexity of human decision making all these events happen simultaneously and are not easily distinguishable from one another. Not all component parts are of equal importance, however, nor do they have equal influence on the shaping of family interactions. Only by analyzing a sequence in view of a system's particular elaboration of its component parts can one establish the relative weight and importance of each component part in a sequence. Normally, family members do not experience the component parts of system process in any logical progression, though a logical progression does exist in the form of a prototypic feedback loop, as illustrated in Figure 5.

To show how this information-processing loop works, we take the early morning sequence cited above and break it down into its individual acts. Our analysis of this sequence demonstrates how the five component parts of the distance-regulation model we

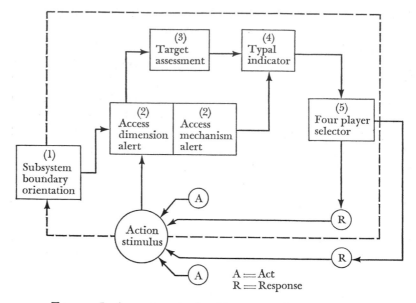

FIGURE 5. A prototypic family process feedback loop.

present in this book directly articulate the various operations of the family-system prototypic feedback loop. In our analysis, we assume omniscience about the family and its individual members. In addition, these members accurately recognize each other's actions and signals. The result is a deliberate simplification of process on our part, for we have eliminated the many kinds of special issues that arise whenever processes of nonidentification and misidentification occur, issues we prefer not to deal with in this introductory presentation of a distance-regulation feedback loop.

Step One: Components in Readiness

A small child stands outside his parents' bedroom door on Saturday morning. He knocks on the door. The boy's knock is equivalent to the action stimulus of our feedback loop, the act that begins a sequence. The knock itself is an act with its own antecedents. If these antecedents were known, we could analyze the operations of the boy's internal information-processing loop prior to his knock. Since we do not know the specific antecedents, however, we shall wait until the next act in the sequence to make our analysis of the prototypic feedback loop in operation.

Whether the initial act of any sequence is designated as cause or effect is always arbitrary. Any event which is the cause for one thing can be the effect of another. The child's knock on the door can be taken as effect as well as cause, for the boy's anticipation of what will happen as a result of his knock on the door is based on his previous experience in the same or similar contexts. Correspondingly, what happens on this Saturday may affect what he does in later contexts. In this way important antecedent events can exert control over contemporaneous social behavior through a process of feeding or reinserting information about present contexts and events back into the results of past performance. Thus, the initial act in the sequence, the child's knock on the door, is at the moments of conception and execution influenced by his previous experience. His social act is performed as the culmination of a self-regulating feedback, for by the time he has knocked on the door he has completed his processing of appropriate antecedent information.

Remember that the child is a self-regulating system himself as well as a member of the larger family system. As such, he processes information about context along the same basic distance-regulation feedback loop as other family members. The individuals involved in any family sequence may be processing other information as well—daydreaming, thinking of breakfast, recalling a television program from the night before—but insofar as they are processing information about overt family events, they are displaying their systems-consciousness and behaving in accord with the distance regulations and strategies the family system has evolved. It is this systems-consciousness of family players that remains our primary theoretical and operational focus. Within this framework the boy's act defines the social space context for the other players. His knock on the door is the primary antecedent act for them, the stimulus action that triggers their own feedback loop processing.

Step Two: Components in Operation

Both parents hear it. Mother says, "Come on." Since we know its immediate antecedent, this step in the sequence of acts permits us to make a comprehensive survey of the parents' information-processing loop. First, of course, is the actual hearing of the knock, the identification of an action stimulus. Hearing their small son's knock on the door, each of the parents seeks to identify the family-system boundary at which this first act in a sequence of interaction is taking place. On this weekend morning, the parents realize that their son's knock on the door initiates an interaction at the personal-interpersonal subsystem interface. Subsystem boundary orientation, let us remind the reader, is the first component in our theory of family process. It is also the first component of the protypic family-process feedback loop.

The second major component of our family-system model articulates a two-stage operation in the prototypic feedback loop. The first stage, the access dimension alert, is informed by the boundary-orienting component about the subsystem interface at which the action stimulus is occurring. The access dimension alert component of the parents' information-processing loop then seeks to measure the spatial, temporal, and energic aspects of the action stimulus. For example, by measuring the duration and force of the knock, the parents might make a guess about how long or loudly their young son will continue to knock if he is not immediately answered, information which in turn suggests how badly the boy wants to enter the bedroom and how physically close he intends to come to each parent. In this way, the action stimulus is quantifiable within all three access dimensions.

The access mechanism alert (the second stage of this feedback component) evaluates and applies the measurement of the access dimension alert. Figuratively, the access mechanism alert sorts through the access mechanisms and submechanisms of family process until it locates a structure of operation that seems to fit or encompass the present interaction. In this Saturday morning sequence, the mechanism primarily in operation is spatial linking and its submechanism, bridging.

Target assessment, the third component of our prototypic feedback loop, attempts to measure the direction, destination, and goals of family traffic. The question it seeks to answer is, what is being sought? In this sequence, the parents might ask themselves, "What does the boy want from us?" By introducing target considerations, the target-assessment component completes the six-dimension grid on which families regulate their members' access to affect, power, and meaning through the way in which they regulate space, time, and energy. Thus, where the access dimension alert seeks to quantify the space, time, and energy inputs of an action, the target dimension assessor attempts to identify which qualities of the affect, power, and meaning dimensions are being sought. In this sequence, the parents tap a memory bank of foundation images, generated by shared family experience, to identify just what target or targets the boy is seeking to attain. Without such an imagistic memory bank capable of storing impressions of both family and individual traffic patterns, their target assessment would be far less predictable. In the sequence under discussion, the parents realize that emotional nurturance is the primary target of their son's early morning behavior.

The fourth component in our model of family process is the typal indicator. Its chief features include the criterion variables and target ideals of the family typal design, each of which represents an elaboration of the system's homeostatic ideal and core purpose. Guided by the typal indicator, members make a judgment about how closely a particular event facilitates or frustrates a family's typal design. More specifically, one assesses the access alert signal in accord with the family's criterion variables, and compares the target assessment signal to family target ideals. In this way the degree of correspondence between event and design can be closely delineated. When a normal everyday event occurs, the typal indicator can do its job easily and efficiently. When an event that is without precedent occurs, the typal indicator must make a more thorough and detailed reading. Similarly, when an event occurs which is at variance with the typal design and has a lot of energy behind it, the typal indicator is placed under considerable strain. Whatever the particular incident, the typal indicator transmits a comparison signal specifying what action it feels ought to be taken in response to the original act on the basis of its degree of correspondence to the family's typal design. For example, in this early morning sequence, the parents feel their child's behavior, including his implied nurturance request, is in conformity with the family's open-type style. (Since all families employ variety as well as constancy loops, a closed-type or random-type family might make a similar decision, but for different typal reasons. For instance, the closed-type family might decide its design should be modified to permit that particular type of event, whereas, in a random type family, the parents might regard the event as incidence of the kind of behavioral individuality they encourage.)

The four-player selector is the fifth and final component of our prototypic feedback loop. It is here, within the four-player interactional framework, that family members individually make their responses to a stimulus action. In the sequence we are analyzing, mother acts as a follower to her son, accepting the right of his petition. She invites him into the bedroom, granting him preliminary access to the affect target he seeks. Father, on the other hand, remains outside the action, a passive bystander in response to his son's request. As this difference in the parental playing of parts implies, family members may exercise considerable freedom of choice in response to a particular comparison signal. Indeed, the presence of such freedom is one of the key differences between complex information processing social systems, such as the family, and more mechanical systems. The effector function of the ordinary household thermostat does not have such freedom. It executes what the error signal of the comparator tells it to do. In our model of family process, it is clear that the effector function, or four-player selector, has more leeway. Even in the simplest of sequences such as we are describing, family players can exercise a great deal of judgment about the innovation, variation, and stability of the parts they play—whether they are played voluntarily or because of systemic induction. In short, it is within this component part that each individual works out his own psychopolitics toward the family and its typal design.

A further complexity concerning this fifth component part of family process must also be addressed. Throughout the course of the feedback loop, following the action stimulus of the knock on the door, each member's bystander function has been active. In a sense, the boundary orientation, the access dimension alert, the target assessment, the access mechanism alert, and the typal indicator each represents a different analytic aspect of the bystander function. Every family member embodies that function in his own way, perceiving system events and generating images from a memory bank of shared experience in order to make sense of those events and develop an appropriate response to them. What this means is that the distance regulation operations of family systems are ultimately dependent upon the self-regulating information-processing behavior of individual family members. When the four-player selector is activated, a significant phase is reached in the operation of the distance regulation loop. An overt behavioral act is made in response to the original social event. It produces a new social event to reactivate the various operations of the distance-regulation feedback loop.

Step Three: Cycle Repeated

The boy enters the room and goes directly toward the bed where he hugs his still half asleep father. Between mother's invitation and the boy's entrance into the room to hug his father, another feedback process takes place. It ends with the boy's response of continuing his move for emotional nurturance. Let us trace, much more briefly this time, the information-processing operations that take place in his mind. The access dimension alert informs him that his mother not only says, "Come in," but that her voice is soft and gentle and still a little drowsy. His target assessment is that nurturance will be provided. His mechanism alert informs him that linking and its bridging submechanism are an appropriate vehicle of access, but that he must be careful not to invest too much energy or he will overwhelm his still drowsy parents, creating a situation in which he will be coercively channeling their nurturance rather than receiving it voluntarily. The typal indicator tells him that his intended move meets the requirements of his parents' open style criterion variables and target ideals as long as he takes into account the opposition-regulation information his mother's voice has transmitted, namely, "Do not come in too hard or too fast." As a result, in addition to continuing his move for nurturance, he chooses in the four-player selector the part of follower to his mother's opposition regulation hints. He enters quietly and proceeds toward his target.

Step Four: Another Cycle

Who groggily hugs him in return. The action stimulus for father's information processing is provided by the boy crossing the room and hugging him. Through the access dimension alert,

Father knows that his son is embracing him, that the boy has crossed the room precisely for this purpose. The boundary orientation is thereby changed. The personal-interpersonal interface is now a physical as well as a social interface. The father also has his target assessment confirmed. The boy is indeed seeking emotional nurturance. With the triggering of his access mechanism alert, the father realizes that his son has completed a crossover to him with mother's permission and that it is now up to him to complete the linking that has taken place by means of bridging, and he does so by responding in turn. The criterion variable and target ideal matchups of the typal indicator suggest that both the boy's action and the father's projected reaction are not only permitted but encouraged by the family's open typal style. The player part selected by the drowsy father is that of the follower. He fulfills his son's move of petitioning for physical closeness and emotional nurturance by hugging him in return. Once again, a new stage is reached as the boy and his mother process the information that the father has placed an arm around his son. In everyday life, the interaction would continue, either as an extension of the same sequence or as the start of a new one. For our purposes, however, the sequence is concluded.

In the foregoing analysis, we have shown that every player in the sequence is a self-regulating system owing most of his or her stable behavior to feedback controls. One of the fundamental principles of the feedback concept is that every event has an antecedent event preceding it. Thus, father's hug is preceded by his son's crossing the room, which is preceded by his mother's invitation, which is preceded by the child's knock, which in turn is preceded by the parents' being in bed on Saturday morning, and other contextually appropriate events. Each of the antecedent events helps to shape and trigger the next event in an unending closed feedback-loop process. Within the loops themselves, we have identified the five major information-processing components of the family system as subsystem boundary orientation, access dimension and mechanism alerting, target assessment, typal indication, and interactional selection. It is by means of their systemic consciousness of the passage of an input signal, through each of these components of the total feedback process, that family members learn to carry out their distance regulation operations of association and dissociation in a stable way, consistent with the family's style and design as well as their own psychopolitical preferences.

Patterns of Family Enablement

The sequence analyzed in the preceding discussion appears to be a successful one. The young boy gains access to the target he seeks, namely physical affection from his father. His father seems willing to provide such affection as long as he is free to continue recharging his energies with a last forty winks. For her part, Mother willingly facilitates the situation. In this way, the three family members work out an access arrangement agreeable to each. In addition, Mother and Father have their typal propensities affirmed. They permit an open-type sequence of action to take place, resulting in everyone's benefit. Furthermore, each of the players seems satisfied with the role he or she is assigned to play in the sequence. In Chapter Ten, we noted that an unsuccessful sequence is not necessarily a signal of strategic disablement, nor is a successful sequence necessarily representative of strategic enablement. Nevertheless, there is a general pattern of connectedness between sequences and strategies, allowing us to ask two basic questions. What clues does a successful sequence provide for an understanding of strategic enablement? What in fact are some of the general features of strategic enablement in families?

Strategic enablement does not mean an absence of system stress. Each subsystem of a family has it own typal goals, which may be either compatible with or in competition with other subsystem goals. There is not a family existing, not even an ideal closed-type family, that doesn't experience some competition of goals and purposes or at least some conflict over the best way to attain those goals. The stress that results from these subsystem competitions is an inevitable consequence of family life. We believe therefore that *an enabling system is one which maintains a distance regulation balance so that no one subsystem or member is consistently and systematically denied actualization of its typal goals.* The two vital concepts in this statement are "balance" and "systematically denied." Family distance-regulation circuits systematically guide individual members along strategic pathways according to a design of what the system regards as ideal. Individual sacrifice is thus intrinsic to family distance regulations, even in the random-type family. Regardless of type, however, an enabling family spreads its demands around so that no one family subsystem or member is singled out for repeated sacrifice to the whole. When a just and enabling balance of subsystem sacrifices is achieved, each member can become psychopolitically free to cooperate with his or her family even though it may require a temporary sacrifice of individual goals. Since all families cannot help but obstruct the bid of each subsystem for maximum actualization at one time or another, such cooperation is absolutely essential to preserving family enablement. Where it does not exist, friction over the goals and strategies of the various subsystems is certain to escalate, setting a crisis chain in motion in accord with the family's typal design. Satir (1967) has identified the "management of difference" as the issue on which most families get into trouble. We endorse her suggestion that the recognizing and affirming of members' differences is the primary task of family therapy. In our mind, distance regulation and the management of difference are in essence synonomous.

Not even enabling families manage to stay on course all the time. All families experience disablement at least some of the time. When disablement occurs, families are faced with the necessity of having to take corrective action. Family enablement is thus directly related to the effectiveness of a family's repair strategies in taking corrective action. We believe that an enabling family is capable of employing strategies associated with other types as well as its own, if need be, in restoring a distance-regulation balance among its subsystems so that all members may actualize their typal inclinations. In order to exercise such freedom, persons playing the bystander part must make available to the family the option of drawing upon strategies not normally associated with the family's typal design. Furthermore, along with Carl Whitaker (1973, pp. 1–2), we believe that an enabling family is flexible in the distribution of its player parts. Whatever its norms, a family in which each member is able to play all four parts effectively is a family with more resources to draw upon, especially in times of crisis, than a family in which members are characteristically permitted to play only one or two parts.

Understanding Family Disablement

Does our distance-regulation model help explain disabling strategies as well as successful sequences like the one explicated above? We believe it does. Each component part in our family model helps to explain the causes of disablement and is applicable to therapeutic treatment of the problems that arise as a result. First, the subsystem component suggests that competition between the subsystems of family can generate ironic displacement effects, that is, unforeseen obstructions of goals for one or more family members.

The dimensions component demonstrates that targets as well as subsystems may be in competition with one another. This component also suggests the presence of historic themes that are of particular importance to individual family members because of distance-regulation patterning in a prior context, frequently the parents' families of origin. When different themes are competing for priority, conflicts over how to regulate members' access to targets can be quite severe, because the priority of targets can often be felt to be morally or ideologically nonnegotiable, so that an element of fate or destiny is introduced into the realm of family process.

The mechanism component refines our conception of access regulation and introduces the notion of modulating mechanisms, which a family employs for keeping on course toward its own chosen destinations. When members fail to make use of these modulating mechanisms in response to strategic disablement, they in effect acquiesce to such disablement.

The typal component of family process suggests several preconditions in relation to disablement: a typal or stylistic competition concerning what the family's typal design is or ought to be, a poor choice of goals, poor communication about what the goals of any particular sequence are, the poor choice of a strategic pathway for gaining access to target goals, and a poor cuing of members as to what the family, according to its typal design, expects of each member in different behavioral contexts. All of these preconditions can be further complicated and exacerbated by the presence of covert metacommunications among members. The typal component further suggests that a family's style of opposition regulation is the prime source of information about family disablement. It is in its mediation of conflicts among members and between members and the system as a whole that a family works out whether its typal ideals become a reality or not. The crisis chain is intended as a conceptual guideline to portray the process of accelerating disablement that occurs as a family's typal design is repeatedly frustrated. It offers a theoretical framework for tracking a disabled system's misuse of its typal design for maximal self destruction through the following stages: (1) a system's probable direction of error; (2) its homeostatic impasse, based on the failure of individuals to agree about their family's typal design; (3) its probable errors of substantiation, based on a perversion of the system's ideals; (4) the ritual sacrifice of an individual member, or, on rare occasions, of the system as a whole; (5) the emergence of runaway in which the system is torn asunder by its members.

The four-player selector shows how disablement can occur if members are too rigidly confined to certain parts. This component reveals that frequently recurring disabling interactional patterns are triggered in response to a theme or set of themes in which at least one member's access to his goals is systematically obstructed. One of the key features of such a resolute and recurring pattern is that it is "stuck." No one can find any way out of it. It is repetitive and circular and can start anywhere in its natural cycle. Often, anyone can start it, providing he gives the correct cue to trigger the stereotypic response of the other(s). Everyone is responsible, and yet, strictly speaking, no one is accountable. Such patterns can be virtually impossible to disrupt or impede, for they are the product of self-reinforcing feedback loops. The destructive impact of such patterns on the whole of family process is indeed great. Its potential is outlined in the crisis chain.

Inflexibility in the player parts is perhaps the most visible feature of family disablement. This inflexibility or rigidity can lead family members and often therapeutic practitioners as well into blaming particular individuals for the disablement of a family. We assert, however, that frequently recurring disabling interactional patterns (or, as we prefer to say, "stuck" patterns) require the willingness of all family members to continue them. Such "willingness" raises serious behavioral questions. How is it that family members can be aware that their family is disabled and still permit the disablement to continue? What permits them to witness and yet continue to cooperate in their own as well as their family's destruction? These are vital questions not only for the field of family process, but for all social system research.

Our four-player interactional model suggests that system members can be prevented from recognizing the self-destructive nature of stereotypic player patterns by a systematic disqualification of the system's bystander function. Through repeated disqualification, members are taught not to "see" what is happening to and in front of them. Instead, members are encouraged to participate in processes of nonidentification and misidentification, denying the reality that is before them, or confusing it with an image that doesn't actually exist. To maintain such denials and confusions, a family's player system must of necessity be further impaired through the frequent repetition of a disabling pattern. Nonidentification and misidentification are far less visible features of disablement than stuck player patterns, but they are no less important, for stuck patterns are often derived and/or maintained on the basis of a failure to identify accurately the target goals and access means of other system members. It is a fact that wherever processes of nonidentification and misidentification go unchallenged, moral confusion and incongruence abound.

Responsibility for Pathology

Do family systems as systems have the power to determine the behavior of individual members? If so, does the system itself have to bear the brunt of responsibility for generating individual pathology? If not, who *is* responsible for the harmful effects families sometimes have on their members? Though the family's control over its members' lives can be very extensive, we believe that its power is somewhat ephemeral, at least in one very important sense. A system's real power lies in its ability to co-opt the power of individual agents.

Without this power the system cannot even exist, much less effect its own ends. The increasing complexity of life, which has stimulated thinkers to generate the concepts of systems theory in the first place, has begun to suggest that virtually any social system is more powerful than the individuals who find themselves living in relation to it. It is, then, no small wonder that theories of individual victimization have begun to gain currency in our culture.

The ascription of responsibility for pathology has always reflected the theory endorsed by the majority of practitioners at the time. When the dominant theory was organic and individualistic, responsibility for pathology was primarily placed on the "sick" individual. When dynamic personality theory became prevalent, therapists began to pay attention to "the significant other," almost always one of the patient's parents, usually the mother. In many persons' eyes this "other" began to bear the onus of responsibility for victimizing the child. With the advent of a variety of social and interpersonal contributions, the locus of responsibility changed. The triad (almost always mother—father—child) and various field forces and social processes emerged as the key elements associated with responsibility for control over human behavior. Several of these theoretical contributions soon overlapped and merged with family systems theory. Now that systems theory is becoming the prevalent mode of thought, there has arisen a tendency to ascribe an almost awesome power to the family system's ability to gain control over the lives of its individual members. In recent years, the explanation, "It is the system's fault" has become a rallying cry for many family practitioners and theorists, often ourselves included.

Since systems theory has come to dominance as a way of conceptualizing and making sense out of the complexity of modern life, one of the effects has been an erosion in the belief that man is the master of his institutions, machines, and selves. There seems to be a growing tendency to relieve the individual from responsibility for actions when those actions are committed as the member of an institutional system. Although we don't mean to underestimate the power of systems to co-opt and coerce individuals, we find it a somewhat dangerous tack to excuse individuals from all or nearly all responsibility for their actions as system members. Our desire to oppose this tendency is both philosophical and quasi-theoretical. We have a definite philosophical bias in favor of preserving at least some aspects of individual responsibility. Our task as systems theorists is to reconcile this bias with the systemic presentation of family process we have made in this volume.

It is the paradox of systems that, while systems control individuals, individuals in turn control systems. Family acts are ultimately individual acts, even when they are a function of system awareness and control. Each of the three basic family process types we have identified, even the closed type, permit and perhaps encourage at least some variation in the playing of individual parts. The presence of such variation suggests a significant measure of individual control and responsibility. In addition, as our model indicates, we maintain that traffic control issues within the family are ubiquitous, the issue of regulating members' access to targets being consistently prevalent at each and every dimensional interface. Thus, the power dimension is but one of six dimensions occupied with the task of distance regulation, and control of this dimension cannot be equated with control over all of a family's process. Furthermore, the dimensions themselves are but one of five family components in our distance-regulation feedback model, each component making its own input and exercising its own control over the system's eventual actions. In this way our model suggests the difficulty to be encountered by any individual or even the family system itself, depending as it does on the co-option of individual members, should the unit attempt to gain complete and tyrannous control over the totality of family interactions.

Finally, it is our contention—partly metaphysical and partly grounded in reality—that the bystander function of social systems can never be completely and permanently disqualified. We believe that system members can never be completely or permanently shut off from felt reality by processes of nonidentification and misidentification. Even the disturbed and disoriented patients who get admitted to state institutions bear witness (though often in a language that is difficult to comprehend) to the realities of life as it is lived in their families. That this is so suggests that there may be more health in the family, even in overtly pathological families than one might suppose at first. It is our position that the first and perhaps primary task of family therapy may be to reactivate the hitherto disqualified bystander function for all family members so that they may more accurately recognize and identify their family's disabling strategies and begin to make plans for the kinds of renovation and change they desire. Indeed, the health of any system may lie in the capacity of its bystander function to be both a check on the system and an enricher of the system, introducing new images to help effect renovation and change, and thus keeping the system vibrantly alive.

In adapting cybernetic principles, we have suggested that human social systems, like their mechanical system counterparts, exercise a high degree of control over those contingencies which determine predicated outcomes. We have also argued that there are limits to systemic control by insisting that the human system embodies certain checks on its actions, which, in a final analysis, are ungovernable. In the first place, no machine, not even the most recent computers, can match the complexity and sophistication of the collection of human minds to be found in a social system such as the family. Not only is a human social system required to process more "bits" of information simultaneously than is the computer, but also it is capable of conceiving new items in the process. In mechanical systems all contingencies are not only known, but controlled as well. In human systems, however, all contingencies are not known, much less controlled. Even in strict control-oriented social systems, elements are present that have the capacity to offset the system's power by challenging its control over contingencies. These elements can either reinforce the system's authority or gain control over that authority. We suggest that the individual member's bystander function is the family's chief ungovernable element.

Chapter 14

Epilogue: The Evolution of a Family

Throughout this volume we have attempted to show how families process information and develop strategies to regulate distances among members. The purpose of this epilogue is to suggest a framework for understanding why families choose the strategies they do by taking a speculative look at how families form. Our primary focus is on the way in which individuals leave their families of origin to meet, woo, marry, and begin to shape new family spaces with one another.

In the preceding chapters we have developed a theory for explaining ongoing interactions in families. This theory has evolved out of an intensive examination of process in a small number of families for a relatively short period of time in those families' life-cycle histories. Ideally, the applicability of the distance-regulation model should be verified through several family life cycles, or better yet, through several generations. Not until such genetically oriented social research is carried out will we truly understand how families come to be what they are, or why one family develops one way while another turns out differently.

Obviously we ourselves have been unable to undertake such a longitudinal evolutionary study of family process, but we propose that there are two basic questions that any such investigation must attempt to answer: How do families evolve into the reasonably stable forms we and other observers find when we study them in full bloom? How do families, together with their stable forms of interaction, change in the course of time? Though our own theory of family process was not formulated in an evolutionary context, it does contain concepts which, when extrapolated, may facilitate an understanding of such process. Certainly it allows us a unique vantage point for speculating about how families get started and how they evolve over time.

Three conceptual features of our prototypic family-process feedback loop presented in the previous chapter constitute a theoretical foundation for such speculation: these are the imagistic memory bank, the typal indicator, and the four player selector. First, the imagistic memory bank is the storage feature of our prototypic feedback loop. Each of the components in the prototypic feedback loop we presented in the previous chapter has its own information storage and retrieval facility attached to it. Each of these components—the orientation to subsystem interface, the access alert component, the target assessment component, the typal indicator, and the four-player selector—receives, generates, and stores imagistic signals unique to its distance-regulation function. In this way each member of the family acquires and is able to apply a storehouse of distance-regulation information about what was, what is, what ought to be, and what ought not to be a part of familial and other social interactions. Second, the typal indicator operationalizes a design for living which puts together a compendium of meanings and images regarding how family members should pursue their target goals both as a collective unit and as individuals. As such it suggests a strategic pathway for pursuit of all future target destinations. Finally the four-player selector helps focus attention on how each person attempts to effect what is expected of him in terms of the family's and his own typal preferences. It is within the four-player model, then, that members learn to play specific parts in relation to other members playing other parts. Implicit in our four-player model is the notion that individuals not only become familiar with the playing of certain parts, but also that these parts continue to be played in social interactions far removed in time and place from the original family household.

Every family passes on to its members its fundamental meanings, its conceptions of how and what to be and not to be, along with a behavioral guide suggesting what targets to seek and what targets to shun. In addition, every family generates and passes on images of how it actually lives, how it regulates distances and controls access to targets, including how it tries to realize the target ideals of how it thinks it ought to be. A family's meanings are its philosophic and moral perspectives and precepts. They are often universal in scope. In content and expression they are a part of the public idiom. A family's images are much more private and personal: they portray and make manifest how these precepts and perspectives are translated into the reality of family life. Inevitably, discrepancies occur between the meanings a family puts forth and the images or internalized representations each member takes away for himself of how these meanings are made manifest in the family. A family's images thus distill and give form to individual and group experience, and, as such, become the carriers of each family's history. Indeed, each family's social future is shaped as much by its central meanings and images as each individual's biological development is shaped by his or her genetic makeup.

Image transmission is continuous from one generation to another. When individuals leave their families of origin to form new families, they carry with them knowledge of what distance regulations in their original households were like, and of the contexts in which such regulations were to be maintained, altered, or qualified. An individual's images, therefore, together with the meanings attached to them, are the moral and procedural bases for resolving differences between himself and all other persons, including his spouse. Following Piaget as discussed by J. Hunt (1961, p. 173), we are here using the term *image* somewhat loosely as an internalized representation of an action made or observed. We also believe that an image can exist in the form of a kinesic imprint, a kind of memory which is muscular and energic. This is perhaps the most basic form of an image. An image may also be a picture of an event, whether literal or symbolic. Another step removed, it exists

as a sentiment or feeling about an event. Finally, an image may
exist as a belief or an idea about an event, a step further away still
from the event itself. All four forms of an image are usually re-
coverable, though sometimes only with effort. Whatever the form,
however, an individual's images, together with the meanings attached to them, are stored in a memory bank, and inform him how
to regulate distance with other people, when and how to play certain parts, and whether to move, oppose, follow, or bystand in regard to specific access and target issues.

The imagistic memory bank also suggests specific strategies
for pursuing particular target themes. In this way a person's images
create something of a thematic continuum from one generation to
another, for the psychopolitics and strategies an individual employs
in response to his family of origin's images and meanings carry over
into the new family, where they help trigger a whole new generation of images. This is not to suggest that either meanings or images
remain the same from one generation to another. Children, as we
all know, can develop meanings and images diametrically opposed
to those of their parents or even to those of their siblings. Just as
each person's distance-regulation experience in a family is different,
so are his images and meanings. The same image may be of high
importance to one member of a family and of low importance to
another. Each subsystem, as well as the family unit as a whole,
evolves its own image hierarchy in the course of time, through
periods of stability and instability, as new distance-regulation strategies are developed to deal with new circumstances. During periods
of stability, the hierarchy will remain the same, whereas in unstable
periods significant change can occur.

We believe that each family member usually knows what
his family's image hierarchy is. Indeed, his own hierarchy is con-
structed in large part as a response to it, even though his own hierarchy may contain quite a different set of images and meanings.
Those images which are high in the hierarchy have a great deal of
energy attached to them while images low in the hierarchy may
have little or no energy attached. The set and order of images are
not the only means for measuring differences between hierarchies,
however. Two family members may share a highly charged image
and yet be in strong conflict over its sign, for the image may have

a high positive energy charge for one person and a high negative energy charge for the other.

The general makeup of the image hierarchy a person takes away with him when he leaves his family may be either symmetrical or reciprocal to the family's image hierarchy: by *symmetrical* we mean similar if not identical to the set, order, and sign of the family image hierarchy; by *reciprocal* we mean different from the family hierarchy either by order, by sign, or by virtue of the fact the set of images is itself quite different. Often, an individual's private hierarchy may be reciprocal to his family's hierarchy, but when he is at interface with the family he chooses to behave as if his images were symmetrical. The actual relationship between his behavior, his "image" in the family, and his private images of himself requires a working out of his own psychopolitics, including the parts he elects to play in critical complementary arrangements with other family members.

The imagistic memory bank is thus linked both conceptually and operationally to a player's positioning in the four-player scheme. In general, a player's images and meanings guide his part positioning while the parts he plays in a family system help determine the perspective from which he will perceive events and the images he will carry away. More specifically, one might expect an opposer to develop images reciprocal to the image hierarchy of his family and a follower to share his family's image hierarchy, that is, develop symmetrical images. Correspondingly one might expect a person with a symmetrical image hierarchy to fit logically into the part of follower toward his family and a person with a reciprocal hierarchy to take up the part of opposer. In such a situation, a continuity exists between a member's image hierarchy and player parts he elects to play.

Such imagistic and operational continuity is not always the rule in families, however. An individual's psychopolitics may dictate that he play a role discontinuous with his image hierarchy. A person may pretend to have symmetrical images and meanings by interactionally playing the follower part, thus masking his true reciprocal image hierarchy. A number of other possibilities also exist. A person playing the passive bystander part has the option not to divulge how his own images and values are similar to or different from the family's official image hierarchy. Or, an active bystander part affords one the opportunity to declare in precise terms and in what ways his images are symmetrical or reciprocal to those of the family. Another possibility is for an individual to mask his reciprocal image hierarchy at least temporarily, and take up the opposer position as a kind of interactional devil's advocate to delineate more clearly the particular images and meanings given high place in the family hierarchy.

We believe that our four-player interactional model helps to illuminate, in large part, an individual's reasons for seeking out and committing himself to an intimate partner. Three general choice patterns seem to exist. In the first and most prevalent, the individual tries to play a specific part or combination of parts with the intended partner that he played in the family of origin. Thus many of us do not so much "marry a parent or sibling," as we "marry a player part," some member (grandfather, sister, mother, brother) with whom we shared a particularly intense complementary four-player arrangement as a child, such as a follower to a powerful mover, an opposer to a "stuck" follower, and so on. The subtle repetitions in the playing of parts adds an element of zest, intrigue, and/or pain to what takes place in the new pair's everyday dealings. For example, when an opposer chooses not merely a follower but a follower with a penchant for victimization, he may find himself transformed into an oppressor-opposer even if he was not originally oppressive. In any case, whether there is an exact replication of an old family arrangement or whether there is a complicated variation on that arrangement, the forming of a relationship with a new partner poses a unique opportunity to regain and extend the familiar family pattern.

In a second, less frequent choice pattern, the individual tries to play out with the intended new partner the part or combination of parts played by one or even both parents in the family of origin. In this way, a person reenacts or recreates the marriage of the previous generation, or at least one key aspect of it. In such a situation, the process is one of adaptation, the playing of a part learned not from direct experience but from observation, which is then internalized and identified as one's own. Even less frequently, an individual may choose a part or seek to play a combination of parts in the new intimate relationship that he or she felt was missing in the interactions of the family of origin. In any courtship or early marriage relationship, we expect to find one or more of these choice patterns shaping the new generation's interactional responses. Again, we believe that most people tend to recreate patterns that are interactionally familiar, and some attempt to reproduce almost exactly a previous relationship.

Courtship players are not normally conscious of playing their learned, induced, or preferred player parts, nor are they aware that the other is playing (or seems capable of playing) the complementary part. Yet we would propose that some significant part of the phenomenon of attraction is the *familiarity* of the preferred combination of parts. Each player needs another person to effect certain kinds of familiar resolutions that are strongly goal-oriented, for the preferred player combinations are associated with key family strategies. It is important to note that interactional goals do not always have to be effective ones, just as the strategies around which the combination is chosen may themselves be disabling. Player combinations are formed as each individual strives toward some target. In the midst of this striving the hierarchy of images for each person and his player preferences converge, facilitating the aura of attraction, reinforcing the sense of familiarity, and encouraging individuals to make the judgment to finalize their decision to live together.

It is our experience that a person's foundation images, the core set of images that make up the image hierarchy he takes with him out into the world to negotiate similarities and differences with others he encounters, derive primarily from his family experience. This is but another way of saying that a person's foundation images are representations of the themes associated with key family strategies, for a family's strivings, intentions, and goals are made clear to individuals through its strategies. The themes that underlie all strategies, the substantive threads that hold the action together and tie it to specific goals, are reinforced through repetition. These important themes help the individual to label his or her images. If the image is a representation of action, the theme gives the action and the image of the action a name. It provides a conceptual framework for pinning it down and associating it with other imagistic representations of other events. It is true, of course, that many lives are affected by extraordinary events, dramatic occurrences that seem to shuffle foundation images into some new order. Also, many people cannot trace certain of their key images to family experiences. For such individuals even the notion of individual reciprocals to the family's image hierarchy does not seem relevant. In this discussion, which is focused on the ordinary, we are not concerned with these special occurrences.

Thus far, we have treated the "matching" of complementary four-player arrangements as quite straightforward. "Matching" is not always straightforward, however. People are not always what they appear to be, especially during courtship. An apparent bystander eventually emerges as a chronic opposer, a follower transmutes into an unmovable mover, and so on. Suitors are usually able to choose from more than one player arrangement for several reasons: first, because most people are, from the predilections derived from early experience, driven toward more than one player arrangement; second, because usually there is more than one possible arrangement between any two attracted people; and, finally, because each suitor is free to choose different people, each offering a different combination. In any case, the different potential combinations are probably internally ranked according to preference. Anything but the primary preferred arrangement produces some degree of pattern dissonance, a consequence of mismatching. Faced with pattern dissonance, the players, if they are to continue the new relationship, are left with a difficult choice. Either a player must give up the part or part pattern preferred in the pursuit of key targets, thereby relinquishing a familiar aspect of the self, or he must try to change the part the partner plays until the preferred combination is realized. Unfortunately, we have no evidence on the distribution of these two resolutions. In a single case we might suggest that the outcome of player mismatching, assuming the players remain in relationship after the mismatch is discovered (as a surprisingly large number do), depends on the primacy of followership versus opposership in the preferred arrangement as well as on the original strategies that spawned the arrangement. For instance, if a follower thinks he has found a mover, but in actuality finds another follower, he might try to become a mover himself, whereas if the supposed mover was really an opposer, he might prefer to reverse the direction of his own traffic to follow and facilitate the action of the opposer.

The emergence of a dominant player pattern in a new relationship is not the only cause of stress in building a marriage. Each partner's typal style is also important, because each person tends to regulate distances in accord with the type of system in which he or she prefers to operate. Typal considerations are probably less immediately accessible to the new partners' awareness and scrutiny than their player interactions, yet they are no less important. Often they emerge after marriage as a fundamental distance-regulation issue. That some typal issues do not arise until after marriage is predictable, for each person's relationship to the other's image hierarchy cannot fully emerge until a considerable number of experiences have been shared, permitting a recurrence of similar distance-regulation issues plus repeated activation of individual and joint strategies for solving them. Only then can two people truly begin to delineate the stylistic differences inherent in their images of loyalty or sincerity or security, images whose importance and sign (positive or negative) they may have previously been able to agree upon. Now, however, in living together they can begin to understand how events similarly labeled by each may be experienced quite differently. For example, a husband's images of random-type security may include the propensity not to lock household doors, a practice which generates or reawakens his wife's closed-type images of physical insecurity. Similarly, a husband's closed-type interpretation of integrity may not permit him to appreciate or even approve of his wife's open-style exchanges with her friends in which everything, including the newlyweds' sexual life, is discussed very outspokenly.

In summary, when a person starts searching for another person or persons with whom to share his life, he looks for someone whose meanings and images, style and typal design, and player part positioning are complementary to his own. Such a search usually requires that each person do a lot of sorting and mapping of the other's behavior against his or her self-reported meanings and stylistic preferences, and against his or her own imagistic hierarchy. This is a truly tricky task, for it is very easy in the process of wooing to misread someone, seeing that person not as he really is but as he is desired to be. Image mapping can be further complicated by the possibility that one or both persons may be accustomed to masking or distorting his or her true image hierarchy, owing to the psycho-political arrangement in the family of origin.

To illustrate how complicated this process of mapping can become, let us pose the following hypothetical example. An elder, academically successful son in a closed type family has been successfully granted mover status by his parents for the purpose of "shaping up" and organizing his random-type younger brother to motivate him toward academic achievement. He then becomes attracted to an only daughter whose primary part is that of opposer to her random type parents. Now suppose the two initially share a high negative image of laziness and a high positive image of achievement. The elder son might recognize the daughter's opposition to randomness and try to place her in the successful mover-follower relationship he has experienced with his younger brother, especially in regard to intellectual matters, only to have her initial following moves give way to opposing tendencies. Gradually, he discovers that the more he tries to lead her into the academic realm, the more she opposes. She, at the same time, might feel confused by his attempts to coerce her toward an acceptance of closed type academic values, especially since she has chosen to follow an open-type strategic pathway toward her own achievement goals. Furthermore, her sense of achievement emphasizes material rather than intellectual success, since she associates intellectualism with her parents' tendency to talk about things rather than do them. In the end, whether they marry or not, each partner may feel betrayed by the other. Anger, confusion, and a strong sense of failure can easily be generated in situations in which two people try to share an intimate space, but each mismaps the other's distance-regulation behavior.

When two people live together for any length of time, they evolve a conjoint image hierarchy in addition to preserving and expanding their own individual meanings and images. As long as the two remain together, this conjoint hierarchy, however discordant or skewed it might be, serves as their dyadic system's behavioral guide. The dyad's hierarchy of images, together with its typal style and its four-player arrangements for gaining access to targets, are all put under great stress by the arrival of a baby. When a child is added to an ongoing system, a disruption of ongoing distance-regulation strategies is inevitable. Suddenly new rhythmic patterns must be negotiated between child and parents, and parent and parent, in a triadic relationship requiring the formation of new distance-regulation patterns. In addition, stress is experienced in the adult pair's separate and joint image hierarchies, for the baby is a bearer as well as receiver of images. The appearance of a child provides the impetus for the emergence of new child-parent and parent-parent sets of images, as well as the reemergence of old ones. These images largely determine the distance regulation operations the new triad will adopt.

At each stage of development in a family's life cycle, new distance-regulation crises appear, stimulating new images and reemphasizing older ones. The development of family and individual strategies at each stage continues to be dependent on the interaction of family and individual image hierarchies as well as on each system's typal and four-player interactional preferences. In his model of individual development Erik Erikson (1963) identifies the issues of primary importance to the individual at different stages of his life. Unfortunately, family theory has not yet advanced far enough so that a similar model of family life-cycle issues may seriously be put forward, for the family as a systems entity has not been genetically investigated to the extent that such a model requires. It is our hope that our model for understanding distance regulations in families, as well as our speculations about family evolution, will help bring the day closer when the presentation of such a life-cycle model might prove feasible.

References

ACKERMAN, N. W. *Treating the Troubled Family.* New York: Basic Books, 1966.

BATESON, G., JACKSON, D. D., HALEY, J., AND WEAKLAND, J. "Toward a Theory of Schizophrenia." *Behavioral Science,* 1956, *1,* 251–264.

BUCKLEY, W. *Sociology and Modern Systems Theory.* Englewood Cliffs, N. J.: Prentice-Hall, 1967.

ERIKSON, E. *Childhood and Society* (2nd ed.) New York: Norton, 1963.

HALEY, J. "The Family of the Schizophrenic: A Model System." *Journal of Nervous and Mental Disease,* 1959, *129* (4), 357–374. Also in G. Handel (Ed.), *The Psychosocial Interior of the Family.* Chicago: Aldine, 1967.

HALL, E. T. *The Hidden Dimension.* Garden City, N. Y.: Doubleday, 1966.

HENRY, J. *Pathways to Madness.* New York: Random House, 1971.

HOFFMAN, L. "Deviation-Amplifying Processes in Natural Groups." In J. Haley (Ed.), *Changing Families.* New York: Grune and Stratton, 1971.

HUNT, J. M. *Intelligence and Experience.* New York: Ronald, 1961.

LAING, R. D. *The Politics of Family.* New York: Random House, 1969.

LIDZ, T., CORNELISON, A. R., FLECK, S., AND TERRY, D. "The Intrafamilial

Environment of Schizophrenic Patients: II. Marital Schism and Marital Skew." *American Journal of Psychiatry*, 1957, *114*, 241–248. Also in G. Handel (Ed.), *The Psychosocial Interior of the Family*. Chicago: Aldine, 1967.

LORENZ, K. "The Function of Colour in Coral Reef Fishes." *Proceedings of the Royal Institute of Great Britain*, 1962, *39*, 282–296.

PIAGET, J., AND INHELDER, B. *The Child's Concept of Space*. London: Routledge and Kegan Paul, 1956.

POWERS, W. T. "Feedback: Beyond Behaviorism." *Science*, Jan. 1973, *179*, 351–356.

RABKIN, R. *Inner and Outer Space*. New York: Norton, 1970.

SATIR, V. *Conjoint Family Therapy* (rev. ed.) Palo Alto, Calif.: Science and Behavior Books, 1967.

TINBERGEN, N. *Social Behavior in Animals* (2nd ed.) London: Methuen, 1964.

VOGEL, E. F., AND BELL, N. W. "The Emotionally Disturbed Child as the Family Scapegoat." In N. W. Bell and E. F. Vogel (Eds.), *A Modern Introduction to the Family*. New York: Free Press, 1960. Also in G. Handel (Ed.), *The Psychosocial Interior of the Family*. Chicago: Aldine, 1967.

WHITAKER, C. "Process Techniques of Family Therapy." Unpublished mimeograph. Madison: Department of Psychiatry, University of Wisconsin School of Medicine, 1973.

WIENER, N. *Cybernetics: Control and Communication in the Animal and the Machine*. New York: Wiley, 1948.

WYNNE, L. C., RYCKOFF, I. M., DAY, J., AND HIRSCH, S. I. "Pseudo-Mutuality in the Family Relationships of Schizophrenics." *Psychiatry*, 1958, *21*, 205–220. Also in G. Handel (Ed.), *The Psychosocial Interior of the Family*. Chicago: Aldine, 1967.

Index

with others, 206-208, 210, 211, 216-220; and matching, 246; and other players, 181-183
Bystander function, 192, 195, 202-203, 216, 218-223, 228, 237; disqualification of, 216, 218, 235, 237-238

C

Calendar time, 42-43, 81, 82
CANWIN family, 137-142
Carrier energy, 40
Cathexis, 90-91
Causal chain: closed-loop, 13, 55, 230; open-loop, 12-13
Centering, 74-77; in closed family, 120; and family type, 171; as modulating mechanism, 103, 105, 108, 109; in open family, 127-128; in random family, 135; and synchronizing, 86, 89
Central regions, 42
Channeling, 72-73, 112-114, 120, 166, 167, 169, 211, 229
Charge-discharge ratio, 44, 91-92, 96, 102
Charging, 93-94
Checkpoints, 70
CLARITY family, 216-219
Clocking, 82-86, 89, 103, 108, 121, 128, 129, 136, 223
Closed family, 119-126; affect ideals of, 145-148; core purpose of, 143-144; distance regulation in, 227-228, 231, 237; flawed versions of, 151-153; institutional preference for, 162; and mapping, 247, 248; and other types, 116-119, 157; strategies of, 164-166, 169-171, 173
Closeness/distance, 42, 59, 61, 120, 127, 149, 230
CLOUD family, 130-134
Committing, 97
Commonplace events, 221-222
Co-mover, 181, 184, 197, 223; ideal, 198-199. *See also* Bystander, Follower, Opposer

Comparator, 13-15, 159, 228
Comparison signal, 227-228
Component parts of family systems: access and target dimensions as, 36, 66; four-player model as, 208; and imagistic signals, 240; for information processing, 11, 12; kinds of, 15; relations of to each other and to whole system, 221-228, 230, 233, 237; strategic relationships among, 20, 21
Conformity, 52
Constancy feedback loops, 14-15, 118, 152, 153, 155, 161, 171, 227
Coordinating, 88
Core purpose, 143-145; and distance regulation, 149-151, 227; in flawed open system, 153; and individual players, 203, 206; in mixed-type families, 157-158; and strategies, 171, 174-176; and typal biases, 162; and typal design, 159-161
Crisis chain, 151-156, 173, 175, 232, 234
Criterion variables, 118-119, 149-151, 160, 171, 227, 229, 230
Crossover, 71, 112, 230
Crowding, 109-113. *See also* Invasion behavior
Cybernetics, 9, 203, 238

D

DAY, J., 5
Decision-making, 104, 132, 139
Depth relations, 50-52
DE SICA family, 109-114
Designing, 75-76
Detaching, 97-98
Direction of error, 151-153, 154-156, 234
Disablement, 176, 232-235
Disabling strategies, 163-164, 173-175, 245; examples of, 6-7, 28, 32-33, 57-60, 62-63, 107-114, 183, 184, 187, 195-197, 209-219